Never Better

Never Better

My Life in Our Times

Tommie Gorman

ALLEN&UNWIN

First published in Great Britain in 2022 by Allen & Unwin
Copyright © 2022 by Tommie Gorman

Allen & Unwin
c/o Atlantic Books
Ormond House
26–27 Boswell Street
London WC1N 3JZ

Phone: 020 7269 1610
Email: UK@allenandunwin.com
Web: www.allenandunwin.com/uk

A CIP catalogue record for this book is available from the British Library.

Hardback ISBN 978 1 83895 782 7
E-book ISBN 978 1 83895 783 4

Printed and bound by CPI Group (UK) Ltd, Croydon CR0 4YY

10 9 8 7 6 5 4 3 2 1

Contents

For Ceara, who never blinks

Beginnings

I was a few weeks shy of my twenty-first birthday. I didn't know it, but I was about to have a conversation that would shape my life. In the 1960s and 1970s, John Healy was one of Ireland's most influential newspaper journalists. He and his family lived in a Dublin suburb, Fortfield Terrace, a fifteen-minute walk from the Rathmines School of Journalism. It was the first third-level education centre in Ireland to provide a full-time course for would-be reporters.

That spring afternoon in 1977, I was sitting opposite Healy in his front room. He was wearing a brown cardigan and breathing heavily, occasionally snorting through a nose that had been damaged more than twenty years before when playing as goalkeeper for the Gaelic football team of his native Charlestown, Co. Mayo.

I was in the lair of a master and he was sizing me up.

Healy was a legend in Irish journalism and a maverick. In his mid-teens he didn't want to return to St Nathy's College, Ballaghaderreen, as a boarding student to complete his second-level education. He decided he would try to get a job as a cub reporter in his local weekly newspaper, the *Western People*. He cycled the thirty miles from Charlestown to its office in Ballina and waited four hours before getting to see the editor-proprietor, Fred de Vere, to ask for a job. Fred listened and made the offer. Healy's starting wage would be £1 per week – slightly less than half the cost of his accommodation.

Healy's mother was against the plan when he got home from his bicycle journey. She was the dominant force in the house – a district nurse who wanted her son to return to secondary school, as she hoped he might someday become a doctor. His father was a milder presence, an insurance agent who would die before he reached fifty. In this instance, he backed his son, and a career in the reporting trade began.

My inquisitor that spring afternoon in Rathmines was in his late forties. A decade before, he had published a devastating series of articles in the *Irish Times*, 'No One Shouted Stop', describing the impact of emigration on communities in rural Ireland. He would pioneer a form of political journalism in Irish newspapers, the role of the commentator, with new edge and a new way of writing.

'How many are in your class, kid?'

'Sixteen. Twelve girls and four fellas,' I explained.

'The boss of the school, my old buddy Sean Egan, tells me you are the only one from Connacht.'

'That's right.'

Healy and his long-time journalist friend, Jim Maguire, were planning to launch a new weekly provincial newspaper. The pair of them had started their careers with the *Western People*, and, decades later, they were plotting a reckoning. Over a number of years, the relationship with their former employers, the de Vere family, had turned sour. Now they were preparing a return to launch a rival newspaper: the *Western Journal*.

They had some local funders backing them. They decided to bypass raising the money needed to acquire printing machinery by outsourcing that work to the modern presses of the Connacht Tribune group in Galway. Their hope was that the clarity of the photographs produced by the Tribune's new technology would give them an advantage over the output from the *Western People*'s traditional hot-metal system.

From his armchair, Healy was sussing out the merits of hiring me. I was from Sligo, the county next door to Mayo, and might be able to generate readers and advertisers. I told him about the six-week placement the previous summer in the *Sligo Champion* newsroom and how the editor, Seamus Finn, was now using my reports of Sligo Rovers away matches against Dublin clubs.

I didn't realize it, but in the course of the conversation, I was acquiring a mentor.

He sat forward in his armchair. 'I see you have a neat patch in the knee of your trousers. Who did that, kid?' He was referring to my best wear, the fawn-coloured trousers, with an ironed crease as well as a repaired small hole in the left leg.

'My granny. She lives with us in Sligo. She is great at darning and knitting.'

He brow tightened. He was watching intently, seeking more information.

'She is from north Leitrim. Her husband died young, leaving her with seven children, including my mother, whose father died before she was born. Granny had relations in America who sent her a sewing machine, and that helped her to rear her family.'

Healy nodded and smiled. I kept going. 'Granny came in from Leitrim to stay with us after I was born, and she has lived with us ever since. We share the same birthday. April 3rd.'

Healy smiled. 'You are from snipe grass, kid. You are hungry. That's good. When do you think the general election will be held?'

'June maybe,' I replied.

'What makes you say that?'

I decided to roll the dice. 'The father of my friend, Bairbre Ferguson, has a big job with an advertising agency who do work for Fine Gael. He was supposed to go on a cruise with his wife, but he cancelled it to be available in Ireland.'

The gamble worked.

With Healy saying there would be a place for me in the new enterprise, he was keen to share advice about the reporting trade: 'By the time you get to forty-five, kid, you should be able to sign your name to the "Our Father" and claim a week's wages.'

'If you want to build a relationship with readers, kid, you have to tell them you are going to tell them, tell them and then tell them that you told them.'

Healy died in his sleep, upstairs in that same south Dublin house, far too young, aged sixty, in January 1990.

At one stage, with his head slightly bowed, he advised, 'Every man should try to do three things in his life, kid: plant a tree, father a child and write a book.' In the shadow of my first employer, I set about the third of those tasks.

1

Sligo: early years

During every life, there will be light and shade and love and loss. Nobody escapes an ambush. You don't sense the bushwhack coming. Things are going swimmingly, and then, suddenly, bang.

In our house, it happened three times. First, with Daddy's death in October 1992. Again, in May 2001, when, alone in our Sligo home, our mother struggled with a piercing headache as she opened the curtains to begin a new day. Our next-door neighbour, Mary Lennon, answered her call for help and was with her in her final moments.

And then, in April 2016, a different version of grief: sibling loss, when Paula, our baby sister, died suddenly. That Sunday evening in April, Paula's neighbour, Brigid, and her daughter, Evelyn, found her dead on the bathroom floor of her cottage, beyond Lissadell, at Maugherow, near the sea in north Sligo. There was medication near where she collapsed, indicating she had tried to calm the brewing aneurysm that killed her, similar to the swift crossing made by our mother fifteen years before.

Paula wasn't married, but she was rarely alone. She rescued dogs and found homes for them. For several years she always had at least two of them in the house with her. She was a community worker and was the manager of a resource centre, in Cranmore, a working-class area of Sligo. It was a challenging job, and she loved it. Her days usually started with breakfast clubs, and her workplace, surrounded by housing estates, hummed with activity through to the evening homework clubs. Sometimes Paula would take groups on day trips, driving them in a big maroon minibus.

You would hear her before you'd see her. She was spontaneous. She called to the doors of loan sharks and warned them to stop sucking people into hopeless debt. The community police liaison officers appreciated her direct ways. For the Halloween festival each November, her home in north Sligo was party central for the children of the area.

On Saturday 8 April 2016, my wife, Ceara, arranged a small family gathering in our house to mark my sixtieth birthday the previous weekend. Sitting together after we had eaten, Paula sang a song she had learned from an Ella Fitzgerald CD. Towards the end, I hit the audio record button on my phone.

> *It's a Barnum and Bailey world*
> *Just as phoney as it can be*
> *But it wouldn't be make-believe*
> *If you believed in me.*

That perfect night was our last time together. I was in Belfast when Ceara phoned to tell me Paula had been found, dead.

Driving west in the dark, a recurring memory was of carrying her down the stairs of our home on Cairns Road, after an asthma attack. She was maybe six at the time, and I was thirteen. Her head was on my shoulder, and her little body was limp in my arms. Oxygen and steroids revived her in Sligo hospital that night. Now I was going to that same place to formally confirm that she was the person in the morgue.

Paula was a gift from the beginning. She was the glue, the angel that became the spirit of our home. She was born in 1963, on 4 July, American Independence Day. Mammy named her after the kind-faced Italian, Paul VI, who was elected pope the previous year. Our brother, Michael, had been born in September 1952; Mary arrived in January 1954; and I came in April 1956 so there was a seven-year gap before Paula.

Our father, Joe Gorman, was born in May 1921. On his birth certificate, his father, Thomas (Tom), is described as a farmer. His mother was Bridget O'Hara. The family lived under Knocknashee (Hill of the Fairies) mountain at Carrowloughan, beyond the village of Coolaney in south Co. Sligo.

Some of Daddy's bachelor uncles on his mother's side established a grocery, drapery and general merchants business, O'Hara Brothers, in the Co. Leitrim village of Dromahair, twelve miles from Sligo town.

Daddy had three siblings. Eamonn went boarding to secondary school in St Nathy's College in Ballaghaderreen, Co. Mayo, and immediately afterwards joined the Holy Ghost Order to become a Catholic priest. Mary went to boarding secondary school in Balla, Co. Mayo, before returning to work in her uncles' business in Dromahair. In his childhood, Jack was badly scalded by an accident with boiling water and his speech was affected. He would spend most of his life on the family farm.

Daddy's education finished after national school, and he began working with his father, building what was a growing business buying cattle at fairs and farms in the west of Ireland and exporting them to Scotland and England.

The entrance to the narrow avenue leading to their two-storey farmhouse at Carrowloughan had a wall with an inset, housing a holy statue. Close to the gate was a three-cornered field. When Eamonn returned for holidays from boarding school, he'd bring a store of sweets. The siblings would go to the field and make four divides of the booty. Daddy often told us the story and encouraged us to do the same.

Our mother, Maureen Harkin, was the youngest of seven children from the townland of Trenadullagh (Through the Leaves), a small north Co. Leitrim farm with a two-bedroomed cottage, five miles from the village of Drumkeeran. Her mother, Ellen-Nora White, eloped to marry her younger husband, Patrick Harkin. He was in his early thirties when he died.

Granny's siblings helped her with the rearing of her five sons and two daughters. Some of the boys went to stay with two of her brothers who lived nearby and who had their own young families. Mammy, her only sister, Peggy, and their brother, Mick, were taken in by their aunts, who were married in Sligo but had no children of their own.

Although she was widowed very young, Granny Harkin never remarried. During the first Christmas after her husband died, she walked in the sleet to visit the cemetery, with one of her sons, Johnny Joe. At the graveside, the boy asked her why wouldn't his father come out and talk to him.

She was resourceful and very calm. She churned butter and made tasty bread, potato cakes and boxty. She was clever with a needle and thread and with her sewing machine. She could add collars and sleeves to an empty meal bag and transform it into a shirt.

There was subsistence farming and no wealth in rural Leitrim, but families and neighbours helped each other. Emigrants' remittances were an important buttress. Granny had two sisters as well as in-laws in the United States. A feature of my mother's childhood was Granny discreetly inquiring from the postman, 'Any American mail today?'

Granny's eldest son, Paddy, and his brother, Jim, were the first of her children to leave. In their teens, they went to work for a neighbour who ran bars in Belfast. They would travel further, to London, and put down permanent roots there. Keevie (Kevin) was the only one to emigrate to America. He got a job working as an assistant cook on the boats that ferried timber from the forests around the Great Lakes. He supplemented his earnings as a barber for the crews. He met his future wife, Mary Carroll, from Killarney, Co. Kerry, at a dance in New York, and they returned to settle permanently in his home place, Trenadullagh.

Peggy, Mammy's only sister, joined the nuns. Their aunt, Granny's sister Dora, was a member of the Cross and Passion order, and in their teens Peggy and her cousin, Maura White, were persuaded to enlist.

Johnny Joe was the only one of the seven to put down roots locally. He had great physical strength and became a ploughman and farmer. He married a district nurse, Kathleen Gilhooly, and they set up home at Tarmon, eight miles from the family home, by the shores of Lough Allen, where they reared their seven children.

Mick was one of the three children who spent time living with his aunts in Sligo. That period away from home together gave him, Mammy and Peggy a closeness that continued for the rest of their lives. Mick's first job was working in a shop in Sligo. In time he became what was known as a commercial traveller. He married a national-school teacher, Nano McHugh. They settled in Sligo and had a family of six.

When living with her aunt Peggy and her husband, Tommy Burgess, Mammy went to school in the Mercy and Ursuline convents. Another of Granny's sisters, Babs, was joint owner of a ladies' clothes shop in Castle Street and married Stanley Mulligan. Mammy began working there, and it was during that time that she started going out with my father. They first met at a St Stephen's night dance in the corrugated-roofed Ballinagar hall, beside the local Catholic church. There was a six-year age difference between them.

By then, Daddy and his father were prospering as cattle dealers. In one photograph taken at a fair, each has a heavy overcoat, a stick and a lit cigarette. In another, Daddy is tall and thin, with a full head of hair, seated at a meeting of the North West Cattle Exporters Association in Sligo's Imperial Hotel.

Their routine was to buy cattle at the scheduled list of fair days in west of Ireland towns, have them transported by train to the ports of Dublin or Belfast and then sell on their stock for a profit at marts in places like Annick, Forfar and Carlisle. Collooney railway station was one of the places where cattle were loaded onto the train. More than a decade after my father died, a man called Jimmy Brennan recalled a childhood memory of seeing him with a massive roll of notes, peeling off some to pay for fodder and overnight storage before the cattle were dispatched on the next leg of their journey.

Father and son would take a berth on the cattle boats to Scotland. In the Glasgow mart, they paid a person to walk behind them and watch for discarded cigarette butts, lest they cause a fire. A lot of the deals were a matter of sums, done in their heads or on the back of a cigarette packet. They stayed at Glasgow's George Hotel and became dependable providers of flowers and Mass offerings at the Catholic church where they attended Mass. After a successful morning selling cattle, their Scotland thanksgiving routine sometimes included a journey to Carfin, a Marian shrine and pilgrimage centre, sixteen miles from Glasgow.

In those years, our father loved fast cars and regularly changed them. He was impulsive, generous and trusting. He and our mother married in Ballintogher church in September 1951. Their first home was the Rockview Bar and the house attached to it on the main street of the village. The liquor licence for the premises was issued in Mammy's name.

The prosperous phase was continuing when Michael was born a year later. By the time Mary arrived in 1954, the family had moved to a large rented house and lands at Hazelwood, three miles from Sligo town.

Early one cold morning, Daddy was having trouble starting his car and Mammy was helping him to push it. As it gathered momentum, he slid into the driving seat, manipulated the clutch and gears and the engine kicked into life. Before he drove off, he looked into the back mirror for a parting glance and saw Mammy jumping up and down on the road. While attempting to help with the pushing, Michael's tiny hands had become trapped in the chrome car bumper. Had Daddy not spotted our mother's despair, Michael's little legs would have been dragged along the road and worn down to stumps. On that occasion disaster was avoided, but there would be sorrow further down the line.

In late 1957, our father made one of his most spontaneous decisions. He announced to our mother that he had made the arrangements to purchase a house, a mile from Sligo town centre. It was the last one, No. 12, of a row of newly built semi-detached three-bedroom dwellings on Cairns Road, called after the rugged rocks that feature in some of the surrounding fields.

The two upstairs bedrooms at the front of the house had a perfect view of Markievicz Park, the Sligo Gaelic football pitch that had been opened the previous year. (It was decades before I had the wisdom to understand that that boy in our father had purchased the equivalent of a corporate box.)

Michael was six when we moved there, Mary was four, and I was two. The pair of them remember spending the first afternoon, enthralled by newness, running up and down the stairs and flushing the toilet in the bathroom. No. 12 Cairns Road would be home for our parents and Granny for the rest of their lives.

In the late 1950s our family fortunes changed. There was a period when Daddy drank excessively, recognized he couldn't handle alcohol and gave it up. There was a time when his health collapsed, first with pleurisy and then from the wave of tuberculosis that ravaged through Ireland for a part of that decade.

His deepest regret, one that remained with him for the rest of his life, was the possibility that he had been too trusting in a business where your word was your bond. His bank account, accessible to several, was flush before his period of poor health began. By the time he was released from hospital, the account was empty.

Before he was transferred to Merlin Park sanatorium in Galway for several weeks of invasive tuberculosis treatment, he spent time at what was a local fever hospital close to Sligo town. Mammy said very little to him while he was being admitted there. Many years later he would recall how she was as stiff as a board when they parted. When moving his clothes from a suitcase to a locker, he discovered she had tucked a naggin of brandy inside a towel, even though she disliked him drinking alcohol. He looked out through the window and saw her alone in the trees, near the smoking hut in the hospital grounds, crying. He never opened the brandy bottle, and he never again drank alcohol.

Sometimes, in later years, as we returned home after visiting his sister, Mary, and her family in Dromahair, he would slow the car at a section of the road close to Lough Gill and say, 'That's where your mother took me from the water when I tried to do away with myself.' Mammy would respond, 'Stop talking nonsense,' and the conversation would change.

A night in January 1963 was one rock-bottom moment. Days before, Daddy had driven his father, Tom, to Enniskillen, for a connecting bus that would take him to Belfast and ultimately to the cattle boat and Scotland. Granda was fire-fighting, trying to rescue the business in difficult times.

The long-distance call to the phone in our front hallway brought news that he was dead. He had suffered a heart attack in the bath of his room at the George Hotel in Glasgow. Granda's remains were brought back from Scotland, and, on a bitterly cold afternoon, he was laid to rest alongside his wife and parents in the family plot at Court Abbey grave-yard, under Knocknashee. The family's time in the cattle trade was over.

With Daddy's health still fragile and the work he had done since he left national school over, Mammy took on the respon-sibilities of breadwinner. With a neighbour on Cairns Road, Doreen McIntyre, she found work on the assembly line of a German technical instruments manufacturer in Sligo town, Filler & Fiebig.

Mrs McIntyre was a widow. Her husband had been the manager of a local Ford garage, and she had two sons, Peter and Ken. She would give Mammy a lift to work in her Anglia car.

Although Mammy was used to our father being the provider, she never gave any sense of being cowed by her changed circumstances. From then on, she became the manager in our household. She had a great sense of humour. Sometimes she would say, 'God never opens one door without closing another.'

Eventually Daddy's health improved, and, after much trying, he found work with a local business, Truline Remoulds, that made car tyres and remoulded used ones. He was given a van, and his job was to visit garages, selling and delivering tyres and collecting used ones, casings, for remoulding. Mammy returned to being a full-time homemaker. Each morning, Daddy would set off with his flask and packed lunch in a square, silver biscuit tin.

He worked on Saturdays, and I'd sometimes go with him. On each journey he would say the rosary and bless himself when passing a Catholic church. He had landmarks along every route, like the crossroads beyond Castlebaldwin on the road to Tubbercurry, where cattle-dealing friends were killed in a car accident. Each time he passed it, he introduced, 'Three Hail Marys for Cosgrove and the son.' He couldn't pass a person thumbing a lift. The engine was between the driver and passenger seats, covered by a rug. To make space for the guest, I'd shift over to the warm berth, closer to Daddy.

One Good Friday, after delivering tyres to Kee's garage of Laghey in Co. Donegal, he returned to the van with a bag of sugared jelly sweets for me. I had three or four of them eaten before deliberately withheld guilt finally forced me to tell him I was off sweets for Lent. 'You'll be all right,' he said, squeezing my hand.

One Sunday afternoon I went with him on a journey into his past. He was seeking to collect money owed to him from the cattle-dealing days. On the way home, we stopped in Longford cathedral to say prayers of thanks for the cheque. In a shop near the church, he bought sweets and allowed me my choice of comic. I picked an expensive classic one, with a shiny colour cover, *Voyage to the Bottom of the Sea*.

Three days later, after I came home from school, Mammy was busy in the kitchen, using the wringer on the washing machine to squeeze the clothes. Her face couldn't hide her disappointment. The debt-settling cheque had bounced.

We were driving past the handball alley opposite Lough Gill one dark night when Daddy stopped in the rain. A man had flagged us down. He was seeking help for his wife who was trying to mind their young baby in a tent by the roadside. Daddy brought them to our house, and Mammy gave them blankets and pillows to sleep downstairs, by the fire. The next day, Daddy went to the local authority and asked for its help with emergency accommodation.

Daddy's weekly wage with Truline was 7 pounds 4 shillings and a penny. Each Friday he would leave the small, unopened brown envelope on the kitchen window, and Mammy would give him some of the coins to buy cigarettes.

A different van, a big red Bedford, came with the next job. Cork firm Suttons had a coal and fuels branch in Sligo, but it also had a tyre depot, and Daddy joined them. With Suttons, the pay was better and Daddy was also entitled to a lunch allowance. A young office clerk, Donal O'Neill, from Cork, was transferred to work in the Sligo office for a few months and became a lodger in our house. Michael and I vacated our room and moved to the couch that converted into a bed in the sitting room.

After a night spent playing 25, the card game, for a turkey prize in Sidney Gallagher's pub, daylight came too soon for Donal. Our granny had assumed the responsibilities to wake him.

'Donal, it's time to get up.'

'I'm up, Granny, I'm up.'

'How could you be up and me here looking at you, still in bed?'

Suttons were good employers. But their strategy became to have Daddy gather as much as possible of the outstanding debt in the area and then shut the long-distance tyres sales depot.

Jobs were hard found in Sligo of the 1960s. Daddy had references to help him with his searches. One was provided by our next-door neighbour, Owen O'Donnell, a vet with the Department of Agriculture.

22/5/66

To Whom it may concern

This is to state that I have known Joseph Gorman of Cairns Road, Sligo for over ten years.

He comes from a good family, is honest, sober, hard-working and a God-fearing man, also he is married and is deeply attached to his wife and children.

I have great pleasure in recommending him, to any person requiring his services.

Owen O'Donnell, MRCVS

One night before I went to bed, Mammy asked for a book in my school bag. She was trying to teach Daddy Irish because it might help when applying for low-skilled jobs in state services. The education project stopped abruptly after they came home, disappointed, from a meeting with a manager in the Electricity Supply Board.

Daddy worked for a time as a general helper in O'Gara's garage in Ballisodare, where in the good times he had bought cars. Granny's sister, Peggy Burgess, was friendly with Mrs O'Gara. In later years, Mrs O'Gara was sometimes name-checked affectionately in television interviews by her grandson, Ronan, the Irish international rugby player.

Daddy's next long-term employment was with the drinks distributors Gilbey's, as a deliveries driver for their Sligo depot. A neighbour from Cairns Road, Tom Keaveney, was a senior marketing manager with the company in Dublin, and he and his sister, Maureen, helped Daddy to get the job. He was measured up for a Magee-made green uniform suit and given a blue Volkswagen van.

The pressure to make ends meet was easing. But his health was also in decline.

His last paid work was as a petrol-pump attendant at the garage of a friend from the Truline Remoulds days, Padraig Branley. The premises was on Mail Coach Road between our home and the town centre. He rediscovered the square silver biscuit tin to house his flask and sandwiches. When the main garage closed after normal business hours, he worked from a small wooden hut with a one-bar electric fire.

I was in my teenage years, and, when walking with pals to the pictures or a hop, I'd steer our journey along a route that avoided passing my father as he filled the petrol into the stationary cars.

With Daddy's health slipping, Mammy resumed the role of main provider. A friend, Mrs Harte, recommended her for work as a nurse's assistant at St John's Hospital. Through that job she was asked to move to the Mercy Convent to help with the care of elderly nuns. It always involved night work, and she would be home from her shift every morning, alongside Granny in the kitchen, getting our breakfast and preparing us for school.

Mammy's final job was minding the children of our neighbours, the Carrolls. There were four of them, and it was a beautiful time because my parents welcomed and loved them like grandchildren.

From the very beginning, Paula was a magic force, creating and requiring love. From opposite ends of the age spectrum, she and Granny bound the family together. Granny lived until she was a few weeks short of her 101st birthday. Her old-age pension sometimes helped to pay the bills. I went through a phase of stealing thrupenny bits from her rosary beads purse, kept in her good coat, hanging in the wardrobe.

Towards the end of her life, she became quieter and spent most of her time upstairs in bed, serene, smiling, always available for visitors. In Leitrim, where she was born, families often had children nicknamed 'Baby' and 'Sonny'. Granny was always known as 'Baby' Harkin. In her final years, Mammy, the last of her seven children, minded her like a baby.

Like the Italian pope she was named after, and our father, Paula had sallow skin. She was still a baby the afternoon when I came home from school and Mammy was sitting in the dining room with our next-door neighbour, Mrs O'Donnell. Mammy's eyes were red from crying. Paula had been diagnosed with asthma.

On another lunchtime, Dr Heraughty's car was parked outside our house and he was upstairs with Mammy, seeing Paula. There was a half-full glass on the mantelpiece. Our aunt, Mary Creed, was a regular caller, and the box of groceries she'd bring from Dromahair usually included a bottle of Lucozade, wrapped in orange cellophane, for Paula. I seized my opportunity and took a slug. It was gone off, and I spat it onto the slack-covered fire. When Mammy came down and I gave out about the Lucozade, she smiled gently. I had purloined a sample of Paula's urine, required for Dr Heraughty.

One afternoon, when she was no more than four or five, Paula was the centre of attention during a visit to Uncle Keevie in north Leitrim. He had a piebald pony, and Paula was gently lifted onto the saddle. Within seconds her lips began to swell, and she morphed into a version of the Incredible Hulk. In time other allergies were discovered. It required just the smell of fish to set them off.

As well as the asthma and allergies, she had eczema. Daddy and Mammy brought her in the van to Longford, where a doctor gave her a cortisone injection. She was prescribed an inhaler, with pellets of powdered medicine. During severe attacks she struggled for breath, but she would always recover.

She was in national school when Daddy got her the dog she craved. It was a mongrel. We used to say it was a black-and-white Heinz – as in the fifty-seven varieties. One afternoon, a Sligo Corporation worker collecting the bins spotted Paula, with her short black hair and the dog in her arms. He asked, 'Where did you get the little bulldog, son?' She was more wounded by the 'bulldog' tag than the 'son'.

In 1970, Michael arrived home at Christmas with a golden cocker spaniel pup for Paula. He bought it with a sizeable chunk of his first scholarship cheque. Surina Queen had detailed papers, setting out her family line. 'Sue' and Paula became inseparable. My sister's love of dogs would continue for the rest of her life.

Beyond our family unit, life immediately outside the front door became our next circle of engagement. On our quiet road, there were children in most of the twelve houses. The games of chasing, football and rounders were uninterrupted by cars, except by parents travelling to and from work.

The footpath was ideal for hopscotch. We learned to avoid the road's three water grates when playing marbles. Haughian's, later Burke's shop, was below the first set of houses, close to the junction with Pearse Road, a mile from Sligo town. We lived at the top end, and beyond our house were green fields, leading to Cairns Hill. Most days, a farmer, Luke Oates, would come with his donkey and cart to fill a barrel of water from the tap, fitted by the local authority, opposite our front gate.

I'd ask him for a spin, and he kept replying, 'Tomorrow.'

Frustrated, one day I said to him, 'Luke, today is tomorrow.'

Using electricity poles to assist the climb over the pebble-dash wall of Markievicz Park was a challenge. It sometimes led to scraped knees or bleeding legs. But the risk brought reward. The grounds, including a spacious green pitch, were the local headquarters of the Gaelic Athletic Association (GAA).

The ban, preventing members of the GAA from playing soccer, was in force. If the caretaker, Bob Acheson, caught us playing the 'foreign game' on the pitch, he would expel us and maybe confiscate our ball. But soccer continued to be our game of choice.

Once, before dressing rooms were built in Markievicz Park, the Sligo county team togged out in our garage. Daddy had agreed to the request, and Mammy gave out to him about the mud left on the stairs by the footballers who washed in the bathroom.

We would climb over the park wall or slide past the stewards on the gates to watch the matches. Some of the most physical contests involved teams from different garda divisional areas and games involving the staff of psychiatric hospitals.

In 1966, to mark the fiftieth anniversary of the 1916 Rising, large numbers of men marched into Markievicz Park and assembled on the pitch. On another occasion, the grounds were used to stage an event involving the Hell Drivers, with men driving off ramps through circles of fire. We were commissioned to collect the rubbish left behind by spectators. The disappointing payment for our day's work was a choc ice from Burke's shop.

Spurs beating Burnley 3–1 in the 1962 FA Cup Final was my first memory of watching football on television in the front room of our neighbours, the McIntyres. From the penalty spot, Danny Blanchflower looked one way and shot the other, sending goalkeeper Adam Blacklaw the wrong way.

One Christmas, Malachy Hannaway, our neighbour from two doors down, loaned us a black-and-white set. Before packing his family into the car to visit relations over the border in Co. Armagh, he carried the television into our house. We prayed that their return would be delayed by snow.

Father Tommie O'Brien bought our first television from John Cunningham's shop in O'Connell Street. He and his sister, Nellie, were living in Texas. They were Daddy's first cousins, but they were more like his siblings because they spent a lot of childhood years together after their mother died.

Father Tommie worked in a parish in San Antonio. When he came home each summer, he moved into our living room, sleeping on the couch. Some mornings I'd watch him use shaving foam and afterwards splash Brut from a green bottle on his face. Most days he'd say Mass on a side altar of Sligo cathedral, and Mammy would have the table in the dining room set, with the good china and a toast rack, for his breakfast. He'd ask me if I ever heard the work 'feck' and smile. He'd play golf in Rosses Point, often with other priests back from America on holidays.

He took Michael, Mary and me on our first train journey, to Dublin. We stayed in Wynn's Hotel, and he brought us to *55 Days at Peking* in the Savoy Cinema on O'Connell Street.

Father Tommie bought a new walnut Bush record player and installed it in one of the alcoves in the sitting room. On Sundays, Mammy would have the doors open and the music from *South Pacific*, *The Sound of Music* and Jim Reeves mixed with the smell of chicken roasting in the oven.

Towards the end of his cattle-dealing days, Daddy bought a two-tone Triumph Pennant, BEI 568. It had been off the road for a number of years when he started working with Truline tyres. He brought it to the tyre depot, and it lay parked up outside for months. Children played inside it during the evenings. It smelled of cat pee. A mechanic, Jim Fallon, managed to get the engine running.

Father Tommie and a neighbour, Tom Keaveney, drove it, chugging over the Curlew Mountains, the 135-mile journey to Dublin. They returned with a replacement from the auctions, a green Cortina, CZH 990. It was the first working family car of better times. The previous owner had taken out the radio. I'd spend hours sitting in driver's seat, shining the seats and dashboard with a duster, admiring the long gear stick with the round black ball on top.

Like Tommie O'Brien, Daddy's brother, Father Eamonn, was working in America. He had been expelled from Nigeria during the Biafran war, and his superiors in the Holy Ghost Order sent him to Twin Cities, Minnesota, and then to San Francisco. He'd base himself in Dromahair with his sister, Mary Creed, and her family when he came home each summer. The two priests had the use of our green Cortina, and they bought its replacement, an oyster-grey Vauxhall Viva.

A number of summers later, Father Tommie had returned to work in America when Father Eamonn took responsibility for sourcing our next car. He brought Paula and me with him when he drove to McAndrew's garage in Ballina. A salesman failed to persuade him to invest in a Triumph Toledo.

As a treat, Father Eamonn brought us to lunch in the Downhill Hotel, and there were linen serviettes and heavy cutlery on our table. By then, Paula was able to read the menu, and she surprised us by ordering a dish unknown to us: curry. The waiter laid rice onto her plate. He then moved to begin supplementing it with the yellow-coloured contents of another dish. 'No thanks, I won't have that sauce stuff,' said Paula, and she proceeded to begin eating the rice. The next day was Father Eamonn's final one in Ireland before the end of his holidays. He traded in the used Viva at Dunleavy's garage. We had our first span-new car.

Father Tommie's sister, Nellie, made her first trip home in the 1960s. A decade before, after she qualified as a nurse in St Vincent's Hospital, my father paid her fare to America, something she never forgot. She married a hospital administrator in Dallas, Jack Finch. He was tall and lean with a tanned face and looked like one of the Kennedys. They had their young boy, Kevin, with them. Nellie was constantly looking for iced water. Lustre orange juice in a tin was sourced for her in a Sligo shop.

Nellie was comfortable in motion. When she and Jack set off on a week-long tour of Ireland, Father Eamonn was a willing driver, used to Irish roads. I was brought along as company for young Kevin. We slept top to tail in a single bed in Dublin's Russell Hotel while the adults saw Jack Cruise and Maureen Potter on stage in the Gaiety Theatre. Jack Finch gave me gambling money, and I backed a winning horse, Glad Rags, at the races in the Curragh and brought home a ten-shilling note.

Visitors regularly came to our home. Granny was a magnet for her Leitrim relations and neighbours, and they would call to see her when passing through Sligo. Two of her sisters, Lily and Nance, settled in America, and, after several decades, they came home for a holiday. Her deceased husband's relatives were more regular transatlantic visitors. For several summers they came home in bright-coloured clothes. They brought Granny with them in a hired car to the Leitrim roads of their childhood.

Granny's eldest son, Paddy, wrote to her each month, enclosing a cheque from the Westminster Bank. Every Christmas, he would send a pound each to the four of us. We persuaded ourselves he was manager of Wembley Stadium, not the person overseeing its network of confectionary kiosks. His reputation was enhanced when Granny went to visit him, his wife, Phyllis, and their three children. She returned with photographs of herself seated in the royal box during the Wembley Horse Show.

Nothing ruffled Granny. In her eighties, after an operation for gallstones, she crossed the Atlantic for the first time and was feted by a network of relations in New York and Buffalo. She came home with her long auburn hair shortened. One of her few conclusions about America was they have very comfortable cars.

My first school, Scoil Fatima, run by Mercy nuns, was a mile from Cairns Road, close to the town centre. In low-babies class, Sister Annette often made beginners welcome by gently lifting them onto the rocking horse in her room. To help me settle, at lunchtime Mary came from the nearby girls' school, and in the schoolyard we sat together, eating bread and jam and drinking milk from a glass bottle.

As six-year-olds walking home from school, in October 1962, we were listening out for bombs we feared would go off at three o'clock because of the Cuban Missile Crisis.

Father Gearty came to check on our preparations for Holy Communion and presented each of us with a holy picture. After the Christmas holidays, on Saturday mornings, Sister Veronica opened the school for special classes to prepare us for our future career as altar servers.

On the way home from her Latin instructions, we'd knock at Glynns' front door on Pearse Road and run away. The day my turn came to approach the house, I walked in the path carrying a large stone, determined to make a loud bang, but Mrs Glynn surprised us by opening the door. Even the heads peeping from behind the gate piers froze in shock. When we held a crisis meeting, after eleven o'clock Mass in St Anne's church the following morning, out of our parents' earshot, it was confirmed that Mrs Glynn had called to the homes nearest to her. An anxious Sunday passed without a ring on our door-bell. Fear dissolved after a new week began.

A pleasing adventure in second class was the time in the cast of an action song, 'The *Saucy Sue*'. Some of us were the crew of the vessel, dressed in sailor suits. A half-dozen classmates, wearing wigs and dresses, were the girls about to be left behind as the ship prepared to set sail. We entertained friends and relations at a packed variety concert. It was a first experience of the excitement generated by performance.

As eight-year-olds, we switched to St John's national school, where there was a five-year cycle, from third to seventh class. Brother Felim was the principal, and the staff included several lay teachers as well as other Marist brothers. The year I arrived, Michael had finished and moved to Summerhill College. The classes were bigger, sometimes with forty or more pupils, sitting in twos in lines of desks. Some of the brothers kept a bamboo cane in their black gowns, to impose discipline.

In the large concrete yard behind the school, boys played in groups until Brother Felim blew a whistle and the different classes assembled in orderly fashion.

In the mornings, Daddy often brought me in his van, and he'd let me out at the Weighbridge, a five-minute walk from the school. He'd rummage through his pockets for a thrupenny bit before driving off towards his workplace. I'd cross the road to Feehily's shop where they sold butter by the ounce and single cigarettes and buy boiled sweets – orange and lemon or menthol and eucalyptus.

Going home one afternoon, I saw a drunk man grab his wife by the hair and bang her head off the footpath. Sometimes, when walking home from school past tougher, stronger boys, it was difficult to not show fear.

At home, Mammy would sometimes spread a newspaper on the carpet and then slowly move a fine-comb through our hair, searching for nits. She would split the white eggs with her thumbnail and shout 'Look at him!' triumphantly at any sign of movement before tossing the paper's gatherings into the fire.

Teresa Gilligan, who had returned from England, was our teacher in fourth class. She introduced us to Shakespeare's *The Merchant of Venice* and cast me as Antonio. Our Irish play, produced by Brother Sebastian, made it to the All-Ireland finals at the Gate Theatre in Dublin, but I scuppered our chances. I played a pirate, but the mop I had for sweeping the ship's deck got caught in the offstage reel-to-reel tape recorder and strangled the sound effects of crashing waves.

Brother Einard recruited singers from fifth, sixth and seventh classes for his choir. Sometimes those who didn't impress during recruitment were dismissed as crows or clodhoppers. One year, we travelled in a bus to a competition, ninety miles away in Mullingar. After we won the first prize, Brother Einard and one of the teachers went to celebrate. A boy playing in the driving seat on the bus let off the handbrake, and it rolled into a chip van, setting it on fire. The local fire brigade arrived promptly and doused the flames. After our chastened chaperones resumed their supervisory duties, we headed for Sligo with the winning trophy.

Brother Einard collected old newspapers and magazines and stored them in a schoolyard shed. Once a year, a truck came from Athlone to collect the wastepaper, and he used the money received to subsidize the choir's activities. Some of the boys, helping in the shed, discovered a *Sunday Observer* magazine with a centre-page colour photo of a nude woman. The find, with vivid evidence of nipples, breasts and pubic hair, attracted a huge audience in the schoolyard until Brother Felim was alerted to the situation. As the inquisition got under way, boys were called from the classroom in twos until Val Harte took the rap for all the culprits. More than fifty years later we are still in his debt.

In seventh class, a school inspector, Mr Daly, arrived on a scheduled visit. He set us a task to write a composition and then left to lunch in the town centre with Brother Einard. When they returned, he awarded me first place for my work but in a sympathetic tone told me that a species other than a giant mackerel might have been a more appropriate rival for the joust I had colourfully described in my story. He presented me with a book about the film *In Search of the Castaways*, starring Hayley Mills.

We didn't know it at the time, but several of the teachers in St John's were sexually abusing some of the boys. In our innocence, we thought our school was a happy place. We had no idea of the evil and the suffering in our midst. Decades later a number of Brothers and lay teachers were brought before the courts and given prison sentences.

*

Michael and I shared a bedroom in Cairns Road. Outside the home, he'd help me with things I couldn't do, like climbing the electricity pole to access Markievicz Park. We would argue over our shared habit of wrapping the bedclothes around us while sleeping. Mammy solved that by replacing the double bed with two singles.

We both loved staying up late to watch soccer on TV, but our Sligo home was a long distance from the BBC transmission masts over the border in Northern Ireland. Sometimes on a Wednesday night, when the images described in Kenneth Wolstenholme's commentary were barely discernible, one of us would go outside in the dark and begin wiggling the television aerial.

'That's much better. Hold it like that. The picture is clear now.'

We took turns in the struggle with imperfection.

Until he left for university, the longest time we were apart was the summer he went to learn Irish in the Donegal Gaeltacht and the holidays I'd spent with our first cousins, the Creeds, in Dromahair, twelve miles away. James, John and Eamonn, were older than me. The bedrooms in their old house were huge and sometimes I shared one with them. We would talk ourselves to sleep. Encouraged by their mother, Mary, they minded me like a mascot. She was Daddy's sister and my godmother. Each visit, she gave me separate rations of spending money and saving money although I sometimes blurred the distinction.

I returned from one of those stays to seventh class in national school with my first pair of long trousers.

The Downeys ran the village post office. One of their sons, Jim, was the London editor of the *Irish Times*. Another son, Tony, decided to stage a summer touring production of George Bernard Shaw's *John Bull's Other Island* and gave me the role of Father Peter Keegan. I was thirteen at the time.

After Leaving Certificate, James, the oldest cousin, got a job in the Munster and Leinster Bank in Westport and bought a Morris Minor. Every weekend, he brought a carload to the Silver Slipper ballroom in Strandhill and always brought me. Way out of my depth, I'd head upstairs to the mineral bar and watch the dancers and the showbands from the safety of the balcony.

For one year, Michael and I were together in the same school. He was in his Leaving Cert year at Summerhill College when I began in September 1969. We had contrasting experiences. Corporal punishment featured regularly during his years. By the time I arrived it was being phased out.

Summerhill is part of the Catholic Church's network of diocesan colleges, staffed by priests as well as lay teachers. Traditionally it would provide a cohort of school leavers for training at the Catholic seminary in Maynooth. Around a quarter of Summerhill's 600 students were boarders, mainly drawn from the surrounding counties of Roscommon, Leitrim, Mayo and Donegal. They stayed in dormitories and regularly complained of being hungry. They needed permission from one of the priests to leave the school grounds.

From the late 1960s, a new school president, Father Tom Finnegan, introduced dramatic changes. He sought to put into practice the philosophy of a former student, Father Edward Flanagan, that there is no such thing as a bad boy. Father

Flanagan's compassionate principles in the orphanage and educational facilities he established in Nebraska were made famous in the 1938 Hollywood film *Boys Town*, starring Spencer Tracey and Mickey Rooney.

Father Finnegan's arrival in Summerhill coincided with a new government policy that guaranteed free access to second-level education. As a result, the intake of day students grew. Staff numbers increased to meet the demand, and many of the new recruits were in their first jobs. For the first time, several female teachers were hired. The use of the cane or the fist to impose discipline ceased to be the norm. Restrictions on boarders' movements beyond the campus were eased. It was chaotic at times in the beginning, but there was no going back.

Father Noel Durr was dean of discipline during our first year. He had been working in Texas and brought back tinted glasses that made it difficult to see his eyes. In his role as civics teacher, he produced another US purchase, a Sony cassette tape recorder with a microphone, and asked each of us to record a brief message about ourselves. Earlier times spent in national-school plays and choirs helped my delivery. In most cases it was the first time to hear a recording of our voice. He encouraged me to get involved in debating.

Michael helped with the scripts for some of those first debates. He used to talk to me about the music of language and encourage me to search for the appropriate words and phrases. One December, when we went shopping with our Christmas money to Enniskillen, he bought some of Edna O'Brien's books. We got the *Irish Independent* in Burke's shop every day. Michael was the one who introduced the *Sunday Times* and the *Sunday Observer* to the house, and he introduced me to the work of Brian Glanville and Hugh McIlvanney. When he and Mary left for university, I had no sense that a chapter of everyday closeness in our family life was ending and that my brother and sister would never fully return.

From university, Michael's influence on me continued. He brought home albums of Bob Dylan, Leonard Cohen, James Taylor and Gustav Mahler. He also had records of Auden, Douglas Dunn and Yeats reading their own work. He shared books by Erich Fromm and Gabriel Marcel. The monthly *Time* magazine Father Eamonn provided for us was supplemented by Michael's subscription to the *Honest Ulsterman*.

During my first weeks in Summerhill, I became involved in a scrap with a boarder from the class next door, Tommy Kelly from Belmullet. I was confident his need to wear thick glasses was a sign of weakness. He quickly had me pinned to the linoleum floor with no chance of tossing him. A small circle of spectators had gathered. He said, 'I'm stronger than you. I can keep you here. Or we can stop now.' I quietly conceded. Soon humiliation was replaced by relief. I had made a friend for life. In time he would be godfather to our first child and I would be best man at his wedding in Munich.

We were separated into classes by subjects. The O1s next door studied two continental languages, while we were the O2s, taking French and commerce. The O6s at the end of the corridor did woodwork and metalwork. Year after year, I'd sit beside Edmund Henry with Frankie Gallagher and Padraig Harding close by. Most days I'd travel to and from school with Austin Jennings. These adolescent years, the bridge between boyhood and manhood, were when lifelong friendships were forged.

The boarders were more open to bonding because they were away from home. Paul Brennan from the Donegal Gaeltacht was the most charismatic in our group. He had long black hair, and he could play the guitar and sing. Two of his sisters, Moya and Deirdre, were boarding in the Ursuline. When we were in third year, Paul, his brother, Ciaran, sister, Moya, and two uncles, Noel and Padraig, won the Letterkenny Folk Festival. They performed as Clannad, short for *clann as Dobhar* (the family from Dore). The prize was to record an album. I still have the autographed copy Paul gave me. One snowy day when we went to play a soccer match against a school in Milford, we met another of Paul's sisters. She had legs like matchsticks and piercing eyes. Later, as Enya, she became the best-selling Irish solo artist in history.

For a time, in the banter of our Summerhill exchanges, we had an unhealthy obsession with 'steamers'. Any gentle or effeminate trait was singled out and ridiculed. With my sharp tongue, I was a leading culprit. We wrongly equated homosexuality with sexual abuse.

Once, in second year, a priest spontaneously drifted into a monologue on sex education and warned us not to be experimenting with bottles or using rulers for measurement comparisons. At the end of his class, we opened the windows and the door for air.

Summerhill was an all-boys school. The Ursuline had boarders and day students, and, like the Mercy, it was girls only. The only local co-educational second-level schools were the Tech (Sligo Technical College) and the Grammar (Sligo Grammar School). We would walk the town on Saturdays, spotting. Autograph books were a handy way of gathering information. The Fav Boys and Fav Girls sections were always inspected. Keohanes had a bookshop in Castle Street. One Ursuline girl listed 'Leonard Keohane' on her Fav Singers page.

The Ritz Café, run by an Italian, Nuncio Caliendo, and his Leitrim-born wife, was a perfect meeting place. Its milky coffee and pineapple pastries were popular. I had my first date there with an Ursuline boarder, Cathy Kenny. I borrowed her tartan Bay City Rollers scarf but had to give it back when she broke it off.

Summerhill's new extension included what the president, Father Finnegan, called the gymnatorium – a mixture of a gymnasium and an auditorium. That's where I featured in two plays, both thrillers: Arnold Ridley's *The Ghost Train* and Agatha Christie's *And Then There Were None*. Excitement pumped through the veins during the performance before a packed hall.

I was a handy tarmac footballer, but, as David Pugh, the physical-education teacher, accurately remarked, 'It's a pity you can't do it on a pitch.' But, through a circuitous route, soccer would become a transformative force during those adolescent years. Father Michael Devine had introduced soccer to Summerhill, and his teams won a number of national titles.

During our Intermediate Certificate year, Father Cyril Haran took over the coaching role. When he was making plans to bring a group to the European Schools Championships in Lille, he invited me to become his assistant. It was the beginning of a charmed life as bagman, fundraiser, selector. Raising the money to fund excursions to France and, later, to England and Scotland was an adventure. It began with 'hops', then 'discos' and sometimes live bands, including Thin Lizzy.

The school caretakers, Ned Coogan and Patsy Flynn, acted as bouncers outside the gymnatorium. To prevent gangs from the town having fights on the dancefloor, belts, knuckledusters and other dangerous implements were deposited at the entrance. One night, the security measures failed when the chains used to weigh down the bottom seams of the heavy drapes were removed and used during a scrap.

For the European schools competition, we flew to France
and negotiated our way through the Paris underground to the
train for Lille. The Algerian team arrived to our shared dormitories in impressive tracksuits but hadn't changed from them at
the end of our week together. One night, the Dutch came home
late and drunk but deliberately made themselves vomit before
sleeping to avoid a hangover. We were on the Continent for the
first time, and we were learning about life.

More trips followed. Sean Fallon, the Sligo-born assistant
manager of Celtic, extended an invitation to a tournament in
Glasgow. The Norwich side included Kevin Bond, whose father,
John, managed several First Division clubs. Celtic's team had
two future Scottish internationals, Tommy Burns and George
McCluskey.

Another time, Father Haran hired a large minibus in
Liverpool, and, after our games there, he drove up to Scotland.
We stayed and cooked for ourselves in Maclay Hall, a University
of Glasgow residential facility, and visited Loch Lomond. It
was during a conversation, sitting alongside him as we drove
along unfamiliar roads, that Cyril Haran first encouraged me
to become a reporter. He had studied journalism in the United
States during a sabbatical. The priest in charge of career guidance, Father John Greene, provided information about the
journalism course at the College of Commerce in Dublin.

We were in Liverpool on one more football adventure in the
summer of 1974 when Father Haran agreed to phone Summerhill
for information about our Leaving Certificate results. The call
box in the long corridor near the first-year classrooms was
answered by an Irish teacher, Father Peadar Lavin. He quickly
relayed the important news. 'Cyril, I'm afraid some of the card
players were caught out.' There was a spontaneous whisper of

'Fuck' from several of our group, gathered around our football manager in the Feathers Hotel. We had paid a heavy price for time spent playing games of poker and 25 between classes. Many of us returned for a further year, to repeat the Leaving Certificate. We called ourselves the 'F Troop', not after the malfunctioning US Army cohort in the spoof western TV series but in acknowledgement of some of the 'F' grades received in the Honours Maths paper.

We had a good soccer team once more that year but came up short in our ambition to win the All-Ireland colleges competition. At the second attempt, experience, a reduction in card-playing and a new maths teacher, Austin O'Callaghan, led to a spectacular improvement in exam results.

There was a silence and an emptiness when we rose from the exam desks and walked out of the gymnatorium for a final time. A special phase of life was over.

2

The first job

That May morning in 1977, Sean Egan, the director of the College of Journalism, insisted that we were having a full breakfast in the dining carriage of the Dublin-to-Ballina train and that he was paying. He planned to use the trip west to visit his mother, a retired school principal, in Swinford, Co. Mayo. But his first task was to accompany me to the job in a start-up newspaper, the *Western Journal*.

I was leaving the course in Rathmines before the formal end of term. The two years there had passed in a heartbeat. During the first one, I shared a flat with my sister, Mary, on North Circular Road, close to where she taught on Stanhope Street. For the second one, I moved closer to Rathmines and stayed with two Summerhill pals, Padraig Harding and Frankie Gallagher, and a College of Journalism classmate, Maurice Gubbins. There were other tenants from Sligo in the house at 43 Raglan Road. We used to call it the Sligo Embassy.

At the station in Ballina, Sean hired a hackney car to bring us to our destination in Garden Street, less than a mile away. On first impressions, the headquarters of the new enterprise, the *Western Journal*, was underwhelming. It was in a rented three-storey building, squeezed between Mullens' newsagents and the bar of Ernie Caffrey, the chairman of the *Journal*'s board of directors. From the newsroom on the first floor there was a heavy smell of cooked food. As the preparations towards launch day built, John Healy was sleeping on the floor and cooking in the cramped premises.

Sean Egan spoke for a few minutes with the managing editor of the new venture, Jim Maguire, before shaking my hand and taking his leave. Maguire brought me into his small office and quickly provided an unexpected but convincing tutorial in realism. His main target market was Mayo, and the enemy was the *Western People* where he and Healy had once worked. Both men knew the readers and the territory. They anticipated a dogfight. Maguire saw the neighbouring county, Sligo, as a potential source of extra pickings. The local newspaper, the *Sligo Champion*, was an institution. Like the *Western People*, it had outdated printing technology and had done the same thing, profitably, for decades, not just years, with no pressure from competition.

Maguire explained how Healy, his partner, was a romantic. But, as managing editor, he was the person who had to balance the books and make the venture work. Money was tight, all the costings had been done, and, as always happens, extra expenses would arise. He had to be ruthless. His job was to make sure the ship didn't sink before it left the harbour. They had done their budgets and put a good team in place. The start-up plans did not include a job for me. Healy didn't have the authority to hire me. He was in charge, and he hadn't cleared it.

With the haymaker delivered, Maguire set about softening the impact. He would start me on lineage, as the paper's Sligo correspondent. I would be paid for every line of mine that made it to the paper. The more of my work that featured, the more I would be paid. If I proved there was a market for the *Journal* in Sligo, in time the situation could be reviewed.

Newspaper sales were important, but advertising was the key source of revenue. Each week's *Journal* would be brought to 'camera ready copy' stage in Ballina, and negatives of each page would then be sent for printing on the modern, web offset presses of the *Connacht Tribune* in Galway. The sale price of each paper would cover just the printing costs and the newsagent's cut. So advertising would be the only way to generate revenue each week.

Maguire brought me on a quick tour of the building. He introduced me to four people, seated in front of keyboards and screens. They were the linotype operators. They would convert the stories provided by reporters into material for the make-up room next door, where each page of the paper, with photographs, advertising, headlines and stories, would be assembled. At the end of the ground-floor corridor, in the darkroom, one of four Maguire children on the staff would operate the camera to convert the made-up pages into negatives, ready for dispatch to the printing works in Galway.

The *Journal* would hit the streets each Tuesday, ahead of the *Western People* (and the *Sligo Champion*) publication later in the week. Jim Maguire was conscious of the finances needed to survive and was determined to avoid overtime costs at the production end. If I could provide early copy each week, in a Sligoman's Diary format of short colour stories that would generate readers and advertising, he would take it. And a music column with record reviews? Maybe he'd take that too.

On the bus journey from Ballina to Sligo, I reflected on my situation. A relationship with a girlfriend, Mary Kerrigan, a year behind me in the School of Journalism, had ended at Easter.

Getting out of Dublin, putting my final exams on hold in order to take up John Healy's job offer seemed like the perfect escape. But, as Jim Maguire had made clear, there was no place on the starting team for me. I couldn't share details of the predicament with my family – finished prematurely at college in Dublin, no exams done, back home with no proper job. I was in a hole, and I would have to write my way out of it.

Political skulduggery provided the opportunity to make my debut in the first edition of the new newspaper. Fianna Fáil was holding a convention at Sligo Town Hall, to select two representatives to contest the general election. Ray MacSharry, already a TD (teachta dála) in the national parliament, Dáil Éireann, was a shoo-in. The contest for the second position was between a former TD and successful factory owner and builder, James Gallagher, and Mattie Brennan, a popular local councillor and farmer, hoping for his first run as a candidate.

Mattie seemed to have the numbers until late in the evening when Gallagher made a dramatic entrance. He brought the delegates from Leitrim into a room, closed the door and promised them that he would endeavour to start a factory with lots of good jobs in their area. His offer secured their swing votes, and Mattie was left crestfallen, pipped at the post. Healy liked my report about Mattie's shafting.

I began my new life working from our home. During our father's successful cattle-dealing days, we had a phone – Sligo 2554 – in our Cairns Road house. When that business ended and money dried up, the phone went. More than a decade later, the connection box for it was still on a wall inside the front door. I set about getting the phone service reinstalled. At the local office of the Department of Posts and Telegraphs, Louis MacSharry (Ray MacSharry's brother) explained that such a request would normally take several months to process. But, because of my work as a reporter, planning to provide stories for national newspapers as well as a new local one, the line might come faster. Until it arrived, the nearest available phone was the call box in Burke's shop at the end of the road.

Martin O'Dea had a full-time job with the Department of Agriculture. But photography was his passion. Both Maguire and Healy agreed that Martin, their fellow Mayo man, could be hired on a freelance basis to provide the *Journal* with pictures from the Sligo area. His work lit up the pages of our paper.

I was working day and night, supplying material all through the production week. It was great fun, working in the familiar surroundings of my home town. Newspaper sales and advertising were taking off. For Jim Maguire, it quickly made financial sense to end the lineage payment arrangement and give me a staff job.

In September, I went to him with a proposal. Sligo Rovers were the League of Ireland champions, and stories about them were an important feature of the paper's growing popularity. Rovers had qualified to meet the mighty Red Star Belgrade in the European Cup. If Maguire would sanction my travelling with the team behind the Iron Curtain to Yugoslavia, the support advertising and extra sales for our coverage could deliver a profit, not just cover the costs. The newspaper man and the business man in Maguire bought the logic.

The foreign trip clashed with the dates to sit the postponed final exams at the School of Journalism in Rathmines. It wasn't a contest. The decision made itself. As Sligo Rovers walked onto the Belgrade pitch, watched by 30,000 spectators, I was on their heels, with a camera borrowed from Martin O'Dea. The team posed for a photograph, and, afterwards, I became busy gathering images of individual players. As kick-off time approached, I looked for my route to the stands but discovered the bridge over the moat circling the entire pitch had been raised. There was no option but to take a place on the pitch, directly behind the goals, occupied by a nervous Sligo Rovers goalkeeper, Alan Paterson. A number of times during the first half he shouted to me, 'How long gone, how long left?'

Belgrade, led by the internationally renowned winger Dragan Džajić, were pressing for the breakthrough goal. Billy Sinclair, Sligo's Scottish-born manager, had decided to play himself as a sweeper and he was scampering around the defensive line, like a fireman stamping out flames. Half time came and the match was still scoreless. Fifteen minutes into the second half, Belgrade scored, and eventually two more goals followed.

The most memorable incident of the match involved Sligo's midfielder, Tony Fagan – 'Fago'. As a youngster on Cairns Road, I knew him as the messenger boy from Kilcawley's shop who'd take a break from his job delivering food orders to play a game of street football with us. He would put me in the makeshift goals between two jumpers and beat whatever collection of neighbours' children played against him. Afterwards he would sometimes give us a few biscuits from his consignment and resume his work.

On the rough surface of Sligo Showgrounds, Fago sometimes tried a drag-back, attempting to deceptively roll the ball with the studs of his boots, but invariably the effort failed. On the carpet-like pitch of the Red Star Belgrade stadium, he instinctively attempted the manoeuvre and left two defenders on their backsides. The crowd applauded in appreciation. Fagan put his foot on the ball and waved.

After the match, several of us found a Belgrade version of a nightclub. Tony Fagan was still in overdrive. He spotted the match referee and his officials relaxing in one of the dimly lit alcoves. The alcohol was very expensive and sold by the bottle. As we were preparing to leave, the waiter who had served our table became animated, and we left with the discussion incomplete. Outside on the payment, Fago pulled out a pen. 'He may have robbed us for the drink, but I have his biro,' he explained.

The *Western Journal* carried coverage of the Belgrade adventures over several pages for two weeks in a row. I came home with two rolls of pictures but forwarded the wrong one, with no action shots, for the first week's instalment. With a deadline looming, the Ballina colleagues used a very large photograph of a bare-chested centre half, Chris Rutherford, spreadeagled on a treatment table in the Belgrade dressing room before the match. The roll with the action shots was discovered in time for the second week's coverage.

*

Mobility was an important option for any rookie reporter. Soon I got a bank loan to purchase my first car, a blue Fiat 128. During the test drive, the salesman in Castlebar shifted nervously in the passenger seat when I built up speed. There was a throttle on the dashboard, and, when pulled, it moved the accelerator closer to the floor and the car raced forward.

It was a pre-fax era, and my means of sending photos and reports to Ballina was via the CIÉ (Córas Iompair Éireann) bus that travelled to it from Sligo each day. I would be ready at the top of Pearse Road, my material sealed into a brown envelope, and one of the drivers, Terence McTiernan or Vincie Philips, would stop his bus and collect the mail from me. Sometimes, when I'd miss the deadline, my young sister, Paula, would jump into the Fiat alongside me, and we'd tear out the road, pursuing the bus. Beyond Ballisodare, heading towards Dromore West, the route had several bumpy stretches, and we'd bounce along until we could overtake the bus and flag it down.

Healy had a bolt-hole on Achill Island in Co. Mayo – Rose Cottage, Dugort – but for most of the year he lived with his family in the Dublin suburb where he first interviewed me. He had a weekly 'Sounding Off' column in the *Irish Times*. His *Western Journal* column came to Ballina station on the Dublin train each week. Healy's friend, Douglas Gageby, was back editing the *Irish Times* for a second time. They had a strong bond and often chatted on the phone a number of times a day. During the time when Gageby was away from the paper, Healy felt isolated. 'It was like pissing into a bottomless well, kid. No feedback. It was as if you were standing over the urinal and you heard no sound coming back. In the end you wondered were you pissing at all.'

He monitored my work and gave regular encouragement.

'Watch the clock in the morning, kid. Forget about it at night.'

'Reporting isn't a job, it's a life. Enjoy it.'

He once called to my parents in Sligo and presented them with a copy of his book, *19 Acres*. It is a searingly honest account of his own kith and kin and their life on a small Co. Mayo farm. It is also the story of countless emigrant families and the realities of their struggles in the United States. He wrote inside the cover 'as a small token of appreciation for the gift of your son who will, one day, write a better book than this'.

One September night, on a road outside Ballyhaunis, memories returned of the car salesman's unease when I bought the blue Fiat 128. Coming home in the dark from the Lisdoonvarna Folk Festival, it shuddered to a halt. The full refund for the expired car and a bank loan financed a yellow Mazda 323, a demonstrator model, and I was mobile again.

The weekend before my first Christmas in the new job, I set off to Fermoy, Co. Cork, to visit Maurice Gubbins, a College of Journalism classmate who would later become the editor of the Cork *Evening Echo*. It was a bitterly cold night, and a 200-mile journey lay ahead, but the road south was bone dry. A tap had been left running along a descending stretch of road near the Black Bull pub between Birr and Roscrea, and the frozen water formed a stretch of solid ice. I saw it too late.

When I hit the brakes, the Mazda took off, bounced off the ditch and careered towards the opposite side of the road. In the distance, a car was approaching from the bottom of the hill, and I wondered, 'Am I going to kill those innocents?' A cassette of Electric Light Orchestra music, compiled by our advertising salesman, Seamie Monaghan, was playing as the vehicle turned over. The roof was now under my knees, and I could smell petrol. The geography of the car had changed, the engine was still running, and in panic I wondered, 'Is this how I'm going to die, looking for my bloody keys?' I managed to find them and switch off the ignition.

The occupants of the oncoming vehicle stopped and helped me after I emerged through the fractured glass of the passenger window. The roof of the Mazda was scrunched and the bonnet and sides damaged. The sympathetic helpers brought me to a Birr hotel where the Christmas gathering of the local Irish Farmers' Association branch was in full swing.

The following morning, in the snow, a local mechanic helped retrieve the Mazda from the ditch. Miraculously, the engine worked. Several Christmas shoppers scrutinized the black polythene in the window space and the Mazda's battered frame as I moved slowly through Athlone on the journey home. It was the drive of shame. In Castlebar, at his garage premises, *Journal* director Cathal Duffy consoled me that I was lucky to be alive and promised to have the car repaired in three weeks.

I hitched a lift to Sligo. In our Cairns Road dining room, two visitors, Mrs Neary and her husband, Tom, were having tea and Christmas cake with Mammy, Daddy and Granny by the fire. I told the story of my 'small tip' on an icy road in Offaly and how the car was left in Castlebar to be fixed.

Tom Neary looked at me. 'You were speeding,' he said. There was no appropriate answer. My expensive third-party insurance was of no use in the circumstances. On top of the bank loan taken out to buy the car, more borrowings would be required for the repair work. One brush with death later, I had become a member of the adult world, debts included.

*

In its first year, the paper made solid progress in Sligo. A local investor, Seamus Monaghan, an electrical contractor recently returned from the United States, put money into the venture. His cash injection funded the launch of a sister publication, the *Sligo Journal*. A second reporter, Jim Gray, was recruited from the *Sligo Champion*. Michael McGarry, a freelancer, became our GAA correspondent under the byline 'McGregor'. We had an office manager, Mary Hopper, and three other colleagues, Vincie Gallagher, Tony McMorrow and Kevin Flannery, selling ads and collecting accounts.

Photographs were proving a great success, and we sprinkled them throughout the paper each week. Ken Keane replaced Martin O'Dea, and on several evenings each week we would attend local functions and gather material. My job was to organize the individual groups for the photographer and then take the names of those featured. Writing by hand in pressurized circumstances was never a strong point. One morning, with a bus deadline looming, I was trying to decipher the details from a soggy notebook and type them into caption format. In one group, the name of one person was missing. So I put down the information at hand, left to right, the names of the posing group, as written on the notebook page. When it came to the final person, for whom I had no details, I typed what I saw: 'the baldy little man with the glasses'. I knew full well that by the time the CIÉ bus arrived in Ballina, I would have traced down some of the event organizers to resolve the identity question.

The envelope went to its destination. But I forgot about my unfinished business. That pressurized day, on the eve of publication, there was no proofreading or guardian angel on duty. That's why the front page of that week's edition of the *Journal* included the photograph and accompanying caption as I had sent it, including the line, 'the baldy little man with the glasses'.

One sunny morning in August 1979, a friend phoned the *Journal*'s Sligo office to say that a loud bang, maybe the sound of an explosion, had been heard near Mullaghmore. He wondered could it be connected to Lord Mountbatten. The paper's front page the following day had a seventy-two-point headline: 'Murder in the Sun'. Beneath it was a photograph from Mullaghmore harbour where the dead and dying were brought ashore. The bomb attack on *Shadow V*, the fishing boat used by the Mountbattens when they based themselves in Classiebawn

Castle each summer, was an international story. As well as killing seventy-nine-year-old Lord Mountbatten, the Irish Republican Army (IRA) also took the lives of eighty-three-year-old Baroness Brabourne, her fourteen-year-old grandson, Nicholas Knatchbull, and fifteen-year-old Paul Maxwell from Enniskillen who had a part-time job on the boat during his school holidays. The *Journal* was on the newsagents' shelves alongside the national dailies. It was a rare occasion when we operated to the same deadline to assemble an authoritative account of the same shocking incident.

Attempting to establish a new weekly provincial newspaper in recessionary times took its toll. The founding managing editor, Jim Maguire, departed and was quickly employed elsewhere. Liam Molloy, the Ballina-based news editor, stepped into the breach. He was an experienced and popular local journalist, a keen angler and a rugby referee. But, after less than a year, he moved to the RTÉ newsroom in Dublin. A letter dated 4 October 1979, from Donal O'Shea, the chief executive of the North Western Health Board, arrived through our postbox on 12 Cairns Road. It opened, 'I would like to extend my personal congratulations to you on your promotion to Editorship of the *Western Journal*.' The word was out. I was heading for the hot seat. I was twenty-three and about to become boss of an organization with more than thirty staff. Some were my contemporaries, but several were older than me, with families. I had no fear that the venture would fail. In keeping with Healy's advice to watch the clock in the morning and forget about it in the evening, I thought that if you worked harder than conventional routines, you would succeed. I loved work, a trait that remained in me throughout my career.

When I moved to Ballina, I found colleagues who shared the wish to keep the fragile venture between the ditches in uncertain times. Patricia Fox and Mary Burke ran the front office, including the telephone switchboard. Phonsie McDonnell, Laura McShane, Declan Maguire and Michael Hegarty were the typesetters. Martin Glacken was responsible for assembling the individual pages in the make-up room. Eamon Maguire took charge of preparing negatives for the printers in Galway. Brendan Maguire, Marie Jacobs and Maureen Howley were in the finance department. Michael O'Brien and Paddy Carr distributed the paper each week and collected accounts.

Anthony Hickey and two graduates from the College of Journalism, Eilís Ward and Bernie Ní Fhlatharta were the news reporters. Damien Sleator and Lorraine Cawley provided the photographs. Michael Judge wrote expertly about agriculture, and Michael Commins specialized in entertainment – particularly country and western music. Each Monday, as the paper was being put to bed, Michael invariably got a phone call from one of his best contacts, Louis Walsh, later the manager of Westlife, pushing one of his bands or projects.

Three people sold advertising – Pat Doherty, Joe Gunning and a character whose arrival in Ballina from Galway coincided with mine: Michael A. McGee. He preferred VSOP brandy when socializing. In some respects, his panache made him an imperfect fit for a west of Ireland town. But he suited our challenge and our predicament. Advertising revenue was essential for our survival, and sometimes, in our circumstances, it required action that bordered on alchemy.

Our rivals, the *Western People* in Ballina, the *Connacht Telegraph* in Castlebar, the *Mayo News* in Westport and the *Sligo Champion*, were all established provincial newspapers. Unlike our situation, they had a profit margin from newspaper sales, and they could rely on advertisers coming to them, ready to pay for a service. In a recession-hit environment, our new upstart publication had to constantly come up with suggestions that might woo advertising. Features on back-to-school, weddings, summer holidays, new business openings, festivals, Christmas shopping in the different towns and villages. Auctioneering advertising was hard to crack. The popularity of Michael Commins's columns helped with the sales pitch to dancehall and cinema operators. Healy and Maguire had an old friend, Michael Foy, at a senior level in the state-owned Irish Sugar Company. A substantial ad from that organization was a welcome staple in many a *Journal* advertising feature.

The target each week was to have the minimum possible number of unsold papers and the maximum acceptable volume of advertising. We knew that advertising revenue usually died during the opening weeks of the new year. Our team came up with an ingenious idea of a directory of local services, involving small display ads for the likes of painters, electricians and chimney cleaners, that would feature in the newspaper each week for a year with payment up front. The plan got us out of a financial hole in January, but it left us with a full, locked-off page of the paper for the rest of the year that would provide no further revenue.

Reality was revealing harsh truths on a daily basis. Our advertising team received commission based on their sales. But when their accounts colleagues went to collect payment from individual advertisers, they sometimes were told that the ad featured in the paper was significantly larger and more expensive than what was ordered.

Late one Monday night I was seated on a stool in Ballina's Oriana bar, doing the tot on the *Journal*'s revenue and outgoings and sharing my misgivings with a colleague. Michael Hogan, the owner of premises, overheard some of the tale of woe. 'Jaysus, if I had that amount of money coming in, I wouldn't be complaining,' he said.

When going for a sandwich at lunchtime, I was taking a route that avoided meeting the local bank manager who had oversight of the newspaper's affairs. I worried that he would soon be bouncing our wages cheques. I invited the four main directors to a meeting in Ballina and asked each of them to bring a chequebook. Chairman Ernie Caffrey and board members Cathal Duffy and Seamus Monaghan turned up for the lunch at the Downhill Hotel. John Healy had a prior engagement in Dublin. I explained the precarious state of our affairs and requested an injection of £5,000 each. Four cheques were written – Duffy chipped in for Healy and said it was the most expensive lunch of his life. The black hole was filled. For now.

Duffy and Healy were long-time friends. In fact, Healy's three most trusted sounding posts at that stage of his career as a national commentator were Duffy, his brother, Gerard, a postman in Charlestown, and Michael O'Malley, the proprietor of Keel post office on Achill Island. When shaping a column for the *Irish Times* or the *Journal*, he would often seek their views.

Ernie Caffrey, chairman of the board of directors, had a business premises next door and was a regular caller to the office. He believed in the project and was a great source of encouragement. He was a member of Fine Gael and was elected to the Senate (Seanad Éireann) and to Mayo County Council for a period in the late 1990s.

Cathal Duffy was a prominent supporter of the rival party, Fianna Fáil. He knew that when John Healy was building his reputation as a political journalist in the 1960s, he developed a relationship with a group of ambitious young Fianna Fáil

TDs. They included Donogh O'Malley, the reforming government minister who introduced free second-level education and died in 1968, aged forty-seven. Healy's friendship with another member of that group, Charles Haughey, dated back to that time.

Duffy and Healy were enthusiastic supporters of the proposed international airport near Knock shrine, the Marian pilgrimage centre in Mayo. When Jack Lynch retired as Taoiseach in December 1979 and Charles Haughey pipped George Colley to succeed him, Duffy and Healy were delighted because they thought the west of Ireland would benefit. In September 1980, Duffy was the main organizer behind the erection of a plaque in Castlebar, on the wall of the house where Taoiseach Haughey was born. The unveiling, in front of a large crowd and a pipe band, was done by the then Monsignor James Horan, the parish priest of Knock, who was the central figure in championing the airport project. Cathal Duffy became chairman of the airport board.

But before that he and John Healy had other dealings with Charlie Haughey. Early in 1980, having won the contest to succeed Jack Lynch as Taoiseach, Haughey was making decisions about his cabinet team. Healy made some discreet inquiries and discovered that Pádraig Flynn, a flamboyant TD elected in 1977, was not in line for promotion. Flynn, a schoolteacher by profession, leased the Sunflower Bar in Castlebar, and photographs of him, sometimes wearing a white suit, regularly appeared in Healy's Mayoman's Diary in the *Journal*, above the caption 'The Sunflower Kid'.

Duffy was crestfallen by the notion that Flynn would not get a job as minister. With Healy's guidance, Duffy drafted a confidential letter to the Taoiseach, making the case to appoint

Pádraig Flynn a minister of state. He said that 'whether it is realistic or not, the Fianna Fáil organization here expect Flynn to be nominated. If this should not happen there will undoubtedly be hurt and embarrassment which will, I believe, in the short term very seriously damage the structure and following of the party here.'

In relation to Pádraig Flynn, Duffy conceded, 'in his earlier days he was often accused of immaturity and flamboyance but he has now developed into a dedicated, painstaking, professional politician'. He concluded the lobbying letter saying, 'above all, he [Flynn] is prepared to learn. We would submit here that he is one of tomorrow's men and a cut and thrust capacity to provide service for his constituency but at the same time to lend a hand at the higher level in shaping and developing National Policy.'

When Charlie Haughey announced his selection in March 1980, Pádraig Flynn was named minister of state at the Department of Transport. He went home to Mayo in triumph, with his official driver, in, as he described it, 'a car with the star' (a Mercedes) and Duffy was heavily involved in the awaiting reception party. Before he died in 2009, Cathal Duffy sent me a copy of that lobbying letter delivered by hand to the Haughey residence at Abbeville, Kinsealy. Duffy went to his grave believing that Charlie McCreevy, another candidate for promotion who would later figure prominently in Fianna Fáil heaves, had been bumped off the minister of state list in 1980 to make room for Pádraig Flynn.

*

One episode that tested my relationship with Healy occurred when he accompanied the Gaelic football team from his native

Charlestown on a trip to the United States. He was the celebrity reporter, accompanying his former neighbours on their trip of a lifetime. He rang our Ballina office from Chicago one evening, insisting that I take details of his latest event of their travels. With the phone wedged between ear and shoulder, I began typing. My intention was to entrust the information to a type-setter downstairs, Michael Hegarty, who usually took charge of Healy's political columns and wasn't slow about making an occasional jaundiced observation.

Healy was describing how at a gala dinner the travelling party had good luck when Co. Mayo brothers, 'big in the construction business here, made a sizeable contribution to club funds'. Conscious that Hegarty, the typesetter, with a sharp eye for detail, would have a view on the anecdote, I added to the page '(more drinking money for the lads, Hegarty)', certain it would be deleted after Hegarty had his giggle or grunt.

The next day, the busiest one in the newspaper's weekly production cycle, Laura McShane, a wizard of a typesetter, was at work before her colleague Hegarty. She was so fast at her craft that her fingers could dance through material, free of needing to read or understand it. Once more, in our strained circumstances, there was no proofreader or guardian angel on duty.

The following day, Healy's account of the Charlestown GAA club tour appeared in the *Western Journal*, including details of the sizeable contribution and the '(more drinking money for the lads, Hegarty)' reference. After Healy's return, when we met and I began to apologize he smiled and put a swift end to my discomfort.

The two publications, the *Western Journal* and *Sligo Journal*, sought to establish a distinctive identity. Coverage of local courts, a staple of provincial newspapers, was not a priority. But featuring local notes from the different towns and villages could not be avoided. The providers received a nominal lineage payment, but, in all cases, the motivation was giving a voice to their community. A local national-school principal, Billy Horan, supplied the Ballinrobe notes. He had immaculate handwriting. Sometimes his young son, Liam, hand-delivered them to our office. Liam became an accomplished journalist.

The Ballaghaderreen notes were provided by a recently qualified secondary-school teacher, John O'Mahony, and his wife, Gerardine. On Monday afternoon, 7 July 1980, John O'Mahony called the *Journal* office in a state of shock. An armed gang had robbed the town's bank, and the members got involved in a gunfight with pursuing gardaí when their vehicles collided at a place called Shannon's Cross. Two officers were dead, John Morley and Henry Byrne, and one of the gang was seriously injured. As happened with the Mullaghmore bombing story, our front page the following day was dominated by a 72-point headline: 'Slaughter at Shannon's Cross'.

A friendship with the O'Mahonys was forged during those times. John went on to manage Mayo's GAA team to an All-Ireland final, Leitrim to their second Connacht championship title and Galway to two All-Ireland victories. I had a back-room role as his video analyst.

One Monday evening in August 1980, there was a brief lull in activity at our Ballina office before the push to put one more edition of the *Journal* to bed. My mother arrived over, unexpectedly, from Sligo. She was aware that RTÉ had advertised the job of north-west correspondent and that I had sent away for an application form. If I was to apply, the deadline was approaching, and she had the form with her. She waited while I filled it in and then took it for the post.

The following month we stopped, briefly, to say a prayer at the church in Edgeworthstown on the way to the first interview. In Dublin, one of those sitting across the table at RTÉ, Mike Burns, said, 'You had your sun in the eyes on your way up and it will be the same on the way home.' He was the boss of the radio news team. A native of Roscommon, he knew what it was like to travel to Dublin from the west and was keen to put me at ease. Before leaving the RTÉ campus, I passed another interview candidate, Pól Ó Gallchóir, already an able Raidió na Gaeltachta broadcaster, who would later become director general of TG4, the Irish-language broadcasting service. When I saw Pól, I concluded that the Edgeworthstown prayers would come up short.

When the letter of 2 October with the job offer from Donnybrook arrived, it sparked enormous joy but other emotions too. John Healy had been the first mentor, the one responsible for providing precarious, never-to-be-forgotten flying hours. Part of me felt I was letting him down, leaving the new provincial newspaper he had started. Many years later, an RTÉ newsroom stalwart, Barney Cavanagh, who quizzed me during that first recruitment interview, told me how Healy had urged them to hire me.

The last time we met, months before he died, was in Strasbourg in 1990. Charlie Haughey figured prominently in that conversation. Healy had a history of not holding back on his views in his columns. Some of his best journalism was from earlier in his career when he was fearless in describing central government's neglect of rural Ireland. He invented phrases and nicknames that became part of our language, such as 'the D4 set', a tag for the well-heeled, self-confident cohort from an area of south Dublin. His description of some in the Department of

Foreign Affairs as 'the hind tit of the British Foreign Service'
ruffled feathers. Every so often he would take a swipe at 'the
mandarins', 'the permanent government', his labels for the
senior figures in the civil service.

When he first moved to Dublin from Mayo, he only drank
milk when socializing. He was full of energy and fearless.
Making waves at national level, he was in his prime. Love of
his native place and his desire to help it probably influenced
his subconscious decision to drift 'inside the tent'. Maybe there
were other reasons too. But, in some respects, the changed status
lessened him because as an outsider he was an awesome force.

Douglas Gageby, the *Irish Times* editor, appreciated
Healy's talents. They were from different backgrounds, and
they provided each other with knowledge and insights that
added to their understanding. Aside from his access to the
boss, or maybe because of it, Healy didn't have many friends
or admirers in the *Irish Times* during the 1970s. His relationship with Charlie Haughey and his frequent references to him
rankled. Healy's views about the controversial Fianna Fáil
leader placed him in a minority position. His output became
predictably repetitive and marginally relevant. But every once
in a while, he would produce a belter of a column on issues
as diverse as the opportunities of afforestation, the Japanese
economic model or the potential of the European Union (EU).
His book, *19 Acres*, was published with the support of Kennys
Bookshop in Galway in 1978.

When writing *19 Acres*, Healy discovered he didn't have to
pay tax on his earnings from the book, thanks to legislation
introduced by Charlie Haughey. The years passed, and Healy
found himself faced with an income-tax bill, mainly related to
his work as a newspaper columnist. He approached Charlie

Haughey and wondered could a legitimate case be made for the material to qualify for tax-free status. He was given no succour.

In 1990, it was Ireland's turn to take over the six-month presidency of the EU. Given Healy's long interest in European affairs, Haughey saw him as an appropriate person for the temporary role of adviser on issues linked to the European Parliament. For Healy, it meant a trip to the plenary sessions of the parliament, in Strasbourg, one week per month for the six-month period. It didn't go down well with some of Healy's critics in 'the permanent government', particularly with elements of the Department of Foreign Affairs, who considered he was encroaching on their patch.

During what was our final meeting, Healy described in detail the combative episodes he had endured. 'I was shifted out of the office I had in Strasbourg, kid. In the end some feckers even took my bottled water. It was gone when I arrived.' He insisted I have a *dame blanche* for dessert, and the tears flowed down his cheeks as he spoke. But a smile returned as he began searching through his wallet. He pulled out a cheque, no longer of monetary value as it was marked 'paid'. But it mattered to Healy, because it was proof of his fee, legitimately earned for his work as an adviser. According to Healy, it was for an amount that corresponded to his outstanding income-tax bill for which no tax-free status could be entertained. Healy chuckling, 'Good old CJ' – that's my final memory of him.

3

The north-west years

Bunny Carr was the person who opened my eyes to the power of broadcasting. The lesson was delivered on the first floor of the Allied Irish Bank in Stephen Street, Sligo. In the 1970s, RTÉ had a rented office there and occasionally used it as a radio studio. Bunny was presenting a live mid-morning radio magazine programme during the summer months. RTÉ's keenness to fly a flag in the regions took him to Sligo.

The programme's running order included Bunny having a chat with Seamus Finn, the editor of the established local newspaper, the *Sligo Champion*, and me, as the representative of a new rival publication. Observing close-up the host purr through the gears that day was a revelation. As the presenter of the 1960s RTÉ television quiz show *Quicksilver*, with its famous phrase 'Stop the lights', Bunny was a presence from our childhood. He went on to start a public-relations and communications training company, Carr Communications.

Here he was, across the table from us, effortlessly steering a conversation that was heard by hundreds of thousands of ears. When the time came to conclude our contribution, Bunny thanked us on air, introduced a piece of music, and, after it kicked in, he wished us well as a researcher led us from the room.

Our two-year course at the Rathmines School of Journalism from 1975 to 1977 had focused on print journalism. We tracked the national newspapers. We devoured the details in the book *All the President's Men*, explaining how *Washington Post* journalists Bernstein and Woodward brought down the administration of US president Richard Nixon. When the sixteen students in our class sought summer placement work at the end of first year, none found a berth in broadcasting. Just one from the class ahead of us, Joe O'Brien, got work experience in RTÉ. At the time, Ireland didn't have a network of independent radio stations. RTÉ had a monopoly in the broadcasting space, and it didn't feature in our thinking. The brief brush with Bunny Carr planted the seed of a reporting path beyond newspapers.

RTÉ took a gamble hiring me as its north-west correspondent. I was twenty-four, with three years' experience in provincial newspapers. I hadn't worked as a reporter with RTÉ in Dublin or for a national newspaper. My pulse quickened when I walked through the front doors of RTÉ to begin my new working life in November 1980. That sense of excitement was still there every time I drove into the Donnybrook complex over the next four decades. The starting salary was £9,106 a year. After three years in a fragile, start-up local newspaper, where I sometimes had misgivings when signing the wages cheques, the fortnightly salary transfer from RTÉ to my bank account never lost its sense of the miraculous.

But the magic came from the work and the way of life it provided. The first formal training involved joining a programme for newly recruited production assistants. They included Moya Doherty, a future chairperson of RTÉ. Going home from work on a bus one evening I met another recent recruit, a continuity announcer, Eileen Dunne, who became one of RTÉ's most respected newscasters.

I spent periods observing how different units of the newsroom operated. Mike Burns, the head of radio, was keen to make me feel welcome in my new surroundings. He called me into his office and told several anecdotes about the entertaining nature of the trade. He unscrewed the mouthpiece from the phone on his desk and removed a fitting. He explained this was the voice box and that the crystals inside tended to get stuck together after regular exposure to damp breath. He bounced the fitting off the office carpet, several times, to loosen the crystals. This, he assured me, improved the functioning of the voice box.

Burns then went on to recall how, on a major story in rural Ireland, competing reporters had access to only one public phone booth. One of them discreetly removed the voice box from the phone and slipped it into his pocket. While the others went haring off to find a working facility elsewhere, he inserted the missing piece and made full use of his advantage.

After a number of weeks observing, I was asked to prepare a short voice report for the back end of a minor radio bulletin. My script would be based on information from a press release, using one of the ground rules of the craft: three words per second. Sound engineer Jack Butler remained patient through the dozens of failed efforts. He would press the record button, I would start talking, fluff, curse and panic. He'd stop, say 'Not to worry . . . after five', and we would start again. Following half an hour of failed attempts, an acceptable 45-second effort emerged and I made my broadcasting debut.

The next training module involved travelling beyond the RTÉ compound to observe experts at work in the field. The day I arrived in RTÉ's Galway studio, Jim Fahy was editing a programme for his *Looking West* radio series with producer Padraig Dolan. Jim was in love with the craft of storytelling. His warmth was disarming. Our lifelong friendship began during those days.

RTÉ's Belfast office was on the ninth floor of Fanum House, on Great Victoria Street. We had visited the city once, in childhood years, to visit Granny's sister, a Cross and Passion nun. But this was my first trip to Belfast as an adult. The northern editor, Jim Dougal, worked with five journalists: Poilín Ní Chiaráin, Michael Good, John Deering, Denis Murray and Cathal Mac Coille. The bureau had two camera crews, sound engineer Gerry McCann, office secretary Arlene Williamson and a driver-cum-fixer, Robbie Paterson. It was an impressive news operation, spending most of its time covering what were called 'the Troubles'. Jim Dougal had presence and management skills. Each morning, at a meeting in his office, the tasks were assigned. The BBC offices where film was processed was a five-minute walk away. The material was then cut at the office of a freelance editing company, Greendow, and brought back to the BBC for sending down the link to Dublin. Before my visit ended, Jim Dougal had a question for me about the divide between his turf and mine. He frowned but said nothing when I told him I understood that I would be expected to cover Derry in my role as north-west correspondent.

When the Christmas roster was being prepared at Donnybrook, I volunteered to come back early. My assignment on New Year's Eve was to attend the ceremonies at Christchurch Cathedral and to send back information to a copytaker over the phone. A reference to the event would be included in radio bulletins. I walked the streets, several times, observing the revellers and estimating the numbers. Maev-Ann Wren, a journalist from the *Irish Times*, was on the same marking. We met for the first time. At midnight, the bells rang, officially acknowledging new beginnings.

Letterkenny, Co. Donegal, was the designated base of my new working life. RTÉ's rented offices there included a radio studio with a mixing desk and two large reel-to-reel editing machines, overseen by Vincent Conlon and Jimmy Breslin. They also worked with the Irish-language radio service, Raidió na Gaeltachta, and maintained the network of RTÉ transmitters in the region.

I didn't realize it or couldn't succinctly articulate it at the time but soon into those years I learned a rule that remained unchanged over the next four decades. To succeed as a journalist in the field, one needs stories, resources and outlets. In the north-west, the stories were there to be mined. The challenge was to acquire the resources to gather them and then secure the outlets to share them.

Jimmy Eccles in Sligo and Joe McGarrigle in Donegal shot mute pictures, without sound, on a freelance basis. The lack of a full-time camera crew based in the region was a major disadvantage. Occasionally staff crews from Belfast or Galway or freelance crews could be borrowed, if the story justified it. Good fortune arrived in the shape of an RTÉ producer, John Blackman, who was keen to gather television stories from the north-west for a twice-weekly, half-hour magazine programme, *Ireland's Eye*. Blackman was an Australian producer who fell in love with Ireland after he came over from the BBC in London when RTÉ's second channel, RTÉ2, was being established. He became my teacher in the language and techniques of television. He would arrive with a team of colleagues, usually including a cameraman, assistant cameraman, sound recordist, electrician/ lighting engineer and production assistant.

Blackman taught me how images and sound are the spine of a television story and the reporter's script must enhance but not contradict or simply repeat the information provided by the pictures. Radio is different. It doesn't have the advantage of images to help convey information so that work must be done by the words used and how they are delivered. Blackman was caring in how he sought to relax me and to shed my self-conscious side.

Years later, I heard Seán Duignan say there is an element of acting in television and radio journalism. Down-the-line conversations, known as Q&As (questions and answers), were a standard radio technique when I joined RTÉ. But the television version, with a newscaster throwing questions at a journalist in the field, was rare. The standard format used to convey news was packaged reports. But, driven by satellite technology and improved links, that would change. I was well into the second half of my RTÉ career when the nervousness before live television appearances ceased. By then, live television as well as live radio contributions were almost a daily occurrence. The change coincided with me telling myself I was about to have a brief chat with my neighbours and it was vital to talk in terms they understood.

It misrepresents television to suggest it's a matter of 'It's not what you say but how you look'. But there is an element of truth in the phrase. Keen to not look tired or ill, I always sought to dress sharply, in a formal rather than casual way. My mother-in-law used to look out for how well-ironed my shirts were. Some of them came in Nordstrom boxes from my relation, Nellie O'Brien, in Dallas.

During those early months, I shared a rented house in Letterkenny and occasionally crossed the border to Derry, where RTÉ had a small, rarely used office, over the sweet shop of Sidney and Una Bradley on Great James' Street.

My gradual immersion in the new working environment ended dramatically during Easter 1981. On Easter Sunday afternoon, I played football on Rosses Point beach, where such a kickabout match takes place every Sunday of the year. That night, RTÉ carried reports of how two teenagers had been knocked down and killed by a British Army Land Rover during rioting in Derry and that confrontations were continuing. A quick phone call to the news desk confirmed I should be heading north.

More than four decades later, it is difficult to explain what was about to unfold. Our family home in Sligo was thirty miles from the Northern Ireland border. Derry was ninety miles away, Belfast 130. From the late 1960s, we read accounts of the Troubles, and we became familiar with the daily radio reports and television accounts of death, injury and turbulence. We remembered a summer when refugees from under-siege nationalist areas of Derry and Belfast were given temporary accommodation in the vacant dormitories of two local schools.

But I was utterly unprepared for the full-on, vivid tableau of mayhem I encountered a two-hour journey up the road that Easter Sunday night in Derry's Bogside. The smells, the sounds, the anger, the sights of burning vehicles and a British Army helicopter beaming down light from the night sky were like material from the film *Apocalypse Now*. Even though my home was less than two hours away, this was a completely different world. Two teenagers, eighteen-year-old Jim Brown and nineteen-year-old Gary English, died that weekend. They were run over by a speeding British Army armoured vehicle.

In Derry, as in Sligo, the sun shone that afternoon. The annual Easter Republican commemorations took place, and afterwards youths became involved in stone-throwing confrontations with the British Army. The squabbles that escalated into death took place in the nationalist area, below Derry's city walls, where nine years before British paratroopers had fatally injured thirteen civilians on what became known as Bloody Sunday.

Anger about the loss of life gathered momentum. The following morning, the requested RTÉ crew arrived from Belfast. Young men in balaclavas were hijacking cars and setting them alight in the Bogside. We followed a group through a maze of alleys and found them pouring petrol, from the tank of a stolen car, into a line of assembled bottles, each with a clump of rag intended for use as a wick. One of the masked gang had a revolver stuffed into his trousers. He pulled the weapon into his hand, pointed it at the lens of cameraman, Johnny Coughlan, and told him to 'Fuck away off.'

Further up toward the Creggan, young men in balaclavas were inspecting the barricade they had built and adding new debris to it. Pumping with adrenalin, with the innocence of a stranger, I asked several questions. This time no weapons or threats were produced. The barricade-builders told how the Brits were not welcome, there would be no peace until they left, and, in the meantime, the Brits would pick up the damages bill for destruction on the streets. I hastily recorded a voice track, and the crew sped off to Belfast where the material would be processed, edited and sent down a link to Dublin for the night's television bulletins.

A pale version of our work made it to air. The next day, the senior colleague who removed the graphic scenes with the petrol-bomb makers explained how they could have provided lessons to impressionable young viewers south of the border. I was also told why the interviews with the masked barricade teams didn't feature. They could well have been members of a proscribed organization. Transmission of their interview would have breached Section 31 of the Broadcasting Act.

Strife took hold of Northern Ireland that year. On 5 May, at the Maze prison near Lisburn, twenty-seven-year-old IRA member Bobby Sands died after sixty-six days on hunger strike. Nine more lives would end in the same way. Patsy O'Hara from Derry city was the fifth to die on 21 May. The tenth and final death – Michael Devine, an Irish National Liberation Army (INLA) member from Derry – occurred on 22 August.

I bought a small two-storey terraced house on Strand Road in Derry, beyond a Royal Ulster Constabulary (RUC) station, with a bookmaker's shop next door. Radio Foyle, the local service of BBC Northern Ireland, was around the corner. All of its staff were helpful to the rookie newcomer from over the border. One, Noel McCartney, and his wife, Jean, practically adopted me and regularly invited me to their home for Sunday lunch.

One night, McCartney agreed to come with me, touring the sprawl of nationalist housing estates on the outskirts of the city to check if the rioting had subsided. At a makeshift barricade in Carnhill, a man approached our car. Beyond the lowered window he produced a pistol and pointed it towards my head. He was proposing that we would drive by the Strand Road RUC station with him in the back seat. I stuttered that we were reporters and no journalist had ever been killed in the Troubles. He looked closely at us, twigged the southern accent and then recognized Noel McCartney. After a scowl, the gunman abandoned his drive-by shooting plan. As we drove back towards the city centre, McCartney admonished me for persuading him to come along on a foolish escapade. Minutes later, as I attempted to get out of the parked car, I couldn't find my legs. The adrenalin had run dry.

In theory, Derry was a city, but it sometimes seemed no more than a village. Anthony Mascarenhas discovered that. He was one of the dozens of international journalists who came to Derry during that raucous summer of 1981. He was working for the *Sunday Times*, and, a decade before, he gained world attention for exposing the brutal actions of Pakistan's military during the independence movement in Bangladesh. He told me what happened to him as he left the city cemetery in Derry's Creggan after the paramilitary funeral of a hunger-striker. The rain was pouring down. A young woman asked for a lift in what was his hired car. Despite a huge security operation in the city, there was no British Army or RUC checkpoint halting traffic at the bridge over the river Foyle.

Mascarenhas was heading towards the Everglades Hotel, where most of the visiting reporters were staying. On the far side of the bridge, as the woman took her leave from the stationary car, a handgun fell out of her bag. Mascarenhas quickly worked out that it was probably one of the weapons fired at the graveside by the masked colour party. His passenger heard his swear word as she walked off into the rain.

In those decades, government legislation prevented RTÉ from broadcasting interviews with Sinn Féin members or individuals linked to paramilitary organizations. But seeking information from the Sinn Féin office in Derry's Cable Street was part of the work routine. Most Sundays, I'd go to Mass in Irish at the Nazareth House church in Bishop Street, where the ceremony usually included the work of the Irish composer Seán Ó Riada. Mitchel McLaughlin, a regular Sinn Féin contact, was often among the congregation. Sometimes Martin McGuinness attended. He'd occasionally nod in recognition and always made a swift exit.

In Derry, especially on the west side of the river Foyle, nationalists were in the majority, and the conflict was between Republican paramilitaries, mainly the IRA, against the British Army and the RUC. The Unionist/Loyalist population was such a minority that the green-versus-orange dispute rarely surfaced. Belfast was entirely different. The opportunity to edit TV packages brought me there on a more regular basis. Driving through parts of it in a southern-registered car, particularly in darkness and speaking in a southern accent, left one feeling vulnerable.

Maev-Ann Wren, my friend from the bell-ringing at Christchurch Cathedral, was now working at the *Irish Times* office six floors below the RTÉ base in Fanum House. She was replacing Fionnuala O'Connor, who was on a sabbatical in the United States. Two of her senior *Irish Times* colleagues, Ed Moloney and Andy Pollock, were investigating allegations of organized child sexual abuse at the Kincora Boys' Home on the outskirts of the city. Maev-Ann was a Dubliner, not long out of University College Dublin (UCD). Even in what was an intimidating environment, she was fearless.

One dark Sunday night, she went to a service at the Martyrs Memorial Church of the Free Presbyterian Church on Belfast's Ravenhill Road. She was there to observe if the Revd Ian Paisley made any references to the Kincora controversy from the pulpit. She sat quietly among the congregation, with a small tape recorder hidden from view, to guarantee the accuracy of her record.

Work brought opportunities to witness close-up the unbearable cost of conflict. Eleven-year-old Stephen McConomy was playing with his friends on the street in Derry's Bogside on 16 April 1982. A British Army armoured vehicle was passing through the area. The soldiers manning it had the option of using what were officially called 'baton rounds' but what in reality were four-inch long, half-inch diameter plastic bullets to deter stone-throwers. One such bullet fired from inside the Saracen vehicle hit Stephen on the back of the head. He fell to the ground, bleeding, dressed in the suit that he wore when making his confirmation three weeks before. He was transferred from the local Altnagelvin hospital to the Royal Victoria in Belfast.

Three days after her son was struck by the plastic bullet, Marie McConomy gave permission to switch off his life-support machine. Stephen was her eldest boy. She had two other sons, Emmett and Mark, living with her in a local-authority flat in Dove Gardens. Several weeks after she buried her child, when Marie feared there would be no proper investigation into the circumstances of his death, she was considering starting a hunger strike to highlight her grievance. I visited her in her home and, before switching on the tape recorder to begin a radio interview, I queried the value of any such drastic action, given what the Bobby Sands-led hunger strike had delivered. She looked at me directly and said, 'Thomas, have a look in my fridge. There's not much difference being on hunger strike and being off it.'

As with Marie McConomy, interactions with Edward Daly, the Catholic bishop of Derry, made a lasting impression. He was the priest with the bloodstained handkerchief attempting to bring a fatally injured Jackie Duddy for medical attention while some members of the Parachute Regiment were still shooting on Bloody Sunday in 1971. Those images and the then Father Daly's testimony gained him international attention and probably guaranteed that for the rest of his life he would be bonded with Derry.

As the senior representative of the Catholic Church in the city, he regularly found himself in difficult situations. Banning paramilitary trappings inside church grounds brought him into conflict with Republicans. He never flinched from calling out what he saw as injustice or inappropriate behaviour by the state, including the RUC and the British Army.

On 6 December 1982, he was visiting parishes beyond Derry city when the Republican paramilitary organization, the INLA, placed a time bomb at the Droppin Well disco in Ballykelly. The explosion killed eleven British soldiers and six civilians and injured thirty people. The premises was targeted because it was frequently used by British Army personnel stationed at the nearby Shackleton Barracks. Five of the civilians killed were young women, and three of them were teenagers. The rescue services worked through the night. The last survivor was freed at 4 a.m., but almost a further seven hours passed before the last of the bodies was recovered from the rubble.

When I went to his home, beside St Eugene's Cathedral, to interview Bishop Daly, he began explaining how he heard the first details of the bombing. Suddenly, he began to tremble and started to cry. I switched off the tape recorder and gave him the time to weep.

Bishop Daly was the person who encouraged me to research the story of Billy Page and Thomas O'Hagan. They were two Derry teenagers convicted for their role in the murder of a British Army soldier. Private Michael Ryan was shot dead by a sniper as his vehicle patrolled through the streets of nationalist Derry on St Patrick's Day 1974. Because the pair were so young, they fitted into a special category of prisoners, those

who could be detained indefinitely at the secretary of state's
pleasure (SOSP), until the authorities thought it appropriate to
release them. Bishop Daly believed there were significant issues
around the circumstances of the teenagers' trial and conviction.
He also had concerns with the SOSP system.

Prompted by his views, I visited both young men in the Maze
prison. I also discovered that another person who had issues
with the SOSP policy was Peter Robinson, the Democratic
Unionist Party (DUP) politician usually seen by the side of
party leader Revd Ian Paisley. I met Peter Robinson for the first
time in Belfast and interviewed him. He seemed a cold fish, but
he was forthright in his views about the SOSP question. They
were a mirror image of those held by Bishop Daly.

I had no personal experience of hearing a British perspective about young life taken away by the Troubles, but that
was about to change. The next stage of my journey brought
me to St Marie's Cathedral in Sheffield, where the brother of
the murdered soldier worked as a Catholic priest. At the paro-
chial house, close to the Crucible Theatre where the World
Snooker Championship is played, he talked to me about his
loss. Father John Ryan's vocation would later take him to
South Africa. At their home in Leeds, I met Private Michael
Ryan's parents. His photo figured prominently in their living
room. They were still grieving him. His father was a retired
police officer, and the family had Irish roots.

Before I left, Mrs Ryan asked me to tell the parents of the
two teenagers convicted for their role in the killing of their son
that she bore them no ill will and that she hoped their sons
would soon get news of a prison release date. Back in Derry, I
passed on the message to the Page and O'Hagan families. Six
years later, I received a Christmas card from Mrs Page with

the message 'Billy got wed last May. He is working hard in the hospital. He is going to be a dad in April, all being well.'

December 1982 completed two years working with RTÉ. Instinct brought me home to the Sligo nest for the festive season. As he did every Christmas Day, the head of news, Wesley Boyd, phoned to say thanks for the year's work. The following night, the wonderful fiddler Ben Lennon and some of his family and friends were playing at a session in Rossinver, Co. Leitrim. That's where I had my first conversation with Ceara Roche.

She was up from Cork with her mother, Chris, visiting two of her sisters in Sligo. She was twenty-two, a dairy-science graduate from University College Cork (UCC), on a product-development course in Dublin. In between the tunes, we chatted, and she had a great sense of fun. She had brown eyes, and she was beautiful. One story she told was how she had spent her sixpence pocket money as a child. Quality mattered. Unlike her sisters, who filled up on gobstoppers and penny sweets, she would make a single purchase of an eight-square bar of Cadbury's Dairy Milk.

Passing Granny's half-open bedroom door at 3 a.m., I knew she would be awake, ready for a quick chat. 'I met a girl tonight, Granny. I think this might be the one,' I said.

The instant reply was delivered with a half smile. 'You daft eejit. That's not the first time you've said that to me.'

A second truth was that, many years before, in another part of Leitrim, my father and mother met for the first time at a St Stephen's night dance.

Like many trades, journalism can be more than a job. If embraced, it can shape a life. Early in January 1983, I was in Dublin, visiting Ceara, when the news broke that the Fianna Fáil Sligo–Leitrim TD Ray MacSharry was implicated in a controversy. It was alleged he had secretly recorded a conversation with a colleague, Martin O'Donoghue, while they were in government. Gerald Barry from the *This Week* radio programme decided I would have the best chance of getting an interview with the local TD and asked me to pursue it. Ceara agreed to come with me to Sligo on a Saturday morning, on the understanding that I would have her back by 8 p.m.

The bugging story was gathering momentum. Accounts of unorthodox activity had been discovered in departmental files and made public by the minister for justice in the new Fine Gael-led government, Michael Noonan. MacSharry's defence would be that his actions were to protect him from suggestions that he might be open to financial inducements. I called to his home a number of times and the interview was postponed. Eventually it was done – there were no significant revelations, but it was the voice of a central figure in a national story.

Heading towards Dublin after 10 p.m., the fuel needle in my Volkswagen Jetta was in the red zone. The filling stations on the outskirts of Sligo were all closed. But there was light from a small garage near Drumfin, where the owner was carrying out late-night emergency work on the vehicle of a friend. The diesel problem resolved, I resumed the journey with Ceara asleep in the front seat. I didn't know it, but her delayed return meant she was a 'no-show' for an 8 p.m. date.

On the last weekend in January, Ceara thumbed lifts from Dublin to Strabane and came the final leg of the journey to Derry by bus. It was her first time in the city. It was also the first time someone had made such efforts to visit me. Ceara accompanied me in the sleet to the march marking the tenth anniversary of the Bloody Sunday deaths. In February we watched Ireland play France in the Five Nations Championship. Ceara loves rugby, and it was a thrilling game. Ireland won 22–16, thanks to two tries by Corkman Moss Finn and four Ollie Campbell penalties.

We were squashed like sardines on the Lansdowne Road terraces, behind where Serge Blanco covered the back field for France, and in the heat and the excitement, Ceara felt faint. Three pals, Peter Smith, John Neary and Eddie O'Hehir, helped to get her beyond the crowds to the fresh air. In the euphoria of the weekend, Ceara and I talked for the first time about getting married. We could never figure out how the conversation started. It just happened.

That Easter Sunday, Sligo Rovers played Cobh Ramblers in the semi-final of the Football Association of Ireland (FAI) Cup. Daddy and two pals came on the long journey to Flower Lodge in Cork. Ceara and her mother were waiting for us outside her aunt's house, opposite the entrance to Flower Lodge stadium. After meeting Ceara's mother in the parked car, Daddy quietly said to me, 'She is a looker.'

Deep into injury time, Sligo's often-maligned striker, Mick Graham, rose like a salmon and headed the equalizing goal. Over the next fortnight, three further games between the sides took place before Sligo eventually saw off their brave opponents 3–2 in a packed Showgrounds. Sligo went on to win the cup final for the first time in the club's history. Ceara was with me on the terraces in the rain when Harry McLoughlin curled home the decisive score.

Journalism continued its work, influencing my future. RTÉ's Cork-based southern correspondent, Tom MacSweeney, was on annual leave that Easter, and I jumped at the request to cover for him. The diary markings included the annual conference of the secondary-school teachers' union, the Association of Secondary Teachers, Ireland; industrial relations issues at

Waterford Glass; and a preview of a Cobh Ramblers–Sligo Rovers match. It was my introduction to the Waterford-based RTÉ camera crew, Donal Wylde and Jim Wylde and the start of a friendship.

It was also the first time spent with Ceara's mother, Chris, at their home on the Douglas Road in Cork. She was very welcoming. Her husband, John, a GP, had died at the age of thirty-eight when he suffered a heart attack on a golf course. When Chris was widowed, she had four daughters, with Ceara, the youngest, only eleven months old. She went back to work, in the radiology department of a local hospital. She was the busy manager of a centre for the physically disabled (Lavanagh Centre) when I met her.

We were in Jacques Restaurant on Oliver Plunkett Street, queuing for lunch on a Saturday afternoon when I asked Chris about marrying her daughter. She went silent, smiled and decided she would sit down, break out and have a cigarette. All the preparations were in place for her second daughter, Yvonne, to get married in May, so she was against the notion of another wedding in late summer. But she gave her blessing to the idea of a day out in the autumn. She was a remarkable woman – I soon began calling her the Duchess of Douglas.

Ceara and I were married in Sligo on 21 October. Ceara's brother-in-law, Rory, took pleasure in telling the guests that the bride and groom had spent, at most, thirty days together during their courtship. Outside Ransboro church, Granny pulled me aside and presented me with her wedding ring. The reception was held at the Sancta Maria Hotel, Strandhill, owned by one of the great Sligo GAA players, Nace O'Dowd, and his wife, Bridgie. When Dr Joe Sorenson, a great friend of Ceara's mother, spotted the arrival of the mushy peas to accompany the generous helpings of roast beef, he whipped off his jacket, formalities were abandoned and he got set for a long evening.

Two months later, Ceara and I were sitting in the car outside Ballinamore garda station in Co. Leitrim. She had knitting needles with her as she was making a jumper. In that first phase of married life we were relative strangers, and we were determined to spend time together. It was day twenty-three of the search for the armed IRA gang that had kidnapped a supermarket executive, Don Tidey, near his Dublin home. The motive was to raise funds to finance their ongoing paramilitary campaign. I had reported on a number of inconclusive searches in border areas. There was no indication a breakthrough was imminent. Ceara came with me for what seemed like another day of monitoring work.

The RTÉ camera crew over from Galway, Colm O'Byrne and Des Byrne, was gathering pictures of the activities in fields beyond the town. We had a good view of the garda station when the unexpected flurry of activity started. Don Tidey had been found during a shoot-out. There were injuries. Maybe fatalities. I asked Ceara to run to the phone box nearby. When the operator put her through to RTÉ's news desk, she asked for the news editor, Eddie Liston, and told him that Don Tidey was free. In the meantime, I was searching for information about what had happened and a freelance cameraman, Paddy Ronaghan, was en route from Cavan to help.

Don Tidey was brought to the garda station in a nearby town, Ballyconnell. Paddy Ronaghan managed to get pictures of him. A garda trainee, Gary Sheehan, and an Irish Army soldier, Private Paddy Kelly, had been shot dead by the gang before they made their escape. My pleas for an interview, even one question, with Don Tidey were refused, but the most senior garda officer in the area agreed to talk. When I asked Chief Superintendent James McNally for his views about the IRA kidnappers, he said, 'They are a shower of desp— . . . desp— . . . desperadoes.' Afterwards, he told me he had been on the cusp of calling them 'desperate bastards' but found the unusual alternative at the last minute.

Before the night ended, two colleagues, Jim Fahy and Charlie Bird, arrived to supplement our team. But the IRA gang members had escaped from the area, and none of them was ever convicted and sentenced for the killings.

There was a technical flaw hampering RTÉ's coverage of that international news story. All the television material gathered in Co. Leitrim was driven, at speed, to Dublin. At RTÉ's headquarters, the film had to be processed and edited before it was ready for transmission. The BBC had switched formats from film to video. Its reporters and camera crew were able to drive to nearby Sligo and use RTÉ's new transmission network to instantly send the video images to London and Belfast. The BBC was able to provide a more up-to-date account of the story we broke.

In the weeks after the Don Tidey release in Co. Leitrim, RTÉ's news and current-affairs division began to roll out what was a revolutionary change. Its new electronic news-gathering policy meant video replaced film. Images could be viewed immediately after they were recorded. News reports could be edited and assembled at regional centres and dispatched via a network of links to Donnybrook for transmission. Because Sligo was one of the hubs in the transmission links chain, it became RTÉ's headquarters in the north-west. A crew, Tony Cournane and Tony Finnegan, were appointed to work with me. Two technicians, Gerry Murray and Jim Gartlan, were trained in television and radio editing, and Catherine McConville was hired as a researcher.

I was coming home, after three Derry-based years. The logic of RTÉ's northern editor Jim Dougal was irrefutable. It wouldn't be possible to provide authoritative coverage of Derry from a Sligo base, and the day-to-day responsibility for covering Derry reverted to his Belfast staff. My work beat would be Sligo, Leitrim, Donegal and two other border counties, Cavan and Monaghan. Ceara and my mother found a house for sale under Knocknarea mountain, near Strandhill. It was a mile from the church where we were married, and a new chapter of our lives was about to begin.

The opportunities provided by the electronic news-gathering strategy encouraged RTÉ to increase its presence in the regions. It now had correspondents in a number of centres – Tom MacSweeney in Cork, Michael Ryan in Waterford, Michael Walsh in Limerick, Jim Fahy in Galway – as well as the north-west and Belfast offices.

I found Donegal to be a fascinating county. Home for over 120,000 people, bordering Northern Ireland and the Atlantic Ocean, next stop America. It has that sense of a place apart and often feels every centimetre of disconnection from the administrative authorities in Dublin. Yet, throughout my years working in the region, Donegal kept producing individuals and stories that deserved to be part of the national conversation.

The port of Killybegs is the fulcrum of Ireland's fishing industry. Joey Murrin was a dynamic, authoritative representative of the sector. Joan McGinley, a fisherman's wife, started and ran the successful campaign to base a helicopter rescue service on the north-west coast. A hospital in Dungloe, run by a Mercy nun, Sister Mercedes O'Donnell, was the most inspirational example of community health-service delivery I saw in forty years of journalism.

Some stories from the beat couldn't be shared. Colm Browne was a Cavan-born plain-clothes detective who would often show up at crime scenes. One weekend, he phoned with a message to meet him in Smyth's pub, Butlersbridge, but to come without a camera crew. The intriguing request was too good to turn down, but choice became a problem at the arranged rendezvous point. Smyth's pub, on one side of the street, was full to overflowing at half eleven in the morning. 'Why is there such a crowd here?' I asked a busy man behind the bar.

'Oh, they are here for a wedding,' he replied. There was no sign of the detective among the wedding party.

Across the road, in another Smyth's pub, again there was barely standing room. 'Why are so many people here at this time of the morning?' I inquired.

'A funeral. They're coming from a funeral,' was the reply.

Eventually, I found Colm Browne, lodged in a corner. He introduced me to the man with him as the Daggler. Colm had a basket near his feet, and, after he picked it up, we headed out the front door. I followed my guide along miles of twisted roads until eventually we drove through an open gate into a field and over a hill. Hundreds of people, including many from over the border, were gathered below. I was asked to give my word of honour that there would be no reporting of the activity in the field: organized cockfighting. We found a vacant spot on the warm grass, and my host removed the makings of a picnic from the basket.

*

Five nights a week, immediately after RTÉ's six o'clock television news programme, Peter McNiff and Andrew Kelly provided a platform for regional material on a magazine programme, *Countrywide*. It was the ideal outlet for stories that required more time than the standard ninety seconds to maximum two minutes format that applied to news bulletin reports. Peter encouraged me to compile a long feature about the impact of emigration in the north-west. We filmed young men boarding buses for England and told of football clubs in rural areas that could no longer field a team. Years later, the images regularly featured in John O'Regan's popular series *Reeling in the Years*, based on the RTÉ archives.

Another long piece from the north-west used by *Countrywide* was the story of the Gillespie sisters, Ann and Eileen, who had served prison sentences after they were convicted for a role in the IRA bombings of Manchester. The sisters returned home to west Donegal after they served their sentences. (Ann would later marry Fianna Fáil politician Pat 'the Cope' Gallagher.) In their interview, they talked about their times in prison where the inmates included the Moors murderer Myra Hindley. They became emotional when they recalled not being given temporary release, on compassionate grounds, for a parent's funeral. They were both adamant that they were innocent of the charges for which they were convicted and said they were not members of the IRA. Before transmission, the Gillespie sisters feature was vetted by the head of television news, Rory O'Connor. He was a Kerryman, a qualified barrister as well as an experienced newspaper journalist before he moved to RTÉ. He was succinct in giving the piece his imprimatur: 'Jesus, it's very raw, but it's true. Put it out.'

The region where I worked formed a significant part of the border with Northern Ireland. Joe Mulholland, the head of current affairs in television, was a native of Co. Donegal. He was aware of the constraints that Section 31 of the Broadcasting Act placed on RTÉ. It prevented the broadcast of interviews with representatives of paramilitary organizations. But he was keen to know more about what was happening within organizations like the IRA. His curiosity increased after an incident close to where I lived. That prompted him to make contact with me and to ask that I discreetly try to find out more about what was going on.

Early on Sunday morning, 25 January 1986, the gardaí seized 140 guns and ammunition at three hideouts in the north-west. They were acting on information. It was the largest haul of IRA weapons since a trawler, the *Marita Ann*, was intercepted with seven tonnes of arms on board, off the coast of Kerry in 1984. That cache had been dispatched from Boston – it was linked to the notorious Irish-American gangster Whitey Bulger. One of those convicted for his role in the gunrunning operation, Martin Ferris, subsequently became a Kerry-based Sinn Féin TD. The weapons found in the north-west included Soviet-made Kalashnikov automatic rifles and East German guns. The green crates into which they were packed had markings linking them to the Libyan armed forces.

Seventy of the guns were discovered in Croghan, near Carrick-on-Shannon, and forty more were hidden near a house in rural Mullaghroe, on the Sligo–Roscommon border. The remainder were located in a shed, close to a neighbour's house, two miles from where we lived, near Strandhill. Members of special garda units dealing with subversive activity had been hiding in fields beside our home before they made their raids early that Sunday morning. That lunchtime, I interviewed the officer in charge of the Sligo–Leitrim division, Joe Wilson. (Three decades later, his grandson, Ruairí Ó Murchú, was nominated to successfully replace the party president, Gerry Adams, when he retired from his political roles, including Louth TD, in February 2020.)

On the Sunday morning before the gardaí moved in to seize the weapons, over the border in Derry city, a van pulled up at the address where Franko Hegarty lived with his partner and children. He was brought away by British security-forces personnel to England. In the days immediately after the successful garda operation, IRA suspicions fell on Franko Hegarty. He had an interest in greyhounds, and the hobby gave him cover to travel throughout the island. He spent several weeks protected by his minders in England, but he missed his family and his life in Ireland. Soon after he returned, he went to a prearranged meeting with the IRA. His body was subsequently found, dumped on a road along the Donegal–Derry border. His family, including his mother, claimed that Martin McGuinness, the most prominent Republican in Derry, had given assurances that Franko Hegarty would be safe if he returned. Martin McGuinness always denied those allegations. Joe Mulholland encouraged me to discreetly pursue my contacts with Republicans for information about the weapons discovered in the north-west. My efforts drew a blank.

It was almost two years before one possible reason for the wall of Republican silence emerged. In October 1987, off the coast of Brittany, the French authorities intercepted the *Eksund* vessel with 150 tonnes of weaponry on board. It included 1,000 AK-47 rifles, ten anti-aircraft machine guns, one million rounds of ammunition and one million mortar shells. The haul was the largest IRA shipment ever intercepted. It subsequently emerged that during the previous two years Libya's Colonel Mu'ammar Gaddafi had successfully dispatched several huge consignments of arms to the Provos and that the weapons found in the north-west were from that supply chain. Even though the gardaí seized material confirming a Libyan link in January 1986, the supply route went undetected and remained active until it was rumbled with the interception of the *Eksund* by the French naval authorities.

My contacts with Republicans stalled until a quiet Friday in August 1987. A knock on the dining-room window of our home interrupted our viewing of a late-night film. The caller had a Quinnsworth plastic bag under his jumper. He asked me to take it and to read the document inside. It was an official garda document marked 'confidential'. It set out some of the security arrangements for the visit of the British ambassador (Nicholas Fenn) and his wife from 9 to 12 August when they would be holidaying at the home of Mr Dermot Kinlan, SC, near Sneem, Co. Kerry. The document, according to my unexpected visitor, was evidence that the IRA was able to receive sensitive information from within the British–Irish security services. He left our home and tracked into the darkness.

After a sleepless night, I got up and began follow-up work. The document had come into my possession on foot of activity first commissioned by the head of current affairs, Joe Mulholland. He had been promoted to a different role in RTÉ, and Eugene Murray was his replacement. The vital element of the story was the document. I dispatched it, marked 'urgent', by train to Dublin for collection by RTÉ's current-affairs boss.

In August, the quiet holiday-news season, *Today Tonight*, the flagship programme, was reduced to one programme per week. I was asked to come to Dublin to be a studio guest, in order to give some background to my story. No details about the garda document leaked until RTÉ contacted the authorities, informed them about the material and sought a reaction. When

I arrived at the RTÉ studios, two hours before the scheduled programme time, I became the driver of a runaway train.

Foolishly, I hadn't worked through my line-management structure, the news division. Eugene Murray, the head of current affairs, wasn't on duty, but a senior producer, Paul Loughlin, was in charge. The legal position was that RTÉ had to be careful not to breach the Official Secrets Act so I had to reflect that caution in my comments. And, once the programme was over, two garda officers would be ready to interview me.

In the RTÉ make-up room, a second guest alongside me was having powder applied. It was the security correspondent of the *Irish Times*, Seán Flynn. In a later phase we would become close friends in Brussels. But during that first meeting he told me his garda and political sources were rubbishing the story, telling him the document didn't come from the IRA. ITN led its *News at 10* bulletin that night with an account of 'an embarrassing security breach'.

The days that followed were the bleakest period of my working life. The official version put out from government and garda sources was I hadn't received the confidential garda document from the IRA but it had come from some disgruntled leaker within the garda system who would be tracked down and identified. A garda investigation was under way. The culprit would be swiftly caught. I was advised to say nothing more until the investigation was completed.

There were many lows and landmines to be managed. The two senior garda officers who interviewed me did so on an informal basis, in a Rathmines pub immediately after the *Today Tonight* programme. In Sligo, a serving garda officer, a family friend, went to my relations and told how he had colleagues down from Dublin seeking information about me. He said he was disgusted by what was happening and recommended that I be advised to be careful in all conversations over the phone and to carry no sensitive material in the car.

As the reporting of the ongoing garda investigation continued, I received word that my Republican contacts were keen for a late-night meeting in the car park of Collooney train station. Were they worried I would reveal my sources? Were Ceara and I under threat? Should I turn up? In darkness, taking a route that allowed the opportunity to check if I was being followed, I drove to Collooney and waited in the empty station car park for over an hour. If someone was there, watching, they didn't show up.

On Saturday, 14 August, we drove to the wedding of two friends, Declan and Julie, in Dungarvan. Messages awaited us in Lawlor's Hotel from journalists, seeking a comment, as there were briefings suggesting the net was closing in. Two men, suspiciously like plain-clothes detectives, were sitting in the reception area. In Templemore, on the way home, I stopped the car because I thought my heart was going to burst. Every time I pass through the town since I remember the sense of vulnerability from that time.

On 27 August, RTÉ's security correspondent, Tom McCaughren, sent word that I should watch his output. His script that evening included the lines:

Sources close to the investigation dismiss recent newspaper reports that a person at Garda Headquarters in Dublin is to be charged shortly in connection with the leaking of the document. While it was known last week that they were concentrating on one particular department at headquarters, they say they still have not traced the source of the leak. Furthermore, the same sources now say it's doubtful if the gardaí will be able to bring the investigation to a successful conclusion.

Nevertheless, security sources are still maintaining, on the basis of their own intelligence information, that the IRA never got possession of the document, as reported on RTÉ's *Today Tonight* programme. At the same time, they acknowledge that RTÉ's north-west correspondent, Tommie Gorman, who originated the story, does have good contacts in the area. In the June issue of the *Magill* magazine, for example, he wrote an in-depth article on the release by the High Court of Donegal man, Patrick McIntyre, whose extradition to the North has been sought.

Tom McCaughren's broadcast was the sign that the dogs were being stood down.

Kevin Healy, a colleague in RTÉ, phoned on one of the worst days, offering encouragement. Mary Holland of the *Irish Times* was also kind. Kevin's close friend, Gerry Barry, was then the deputy editor of the *Sunday Tribune*, under Vincent Browne. The Sunday after the change signalled in Tom McCaughren's report, the *Tribune* carried an editorial under the heading 'RTÉ: Buckling under Pressure'. It stated that soon after the story broke the gardaí had released information suggesting that 'the document did not pass into the possession of the IRA, that the source of the leak within the garda was broadly identified, that even the motive of the person who leaked the document was known – upset over cuts in Garda overtime – and that a prosecution was imminent.' Later, the editorial said, 'It then transpired that the gardaí were not going to have anyone prosecuted in connection with the incident for they didn't know who was responsible for the leak. In fact they didn't have a clue about how the leak occurred and therefore Tommy Gorman's story – that it came from an IRA source – remained intact.'

One unfortunate consequence of that saga is that it influenced the retirement decision of a senior garda officer. Superintendent John Courtney was in charge of the south Donegal area, working out of Ballyshannon, in the mid-1980s. When our paths crossed, he was professional and fair. It was an honour to have his trust. His colleague and friend, Frank Hanlon, was in charge of the press office at Garda Headquarters, and the families holidayed together. He, too, was a thoroughly decent man. After he left the gardaí, John Courtney worked as a security consultant with one of the major banks. The Christmas card from John and Bridie, written with a fountain pen, arrived like clockwork. Many years later, at his home in Dublin, he told me how his affection for his job had been soured by the leaked-document investigation. I didn't ask why, and he didn't elaborate.

A month after the *Sunday Tribune* published that supportive editorial, Vincent Browne offered me the chance to edit *Magill* magazine. I met Vincent and his co-director, Gordon Colleary, in Dublin. They were fully committed to the project they had started a decade before. It was a significant presence in Irish journalism. They hoped to increase monthly sales to 25,000 copies. The proposed three-year contract was a tempting offer. After doubt set in, particularly the move to Dublin, I turned down the chance. But I will never forget how Vincent and Gerry Barry helped me when I was in trouble.

*

Sometimes, in discussions with Republicans during the mid-1980s, the possibility that the IRA might want to end its campaign and pursue its aims through politics was not ruled out. But vicious actions that crushed hope continued. On 8 November 1987, a no-warning IRA bomb exploded close to the war memorial in Enniskillen during Remembrance Day ceremonies, killing twelve people and injuring many more. In the first week of 1989, Harry Keyes travelled over the border from Fermanagh to bring his girlfriend, Anne Friel, to her home near Ballintra in Co. Donegal. He was a former member of the RUC Reserve. An IRA gang was waiting for him. They ordered the woman out of the car. A small pet collie was sitting on the back seat. The man was riddled with twenty-four bullets fired at point-blank range while the dog was let live. It bolted, yelping, into the adjoining fields. We filmed the lane where the killers made their escape.

*

On occasion, RTÉ found opportunities to use its regional resources in an imaginative way. The People in Need Telethon was a very useful initiative. It brought me into contact with one of the wealthiest women in the country, Margaret Heffernan, whose family owned the supermarket chain Dunnes Stores. She was on the board of the organization that aimed to raise funds for worthy causes, built around a television event, based on the Live Aid model. We set up a team of friends and contacts in voluntary organizations in the north-west to develop a programme of fundraising events. The promise that all monies raised in the region would be available for distribution locally was a powerful incentive.

The Industrial Development Authority gave us access to a newly built but unoccupied factory, beside the RTÉ office, to use as a regional studio during the live television show. An RTÉ colleague from Dublin, presenter Ciana Campbell, was assigned to help with our plans. John Sorohan, a senior RTÉ executive, came to inspect progress. He was from a small farm in Co. Leitrim, and his father and brothers became one of most reputable house-building firms in Dublin. He was energized by the conversion work under way at the makeshift studio.

In Dublin, Margaret Heffernan had Maria Mulcahy driving the project, day and night. Maria phoned to say that her boss was keen to visit our working group in the north-west. True to my Doubting Thomas instincts, I wondered about Mrs Heffernan's motives. Dunnes Stores had been involved in a long-running dispute with a group of its workers who sought to boycott South African products because of its government's history of apartheid policies. I wondered was Heffernan's involvement with the telethon charity an opportunity for positive public relations.

She arrived by helicopter to the grounds of the Sligo Park Hotel. I was waiting to collect her. She walked across the grass slowly because of her high heels. She was dressed in red. Her tan suggested she had been on holidays in a warm climate. We were due to meet some of our group in Donegal town, but I made an unscheduled pit stop. The house of my sister-in-law, Mary, was undergoing building work. I introduced my visitor, Margaret, and Mary invited us inside for brunch. We negotiated a way past the planks and bags of cement. Mary whipped up a fry in jig time. Sitting on a dusty chair, in her finery, Margaret asked Mary if she had any marmalade as she loved marmalade with a fry.

Up the road in Donegal town, my prejudices were further challenged. The committee members chatted with her and accepted
her as they found her. On the drive back to Sligo, I asked about
her deceased father, Ben Dunne, who built the Dunnes Stores
empire. It was so obvious that she was very close to him. She
welled up as she told me how he had been mugged on his way to
Mass towards the end of his life. My misgivings about Margaret
Heffernan were unfounded. The perfect end to the project
was the Saturday we gathered at Dorrian's Imperial Hotel in
Ballyshannon, Co. Donegal, and decided how to distribute the
north-west's share of the 1989 People in Need Telethon.

*

There were awkward markings, too. One of them was St
Patrick's Day. Coverage of the annual parades in the region
was an impossible challenge because of the number of centres
all expecting their activities to feature on the special RTÉ
programme allotted to the day's events. An RTÉ colleague,
Colm Connolly, kept a scorecard highlighting the festive clichés
used in our reports. After the 1989 parade, I wondered out loud
to Ceara if I was going to be juggling St Patrick's Day parades
coverage for the rest of my working life.

Before the summer ended, life took one more unexpected
turn. RTÉ advertised internally for a Brussels-based Europe
correspondent to replace Éamonn Lawlor. He was coming home
to anchor a new lunchtime television news bulletin, edited by
Dermot Mullane. Interested parties were invited to submit their
ideas. We didn't need time to discuss it. At the time we didn't
have children, and we were excited by what we thought might
be a one- or maximum two-year posting abroad. It was a long

shot, but the application was quickly dispatched. There was no trip to Dublin for vetting by an interview board. I never found out if others applied for the vacancy. Rory O'Connor, the head of television news, phoned out of the blue to offer me the job. I couldn't believe my good fortune.

4

Brussels

The two Aer Lingus Dublin–Brussels return flight tickets for Ceara and myself in September 1989 cost more than £600 each. We were booked into a hotel for a midweek reconnaissance trip and couldn't avail of the cheaper Apex fares that required a weekend stay. On the first afternoon, Éamonn Lawlor brought me for lunch to meet one of his friends, Liam Hourican. For most of the meal, I sat, tongue-tied, intimidated by the depth of their knowledge.

Hourican had been a respected presence on the airwaves during my teenage years. A former Summerhill College student, he was RTÉ's northern editor during the volatile early phase of the Troubles. He had television presence and authority, enhanced by his facility with language. He later crossed the divide to become government press secretary in a Fine Gael-led government. He moved from there to Brussels, where he had a management role, liaising with the European Commission offices in the member states.

That evening, Éamonn brought us to the village of Rixensart, half an hour outside Brussels. He introduced us to his wife, Marie, and their son, Edward. They guided us around the rented house we were about to inherit. Éamonn was looking forward to presenting RTÉ's new 1 p.m. television news programme. He took me into his confidence and said he hoped to remain in Ireland so my one-year posting might be extended. We flew home to prepare for the move, excited but with a sense of the scale of change ahead.

The first story I covered was an informal meeting of European Economic Community (EEC) foreign ministers, in the city of Chartres, as France had the six-month rotating presidency. Gerry Collins was the Irish representative. He had been the minister for justice two years before when I was in the eye of the storm over the leaked garda document. No formal truce was made, but a working relationship began that continued for years. Two Department of Foreign Affairs staff members, Declan Holmes and Michael Forbes, brought me to dinner. It was the first engagement with diplomats. The next scheduled work marking was a Monday meeting of EEC finance ministers in Luxembourg. I decided to drive there directly and learned a chastening lesson about the size of the new parish.

RTÉ's Brussels office was on the sixth floor of a privately owned building, the International Press Centre, directly opposite the European Commission headquarters, the Berlaymont. RTÉ's space was shared with the radio correspondent of ABC Australia, Lee Duffield. He operated on the other side of a set of glass partitions. John Palmer, the *Guardian*'s Brussels editor, was down the corridor. The BBC had a suite of offices near the lifts.

Duffield had some of the traits of James Bond. Prior to my arrival he had made several trips behind the Iron Curtain and was convinced that historic change was under way. He was an expert in packing a functional kitbag for his travels. It would include toilet paper, pencils, chocolate and chewing gum. He gave me a crash course on how to dispatch taped interviews and reports down a telephone line. He carried several screwdrivers and leads with, on one end, a mini-jack plug for the audio output of a tape recorder and, at the other end, what he explained were crocodile clips. He unscrewed the plastic cover on the telephone mouthpiece and showed where to attach the clips to two tiny horseshoe connections. If the phone was a moulded unit, and a penknife couldn't prise it open, the crocodile clips could be attached to the two relevant wires in the junction box, fitted to the wall. For years afterwards, in hotels and media centres across Europe, the Duffield method was used to file audio reports, leaving behind an international trail of damage.

Duffield encouraged me to travel with him to Greece for the November 1989 general elections where the eighty-year-old Socialist Party leader, Andreas Papandreou, was seeking a return to power. The Greeks, like the Irish, were significant beneficiaries and competitors for Brussels aid, and that, plus the Papandreou factor, made for an interesting story. The night that we arrived we went to a reception for visiting journalists, hosted by the Athens News Agency. Throughout the next day, there was no sign of my travelling companion, and I continued news-gathering, with the hired, several-member-strong Greek camera crew.

Unknown to me, many hundreds of miles west, tension was building in Germany. Thanks to his hasty exit from Athens, Lee Duffield was among the journalists in situ to report on the fall of the Berlin Wall. He felt bad for failing to alert me to the major story coming to the boil in Germany.

Six months later, it was my turn to feel ashamed. On the evening of 27 May 1990, two Australian tourists, twenty-eight-year-old Nick Spanos and twenty-four-year-old Stephen

Melrose, were shot dead by an IRA gang outside a restaurant in the Dutch town of Roermond, in front of their partners. The couples were based in London. They came over by ferry to the Netherlands on a holiday break. The killers presumed that the young men with neat haircuts and an English-registered car were off-duty British servicemen, stationed over the border in Germany. I had to phone Lee Duffield to tell him about the circumstances in which his two compatriots were killed.

Within weeks of the fall of the Berlin Wall, the opportunity arose to catch up on the unfolding end of the Cold War story. With John Downing of the *Irish Independent*, I set off from Brussels for Czechoslovakia where the protests were gathering momentum. At a border post, armed guards took several minutes to check our entry visas. The quality of the roads changed dramatically after we crossed from Germany. We picked up a young couple who were hitching a lift to the demonstrations in Prague, sixty miles away. Language was a problem, but they became animated when we showed them reports about their country in the international newspapers. We stopped in search of something to eat. In a dimly lit restaurant an elderly woman brought us bowls of what seemed like dumplings, floating in greasy liquid.

During the following days, half a million people packed into Wenceslas Square and the centre of Prague. Václav Havel and other dissident leaders were hosting meetings in some of the city's theatres. The receptionist in our small hotel came with us to one of the demonstrations. She cried as she described how her father had been a diplomat during the Prague Spring of 1968, but, because he supported Alexander Dubček, he was redeployed as a school cleaner when the Communists restored control. When we took the return road to Germany the following week, the border post where our visas had been checked was now completely abandoned. An administration had crumbled. We had witnessed, close-up, the Velvet Revolution.

*

On 1 January 1990, it was Ireland's turn to take charge of the six-month presidency of the EEC. Taoiseach Charles Haughey and his Fianna Fáil–Progressive Democrats coalition prepared for their time on centre stage. In population terms, after Luxembourg, Ireland was the smallest of the twelve member states. It was also one of the poorest. Along with Greece, Portugal and Spain, it was benefiting from access to a stream of wealth transfers from Brussels. After a press conference in Brussels, I said to Charlie Haughey how the latest statistics showed Ireland to be getting several times more than it was contributing to EEC coffers. He replied, 'That's good, and we need more.'

Hindsight provides a chance to revisit that six-month period of the Irish presidency. It wasn't understood at the time how much Europe was being reshaped and reorganized by circumstances beyond the control of even its most powerful countries. The case can be made that Haughey, his administration and his advisers found themselves in charge of a high-speed train, and their significant achievement was to prevent it from crashing. The provisions that facilitated German reunification were put in place during that period.

State papers, released for the first time in 2020, gave an account of Haughey's meeting with the European Commission president, Jacques Delors, at the start of Ireland's presidency that January. Notes taken by the government secretary, Dermot

Nally, recorded the Taoiseach hoping that in the future there could be cheap air travel, open borders, a single currency, energy interconnectors and fast ferries. Delors added to the list free movement of students and workers as part of a citizens' Europe. They agreed that the June summit in Dublin should have a statement on what Europe means to the ordinary citizen.

But more powerful priorities were building momentum, all of them linked to the collapse of the Berlin Wall and the disintegration of Cold War structures and certainties. After the momentous Berlin events in November 1989, a sticking-plaster administration was in nominal charge of East Germany. During what were their first free elections, in March 1990 voters dumped it and overwhelmingly backed a coalition that promised speedy reunification.

Britain's prime minister, Margaret Thatcher, was one of several European leaders who had reservations about a reunited Germany. She worried about the prospect of a more powerful country, and she also had concerns for the reformist leader of the Soviet Union, Mikhail Gorbachev. In a private meeting with Haughey in December 1989, she said, 'I am sorry for Gorbachev. He doesn't want German unity. Neither do I. Even as things are, Germany has a trade surplus with every country in the community.' Part of Thatcher's (unjustified) concern was that a united Germany might seek to gain additional territories it had lost after the Second World War. France, Italy and the Netherlands were among the other member states anxious about the pace and nature of dramatic change. The pragmatic French president, François Mitterrand, was among the first to conclude that reunification was inevitable.

Conscious of the pace of change in Germany, in April 1990, Ireland took the unusual step of calling an unscheduled early summit of EEC leaders. Haughey afterwards told me how the raw tensions about German reunification broke out for a time during that gathering. German Chancellor Helmut Kohl and Mitterrand came to that Dublin gathering with an agreed Franco-German position to accelerate progress towards deeper cooperation at EEC level. The French saw the proposal as a practical way to embed a reunited Germany in more powerful European structures.

When Margaret Thatcher reported to the Westminster parliament about that Dublin summit, the Labour opposition leader, Neil Kinnock, pointedly asked her had she been consulted in advance by Kohl and Mitterrand about their proposals. He said, 'Is it not plain that the prime minister has made herself merely a spectator, the lame duck of the Community, and she has only herself to blame?' In her reply, Mrs Thatcher told of her surprise and disappointment about the absence of consultation. She also said, 'The document that they put before the Council on political union talked a great deal about political union without any definition whatsoever.' Some of the first steps of Britain's Brexit journey were taken during those days.

Significantly, too, on Germany's future, Ireland took a fundamentally different view to its nearest neighbour, the UK. Haughey had made his position clear during Dáil questions on 13 December 1989 when he said, 'I have expressed a personal view that coming as we do from a country which is also divided, many of us would have sympathy with any wish of the people of the two German states for unification.' On 18 May, those two German states signed a treaty agreeing on monetary, economic and social union. The economy in the east was falling apart. Preparations were under way for the western German Deutschmark to replace the East German mark on 1 July. The 1:1 conversion rate was a political decision taken by Chancellor Kohl, despite opposition from significant voices in the Bundesbank. It was fixed that the formal reunification ceremonies would take place on 3 October.

By the time Ireland hosted its second summit of EEC leaders on 25 and 26 June, in practice it was a case of formally acknowledging what was under way in Germany. The venue was the refurbished facilities in Dublin Castle. A large international press corps arrived to report on the gathering. The Irish hosts were on a charm offensive. Each press member was presented with a side of smoked salmon and a bottle of Jameson whiskey. A huge media tent was erected to provide food and drink, including draught Guinness. The elaborate hospitality facilities would come in very useful when another unexpected story forced its way to the top of the running order.

After the formal discussions ended, Charles Haughey was in expansive mode, briefing a hand-picked number of foreign newspaper journalists about his views on the summit achievements. He looked up when I made my way into the room and asked, 'Gorman, what's up with you?' I advised that he turn on the television. It was fired up in time to discover that in Genoa, Packie Bonner had saved Daniel Timofte's penalty; David O'Leary then scored past the Romanian keeper, and Ireland were on their way to the World Cup quarter-final.

Haughey reassessed his priorities. He left the gathering and headed for the Dublin Castle courtyard where he danced a jig beside where Seán Duignan was in position to present the *Six One News*. The visitors in the media tent witnessed the first scenes of Ireland going buck mad. The reports from Dublin that night and the following day were about a country in party mode as well as the historic decisions about Germany formally adopted by European leaders. It was my good fortune that one

final chapter of Ireland's presidency required coverage. The
Taoiseach, a number of his ministers and the leaders of the
two main opposition parties, Fine Gael's Alan Dukes and Dick
Spring of Labour, set off for Rome on the government jet for
Ireland's World Cup quarter-final against Italy.

I sat beside travel agent Ray Treacy on a commercial flight
headed in the same direction. He told great stories during
the journey. The pick of them was Treacy's account of the
generosity of Johnny Giles. They had played together for
Ireland, West Brom and Shamrock Rovers. After Ray retired,
a business venture wasn't successful. Giles got wind of it
and phoned him. In the chit-chat, he asked how Ray's post-
football career was progressing, and no flare was raised. But
before he ended the call, Johnny Giles said he'd be putting a
blank cheque in the post and the money could be repaid when
circumstances suited.

The Italian government was due to take over the six-month
EEC presidency from Ireland. A formal pre-match dinner for
the two administrations was set up at a Renaissance-style
palace, the Villa Madama, close to the Olimpico stadium. The
Irish delegation had attended an afternoon reception at the
residence of ambassador Robin Fogarty. As the fleet of limou-
sines pulled into the dinner-venue car park, there was one extra
vehicle in the line. The occupants were the Loughney brothers,
Kevin and Brian, owners of the Kitty O'Shea's pubs in Dublin,
Paris and Brussels, and their friend, Kieran Corrigan. They
had managed to acquire T-shirts with an illustration of the
scene from Shakespeare's play *Julius Caesar* depicting Brutus
sticking the knife into Caesar. It fell to the Irish ambassador
to tell the uninvited visitors there was no place for them at
the dinner table. Before the Irish delegation left for the match,

Giulio Andreotti presented Charlie Haughey with a medal to mark the historic occasion.

Inside the Stadio Olimpico, we were given a special pitch-side position on the tartan perimeter to film 'colour' material, pictures of the seated Irish political leaders included. Our reserved location provided a perfect view of Roberto Donadoni's shot that swerved so viciously Packie Bonner could only parry the ball and Totò Schillaci then steered it into the net. We had a bird's-eye view of Mick McCarthy kicking the steps in anger, shouting, as he descended to the dressing room at half time. One nil was the final score, and Ireland's most successful World Cup campaign was over.

Charlie Haughey went to the team afterwards. Cameraman John Hall did his best in the steam and the sweat of the dressing room to film the suited politician among the tired, semi-dressed gladiators. Those images never made air, but recollections from the night remain lodged in the memory.

*

My initial transfer from Sligo to Brussels in 1989 was on a temporary basis. I had no idea how enthralled I would become. I had landed in Aladdin's cave. I have a colleague to thank for preventing the arrangement from coming to a premature end. Wesley Boyd retired as RTÉ's head of news in 1990, and Joe Mulholland replaced him. Andrew Kelly found a phone in a quiet corner of the newsroom to tip me off that the new boss was coming to visit me with the intention of delivering an end date for the posting.

On the day Joe Mulholland arrived in Belgium, we went for a long walk in the woods at Tervuren. Before he had a chance to deliver his unpalatable news, I took the initiative. We were loving our new life in Brussels. Ceara was working as a medical writer with the pharmaceutical company SmithKline Beecham, at its vaccines plant near our home. I then tried to explain my reasons for wanting to stay in the job and my version of the story I wanted to track and tell.

As I saw it, the farmers were the first to feel the benefits of Ireland's membership of what was then known as the common market. The relationship literally began from the ground up. For the first time, in the 1970s, they received guaranteed fair prices, thanks to the Common Agricultural Policy (CAP). Then different EEC aid packages, including social funds, regional development funds and structural funds, helped to transform the country's infrastructure. In every village and parish, there was a project with a plaque or a sign acknowledging the Brussels contribution. The removal of customs checks and tariffs between member states would make Ireland, with its young, educated, English-speaking workforce, an attractive location for US companies keen to do business within Europe's huge single market. In not just the European Court of Justice in Luxembourg but the Court of Human Rights in Strasbourg, decisions were being made that had a direct bearing on government policy in Ireland. The transformative influence was likely to continue and increase.

This was part of the assessment I shared with Joe Mulholland during our walk. I acknowledged that I couldn't hope to replicate the authority and gravitas of my predecessor, Éamonn Lawlor. I promised I would work around the clock to make European stories relevant and accessible for our Irish audience. To my eternal gratitude, Mulholland was a reluctant executioner.

A Belfast cameraman, Johnny Coughlan, once remarked that journalism is 90 per cent logistics. Looking under the bonnet of the Brussels institutions and learning how the many pieces interacted were the essential first steps in my new working environment. The European Commission Press Service provided a briefing at midday, Monday to Friday. An ID badge, issued to accredited journalists, was required to get past the dapper security personnel at the entrance to the Berlaymont building. Without it, no amount of 'soft soaping' would gain access to the press room below. It has hundreds of comfortable seats and is many times more impressive than the media facility at the White House in Washington.

Like daily Mass-goers, many of the regular attendees had their preferred places. The heavyweights were the print journalists, from the likes of *Frankfurter Allgemeine*, *Le Monde*, *El País*, the *Financial Times*, the *Guardian*, the *Wall Street Journal* and the news agencies – including Reuters, Agence France-Presse and the Press Association (PA). Television and radio personnel were from a lower division.

The Commission had a cuttings service. One of its senior officials, a good-humoured man, Neville Keary, was Irish. He was a brother-in-law of the Fine Gael politician Gemma Hussey. John Downing of the *Irish Independent* quickly nicknamed Neville 'the man with the golden scissors'. Each morning, Neville and his team would examine a selection of international newspapers, identify the important stories and circulate photocopies of the material among the Commission hierarchy.

French was the working language of the press room then. Jacques Delors, a Frenchman, was the Commission president. So too was the head of the spokespersons' service, Bruno Dethomas. It quickly became clear that, to survive, work would be needed to supplement my Inter Cert French and the linguistic shortcuts acquired during summer holidays on French campsites. Attached to the press room was a café, staffed by uniformed personnel, with a spacious circulation area. In practice, that was the souk, where, over coffees and beers, gossip was traded, stories were discussed and plans were made.

The Commission had day-to-day responsibility for proposing, advancing and monitoring EEC policy. The member states, through gatherings of its ministers, known as councils, and summits of its leaders, shaped and decided EEC policy. The most important ministerial councils – from an Irish perspective, foreign affairs, finance/economy (known as eco-fin) and agriculture – usually met once a month. For nine months of the year, those ministerial gatherings took place in Brussels. But, to share the gravy around, in April, June and October, they were held in Luxembourg.

The third major institution, the European Parliament, gave a democratic dimension to what often seemed like overloaded and bureaucratic Brussels structures. The parliament publicly debated important issues and developments. It had to be consulted about EEC policies, and it could seek to influence, shape and at times block them. Its approval was required when new commissioners were being appointed. Its powers have increased in the decades since. The EEC had twelve member states in 1990, and Ireland provided fifteen of the 520 Members of the European Parliament (MEPs). In 2021, the twenty-seven EU countries are served by 705 MEPs, thirteen of them Irish.

The parliament's headquarters were in Brussels, and its various committees met there. But, for one week every month, activities transferred over 400 kilometres south, to the French city of Strasbourg, and the public sessions, debated in the Hemicycle chamber, all took place there. The arrangement dated back to when the institutions were being established after the Second World War. Strasbourg, bordering Germany, a city that was caught up in past power struggles, seemed an appropriate site for a working example of reconciliation.

The MEPs always had a suitcase close by. A few occasionally slept in their Brussels or Strasbourg office. Most stayed in hotels or bought or rented an apartment. They'd try to go home on a Thursday night or early on Friday to spend at least one day per week in the constituency that elected them. Getting national publicity, unless it was an unwanted variety, was often a struggle, so many cultivated local and regional media. They received an allowance to encourage visits by supporters and constituents. As a bus full of excited Irish guests arrived, hungry after their journey, some MEPs would head towards the entrance to greet them and others would make a dash for the nearest lift.

Tiny Luxembourg, population 600,000, 200 kilometres south of Brussels, wasn't restricted to the revenue generated by meetings of EEC ministers for three months of each year. It was also the permanent home of the Court of Justice and the Court of Auditors. It was a sedate place, but its tax incentives attracted international investment, banking included. Dutch holidaymakers, heading to or back from the sun, often made a point of diverting through it for low-cost petrol and diesel.

The members of our small Irish press corps all arrived in Brussels at the same time. Seán Flynn for the *Irish Times*, John Downing from the *Irish Independent*, myself and, later, Katherine Butler, freelancing for the *Irish Press* and *Cork Examiner*. Size gave us an advantage over our colleagues from larger member states. Our small numbers meant we got regular access to the Irish Commissioner, visiting Irish ministers and the Taoiseach.

Each member state has what is called the permanent repre-sentation, liaising with the Brussels institutions and providing an on-the-ground government presence. The Irish operation is run by an ambassador and fellow Department of Foreign Affairs personnel. The permanent representation also includes public servants from departments such as finance, agriculture, environment and health, over from Dublin on three- to four-year attachments. A press officer from the Department of Foreign Affairs, based in Brussels, was our main day-to-day point of contact with the Irish government.

During their Brussels years, Éamonn Lawlor and his *Irish Times* colleague Colm Boland established a hotel, in the village of Remich, as their base camp when covering stories in Luxembourg. It was a slow 20-kilometre drive beyond the EEC institutions, but the hotel looked out on the Moselle river, and the owner, Lucien, was welcoming. It was there we reached what became known as our Remich Agreement. The main provision set out that when one was breaking a major story, colleagues would be given some advance warning so that when the inevitable reaction call came from a news desk, the answer could be, 'I was aware of that, and I'm on the case.' The arrangements applied to only high-grade stories, when, if blindsided, one might be in bother. On all other matters, free-market competitive principles applied. For the most part, the Remich Agreement held. There were exceptions – some because of circumstances and logistics; some for other reasons. But the awareness of not leaving a colleague exposed on a foreign field became a factor in what grew into lifelong friendships.

RTÉ had an arrangement to hire for major stories a freelance Polish cameraman, Andre Kasprzak. He, too, was based in the International Press Centre building. One day he wasn't with me in Luxembourg when an unexpected story broke. A Flemish cameraman and his wife, down from Brussels, came to the rescue. It was a miraculous bounce. Hans Deforce and Andrea Waeyenbergh had recently set up a media facilities company, Headline. They had purchased the latest Sony camera and editing equipment. Their business plan included developing a team of young, enthusiastic one-person and two-person crews. They were on the hunt for clients. They had bought a building in Brussels, with office space. A special part of their pitch included the proposal to provide researchers who would help journalists plan and work up their stories.

Back in Dublin, Fintan Ryan managed RTÉ's camera crews at home and abroad. He listened when I proposed RTÉ would leave the International Press Centre and move to Headline's building at 95 Avenue du Diamant. He noted the financial arrangements involved and the plan to put faith in new technology, one-man crewing and mobile editing in specially equipped vans. Fintan gave his blessing to the idea. RTÉ was Headline's first international client. Others would follow – public broadcasters from Denmark and then Sweden and Finland, TFI from France and, eventually, the BBC. The Headline building became a community where the residents shared and exchanged pictures and stories. Cristina Arigho, a Dubliner and the godchild of Peter Sutherland, became the Headline researcher who worked on most of the RTÉ projects until she was recruited by the European Commission. Thirty years later, when RTÉ's Europe editor, Tony Connelly, was leading the Brussels pack, breaking Brexit stories, Headline was his reliable facilities provider.

*

Every reporter understands the value of access to a key player in a major ongoing story. During my early years in Brussels, trying to find sea legs in a completely new environment, I was fortunate to know Ray MacSharry. My granny and his father were once neighbours in north Leitrim. He knew my grandfather and father from their cattle-dealing days. We were neighbours, from a town in the north-west of Ireland, in Brussels at the same time.

MacSharry had responsibility for the agriculture and rural-affairs portfolio. He oversaw the CAP, the EEC's biggest line of expenditure. He got the Brussels job for a number of reasons. He had been a minister for finance, he had a background in agriculture, and he had served as a Member of the European Parliament. Some thought he had accepted a poisoned chalice. On his watch, the first major reform of the CAP in its history was expected. The EEC's subsidies system would also be in the firing line during world trade negotiations. And farming organizations as well as member states were all lined up to protect their interests.

When MacSharry joined the Commission in January 1989, he was also volunteering for what John Healy once described as 'the danger of following a good act'. His Irish predecessor in Brussels was Peter Sutherland. The contrast between them was striking. Sutherland was born in Dublin, attended Gonzaga College and studied law at UCD. MacSharry left Summerhill College after Inter Cert and started in the cattle trade with his relations. Sutherland served as Ireland's attorney general and became the European Commission's youngest member, in charge of competition. In the role, tackling protectionism, he championed the removal of barriers in the airline, telecoms and energy sectors. He was suave with presence and confidence from his times in the Law Library and Lansdowne RFC.

Circumstances also shaped MacSharry. His default position became set for confrontation. He supported Charlie Haughey during the Fianna Fáil bloodletting. He resigned from the party's front bench over the bugging controversy, left domestic politics and won a Connacht–Ulster seat in the European Parliament. He returned from Brussels to become Mac the Knife, the expenditure-slashing minister for finance in recessionary times.

MacSharry's first significant outing on the world stage as commissioner came during the opening round of the world trade negotiations. At the time, the umbrella body was known as GATT, the General Agreement on Tariffs and Trade. Carla Hills was a lawyer given responsibility by President George Bush to lead the US team. Many international players were involved in the discussions, but the Americans and the Europeans were the heavyweights. The first showdown took place at a huge conference centre on the outskirts of Brussels, at Heysel, beside the Atomium monument, in December 1990. Carla Hills publicly called for the dismantling of the EEC's subsidies system that created wine lakes and butter mountains and distorted world markets. MacSharry advanced in the media scrum, flaying and just about stopping short of telling the Americans to f— off.

With negotiations suspended, the analysis began. The row over agriculture was identified as the obstacle preventing a wider deal on world trade. In the European Commission press room, the efforts began to find out more about the Irish bruiser MacSharry. The team around him – his cabinet members and support staff – was intensely loyal. But he had problems within the Commission and with some member-state governments.

Dutchman Frans Andriessen was a vice-president of the Commission, with the external relations and trade portfolio. Unlike the Irish newcomer, he had been a member of the

Commission since 1981. In the trade negotiations, he and MacSharry sometimes had different priorities.

The Commission president, Jacques Delors, had an excellent relationship with MacSharry's predecessor, Peter Sutherland. Their friendship continued after Sutherland left. Delors had a French take on agriculture, and it sometimes differed to MacSharry's Irish perspective. They both have a stubborn streak.

I once asked MacSharry to take a break from his busy schedule to do me a personal favour. Mike Burns, RTÉ's London editor, was retiring. Mike's long career in radio, followed by a phase in management, was bookended by several years spent in London. Among politicians of all shades in Westminster, he was admired for his ability to socialize long into the night, regaling company while meticulously gathering stories. Colleagues in Dublin were keen for a short farewell-and-good-luck MacSharry message for the Mike Burns retirement video.

The commissioner's secretaries, Jacinta Dolan and Theresa Renehan, found a small slot in his schedule to film the contribution. 'What sort of thing are you looking for?' MacSharry asked.

'Maybe you could talk about Mike's Roscommon roots and his work as a pioneer in broadcasting' was my suggestion. Anxious to get back to his day job, he looked directly into the camera and the recording began.

'Mike, it's Ray MacSharry here in Brussels. I want to wish you every happiness after your long career and all the great work you did. And fair play to you, you never forgot your west of Ireland roots. And, like myself, you were a pioneer and not afraid to show it.'

As he made that final remark, MacSharry looked to the white metal badge in his lapel, worn by members of Ireland's Pioneer Total Abstinence Association, who were committed to avoiding all consumption of alcohol. The misunderstanding had arrived into the world unexpectedly and deserved a life of its own. We left the Berlaymont and sent the video down the line to Dublin. At the retirement function in Ireland, MacSharry's deadly serious delivery, associating Burns with temperance, had some of the audience convinced that Mac the Knife really was a comedian at heart.

In May 1992, MacSharry brokered an agreement in Brussels with agriculture ministers from the member states on the reform of the CAP. After the deal was struck, he walked with his staff from the Charlemagne building to celebrate at Kitty O'Shea's pub. MacSharry, the pioneer, ordered what he called 'American champagne': Coca-Cola. With a strengthened hand from successful EEC negotiations, he turned his attention to the deadlocked world trade negotiations, where agriculture remained the stumbling block. Three days of negotiations with the US representative, Ed Madigan, in Chicago were arranged for November. It was major international news. The discussions were held in a local hotel. MacSharry was staying there. I had a room on the same floor, and several times during a break in the talks, he briefed me, on an off-the-record basis. It couldn't be any better – I had direct access to accurate information on a running story.

The biggest issue he encountered wasn't the stance of the Americans but the pressure coming from Brussels, particularly the president of the European Commission, Jacques Delors. French presidential elections were scheduled for the following year. Given the strength of its farming sector, agriculture was set to be an issue during the campaign. In transatlantic contacts, Delors accused MacSharry of going beyond his brief in his attempts to agree terms with the Americans. The discussions broke down. MacSharry headed back across the Atlantic with the public perception that he had been undermined in his role.

A flurry of activity followed. Jacques Delors was the person who faced the most heat in Brussels. The agriculture row with the Americans was blocking progress on a new world trade agreement. The stakes were rising in the poker game. Three weeks after the Chicago stalemate, with his mandate confirmed, MacSharry returned to the table with Ed Madigan. This time, the venue was Blair House, immediately opposite the White House in Washington. After the final details were nailed down and agreed, MacSharry emerged to a media scrum. He was rushing for a flight to Brussels. His brief, impromptu news conference took place in the exact spot where Taoiseach Leo Varadkar would make one of the most important statements of his career, about the COVID-19 pandemic, in March 2019. I squeezed through a gap among the security team as the EU agriculture commissioner moved towards his waiting limousine. In his hand he had a single page. He gave it to me. It had uneven handwriting, similar to what I'd seen used in my father's docket books that he used at cattle fairs. They were the main details of what became known as the Blair House Agreement, a landmark deal between the EU and the United States on farm subsidies.

*

'The chaps' was the nickname we gave to our British colleagues in the Brussels press corps. Most of them were indeed chaps. They recognized that MacSharry's role in international trade negotiations and CAP reform made him a significant player. His scraps with some of his fellow commissioners, member-state governments, the Americans and even farming organizations added to his news value. The access our small Irish press corps had to the agriculture commissioner made us 'persons of interest' to the chaps. But as well as our usefulness, there were other reasons why the chemistry worked. We spoke the same language, and we had so many shared traits and history.

Brussels was the first place where I began to spend time with some of the next-door neighbours. As happened at many levels after Ireland and the UK joined the European Community in 1973, we got on well together. I became pals with a number of the BBC staff in their well-resourced bureau. We often swapped material, and, out of professional pride and historical baggage, I was always keen to give as much as I received. Its journalists included Jonathan Charles, James Robbins and Graham Leach. Bethan Kilfoil, who worked for BBC Wales, later married John Downing of the *Irish Independent* and became a programme editor in RTÉ's Dublin newsroom. Louise Adamson and Kevin Bakhurst were two helpful news producers; Kevin later served as RTÉ's head of news from 2012 to 2016.

At the time, the *Financial Times* was an established force in Brussels. Lionel Barber (later its managing editor) was its senior person, good at networking. David Gardner was the better writer. He actually got on with MacSharry, a fellow smoker. John Palmer of the *Guardian* was one of the press-room heavyweights, known and trusted from Jacques Delors down. He was brought up in London, but his mother was from Tipperary. He had once taken leave of absence to work for Ken Livingstone on the Greater London Council. At the important news conferences, Palmer was one of the first called upon, and he would begin with the line, 'Two questions if I may . . .'

Like Palmer, Geoff Meade of the PA was an institution. When significant statements were being issued, the PA had to be included, and Geoff also wrote a witty weekly column in the Brussels magazine for expats, the *Bulletin*. Freelancer John Fraser looked after a number of the British tabloids. George Brock worked for *The Times*. Sarah Helm (who later married Tony Blair's chief of staff, Jonathan Powell) was the correspondent of the *Independent*. A twenty-four-year-old Boris Johnson, son of a Commission official, arrived from London in 1989 to represent the *Daily Telegraph*. The *Guardian*'s John Palmer, in a fit of temper one evening, rightly predicted 'that b— Boris Johnson' would one day become the British prime minister.

The rise of Boris was directly linked to the turbulent fortunes of the British Conservative Party and the growth of Euroscepticism. He had a huge influence on both. One significant episode was the evening in November 1990 when Margaret Thatcher overcame Michael Heseltine's challenge to her leadership in a House of Commons vote. She survived it but didn't secure the 15 per cent victory margin to prevent a second contest so, wounded and embarrassed, after some days' reflection, she resigned.

Ironically, as the Westminster votes were counted, Thatcher was in France, attending a function of European leaders to mark the first anniversary of the fall of the Berlin Wall and the German reunification it prompted. That evening, I was reporting on the event in Paris. I booked into the expensive Hotel Concorde La Fayette as it had access to the BBC's live news coverage. As I made tracks to monitor what was happening in the House of Commons, in the hotel lift an elegant woman asked if a blanket was required for my cold bedroom. It seemed a daft question, and the offer was declined. I had switched on the television before I realized I had been propositioned by a high-class escort.

The BBC pictures showed Mrs Thatcher emerging from the British embassy and almost tripping across journalist John Sergeant. The emotion in her voice suggested the Iron Lady knew her eleven-year term in Downing Street was coming to an end. Within Britain's Conservative Party, the pro-Europeans had defeated Thatcher's Eurosceptic faction. But the victory margin was far from decisive.

In Brussels, Boris Johnson became the go-to person for the Eurosceptics. He was energized by his new importance and notoriety. Like many in our trade, he wasn't a good timekeeper. Unlike some of 'the chaps', his knowledge of the intricate mechanisms of EEC institutions was very limited. Slumped into his seat in the Commission press room, he sometimes gave the impression of not wanting to be there. But when he bowled in a question, it usually had edge and was built around the theme of Brussels seeking to create a super-state at the expense of the sovereignty of its members, the UK included.

The end of the Cold War and the likelihood that eastern European counties would seek to join the Brussels club set the EEC thinking. It decided it should deepen as well as widen. In practical terms, that meant moving towards a common currency, a more coordinated approach to foreign policy and more decision-making on a majority rather than unanimity basis. All anathema to British Eurosceptics. And easy pickings for Boris.

Kitty O'Shea's, opposite the Berlaymont, was the favoured pub of the Irish journalists. The British press pack used The Old Hack close by, managed by a former freelance colleague. Calls from their news desks in London querying the latest front-page splash by Boris about a Brussels power grab became the bane of their lives. Reaction to the Boris claims would carry through to the Commission press briefing the following day. The denials were rarely 100 per cent airtight so the *Telegraph* story would get international traction.

Although his British colleagues in Brussels often cursed Boris, they never ostracized him. His wife, Marina Wheeler, a lawyer, was liked. Her sister, Sharon, worked as a BBC journalist in Brussels and later became a press officer at the European Investment Bank. Their father, Charles Wheeler, was a respected BBC Washington correspondent.

The glint in his eye and his half smile gave Boris a like-ability factor. He rarely gave the impression of being 100 per cent serious. But, as a communicator, he had a special gift for crafting headline stories that were almost true.

John Major, Margaret Thatcher's successor, began attending summits of European leaders in 1990. The Maastricht Treaty, which changed the EEC name to the EU and planned for more European integration, was signed in February 1992. Four months afterwards, the Danes rejected that treaty, but, when they received amendments to placate them, they accepted it in May 1993.

During those tumultuous times, Boris became the champion of Euroscepticism within the Brussels press corps. Every member-state delegation held a news conference at the conclusion of a summit. International journalists would head to the British event for the Boris question to John Major. Denmark's foreign minister, Uffe Ellemann-Jensen, believed that Johnson's work was an influence in his country's rejection of the Maastricht Treaty.

The year 1994 provided spectacular evidence of the growing influence and impact of the Euroscepticism that Boris championed. At their June summit in Corfu, European leaders gathered to agree who would be given the difficult challenge of replacing

Jacques Delors as European Commission president. The powerful Franco-German alliance, Mitterrand and Kohl, were enthusiastically championing the Belgian prime minister, Jean-Luc Dehaene. Nine other leaders were also prepared to back him. But the British prime minister, John Major, vetoed the appointment. He was the sole objector and said afterwards, 'I am unperturbed about the arithmetic of eleven to one.' Andrew Marr wrote in the *Independent* on 27 June 1994 that Major 'has steadily been remaking himself as a Eurosceptic' and 'the Eurosceptics' perception that they are now in effective control of the Prime Minister matches the view of him from Paris and Bonn'.

In the weeks prior to the summit, the British public had been warned that Dehaene was a federalist, a supporter of 'big government', a fixer, a plumber who would seek to deepen the influence of Brussels. With Dehaene blocked by the British, the need to find a replacement for Delors intensified.

In advance of that Corfu June meeting, Ruud Lubbers, an experienced former Dutch prime minister, was eliminated from the 'possibles' list. His undoing was his lukewarm stance at the time of German reunification, and, as a result, Chancellor Helmut Kohl refused to support him. One prominent Irishman, who wasn't a prime minister, offered his services. On 17 May, Peter Sutherland, the then head of the World Trade Organization, gave me an interview in his office in Geneva indicating that, if asked, he would be honoured to serve. But, Sutherland's Fine Gael background aside, the Fianna Fáil–Labour coalition didn't think he had a realistic chance of success and gave no oxygen to the notion.

When EU leaders gathered in Brussels on 15 July for a special summit to nominate Delors's successor, they looked around the room and settled on a surprise candidate from within their own club. Jacques Santer, the fifty-seven-year-old prime minister of Luxembourg, was the unopposed nominee. It was reported that when his wife received the unexpected news by phone she cried what were not necessarily tears of joy.

Boris Johnson had a significant role in derailing the efforts to replace Jacques Delors with Jean-Luc Dehaene. By the time Jacques Santer formally took over that role in 1995, Boris had returned to London to begin the next phase of his upward trajectory.

*

The summits of EU leaders had a feel of 'showtime'. The practice was to hold the two-day gatherings in the home of the member state running the six-month EU presidency. The press corps from Brussels travelled en masse to the events. I adopted a policy of staying in the hotel where the Irish delegation was billeted. It usually consisted of the Taoiseach, the minister for foreign affairs and, on occasion, the minister for finance and their officials. Because Ireland was seen as a small country and RTÉ its only television service, no issues were raised when we tagged on to the VIPs, guaranteeing access inside the security cordon.

Often, one or two delegations from other countries were posted in the same hotel. It meant that early-morning interviews with the Taoiseach and at least one other prime minister could be discreetly picked up in a quiet corner of the hotel, after breakfast. After we had our business done, as a delegation left the hotel, other crews would be lined up behind crash barriers, hoping for a doorstep remark.

At a number of summits, the Irish and Danish delegations shared the same hotel. Their foreign minister, Uffe

Ellemann-Jensen, was a most obliging interviewee. A former journalist, he had excellent English, and, during that period when Denmark rejected the Maastricht Treaty, his views were in demand. He was a passionate fisherman, and, after a period when he featured several times on RTÉ, I brought him a present of flies from a tackle and bait shop in Enniskillen.

When pursuing interviewees, realism was important. Ireland had a place in the pecking order. An approach from RTÉ to a representative from one of the large member states had no more than an outside chance of success, unless it suited the politician's interests to oblige.

Like Ellemann-Jensen, Jean-Claude Juncker was another who never turned down an interview request. We were on first-name terms. Juncker was from Luxembourg, even smaller than Ireland. He had good time for Bertie Ahern, through their dealings at meetings of EU finance ministers. One important fact about him was that the most powerful EU leader, German chancellor Helmut Kohl, rated him and trusted him. So as well as being accessible, he had knowledge and influence. Even in the early 1990s, some fingers on his right hand were stained by cigarette smoke. (From 2014 to 2019 he served as president of the European Commission.)

The early-morning acquisition of interviews and pictures guaranteed a good start to summit news-gathering coverage. It also gave us material to trade with other broadcasters who had holes to fill in their schedule. Headline usually provided services for the Danes, Swedes, Finns, French and the BBC so we were players in an active swaps market. The system increased the amount of material available to us. Also, it often resulted in Irish politicians featuring on television screens in other member states.

Being 'inside the tent' – in this case 'inside the hotel' – also created the means to arrange live contributions for RTÉ's flagship radio programme, *Morning Ireland*. The programme editors favoured one of their presenters in Dublin doing the interview down the telephone line. My job was to line up the guest. Usually the No. 2 player, the minister for foreign affairs, was targeted. When he was in the role, Brian Cowen never failed to deliver. One particular night he arrived late and went to bed in the small hours. Declan Kelly was his Department of Foreign Affairs press officer. I feared the minister wouldn't keep the appointment and phoned Declan, several times, as the clock ticked towards the arranged live slot. But, despite his limited sleep, Cowen fulfilled the arrangement. Many years later, in Galway, after a late night at a Fianna Fáil gathering, then Taoiseach Cowen got into trouble for his performance when he turned up for a live interview with the same *Morning Ireland* programme and its presenter Cathal Mac Coille.

With the help of the enthusiastic Headline one-person crews, we developed several habits to increase the RTÉ profile. At important international news conferences, we'd place a microphone with RTÉ branding prominently. We always carried a spare RTÉ ident and would strategically place it to feature in coverage, regardless of whether it was attached to a camera. It always gave a lift to see the RTÉ logo featuring widely on major stories.

A specific form of doorstep interview was another important discovery. The standard arrangement for a major news conference had the principal, sitting alongside a media adviser, deliver a statement and then take questions from the seated journalists. Often the person under the spotlight had worked out some script lines in advance and sought to not deviate

My father, Joe Gorman

My parents on their wedding day
at Ballintogher Church

My father Joe (far right) beside my grandfather Tom, with
two cattle dealers at a fair

My mother,
Maureen Harkin

Back row left to right:
Daddy, Mammy and
Granny. *Middle row*:
Michael and Mary.
Front row: me and Paula

Second class at Scoil Fatima National School, cast of the Saucey Sue Action Song. I'm fifth from the left on the second row from the back

The Summerhill College soccer team in Market's Field, Limerick, 1974. I was bag man and assistant manager alongside Fr Cyril Haran – I'm on the far right of the back row

At Summerhill College with fellow editors of the monthly student magazine, *View*. *Left to right*: Padraig Waters, Austin Jennings, me, Edmund Henry, Martin Queenan

THE IRISH TIMES, MONDAY, JUNE 14, 1976   11

School of Journalism, Rathmines, winners of the Gael-Linn/Irish Times debating competition in Dublin on Saturday (from left): Pól Mac an Draoi (captain), Máire Ní Phiobaire, Dónall O Móráin (Gael-Linn), Tomás O Gormán, Donal Foley (The Irish Times), Máire Ní Anchróga.

Gael-Linn/'Irish Times' debating competition final

FOIREANN ón Scoil Iriseoireachta i gColáiste na Tráchtála, Rath Maoinis, bhain an chéad áit i gCraobh na hEireann de Chómórtas Diospóireachta Gaell - Linn / *Irish Times* i mBaile Atha Cliath san oíche Dé Sathairn. Coláiste na hOllscoile, Gaillimh, a bhí in iomaíocht leo don chraobh sa chomortas nua seo do mhic léinn sa tríú leibhéal. "Go bhfuill Caitlin Ní Uallacháin pósta le fear an ghaimbín" an rún a bhí á phlé.

The debate was chaired by the Chancellor of the National University and chairman of Bord na Gaeilge, Dr. T. K. Whitaker, who congratulated both teams on their high standard. Dr. Whitaker thanked Gael Linn and The Irish

Times for providing the opportunity for the debate. The *Irish Times*, he said, had shown the way for journalism in Irish. "Reading 'Tuarascáil' s part of the week for people who read little elsewhere in Irish—though sometimes I'm afraid to read it myself!"

Dónal o Móráin, chairman of Gael-Linn, expressed satisfaction at the success of the new debating venture. There was a need for a debating competition for third-level students, he said, since the collapse of the Comhchuídreamh. Mr. O Móráin also paid tribute to the work done by The Irish Times and by the news editor, Donal Foley, in particular, for journalism in Irish. "Cá mbeimis i gcúrsaí

iriseoireachta gan 'Tuarascáil' agus sé Donal Foley a spreag agus a chothaigh an colún seo."

Agus breith na moltóirí á cur ós comhair an halla ag Aindrias Ó Gallchóir, leas cheannasaí na gClár Telefíse in RTE, dúirt sé go raibh buntáiste ó thús ag Ráth Maoinis sa mhéid go raibh sé i bhfad níos éasca labhairt ar shon an rúin. Ar an dtaobh eile dhe, bhí buntáiste ó fhuaob liofacht na Gaeilge ag Gaillimh, adúirt sé. Cheap sé go raibh an díospóireacht ar an iomlán ro-liteartha agus ro-stairiúil, ach ghaibh sé buíochas leis a dá fhoireann as ucht oíche agus oíaíd thaitneamhach a chur ar fáil. Ba bheag a bhí idir an dá fhoireann sa deireadh, adúirt sé, ach b'é

tuairim na moltóirí go raibh foireann Ráth Maoinis beagán chun tosaigh.

Labhair eagarthóir nuachta an *Irish Times*, Donal Foley, agus bhronn sé an corn agus cuimne neachaín ar fhoireann Rath Maoinis. Bronnadh cuimhneacháin ar fhoireann na Gaillimhe freisin. Labhair Micheál Ó Cinneíde (captaen), Veronica Ní Cheoill, Seán Ó Cuirráein agus Neasa Ní Eígeartaigh ar son na Gaillimhe.

B'iad Aindrias ó Gallchóir, Micheál Ó Fathaigh, Nuala Ní Dhomhnaill agus Breandán Ó hEithir na moltóirí.

Bhí Séamus Mac Gabhann i mbun foireann Ráth Maoinis.

With the School of Journalism winners of the Gael-Linn/*Irish Times* 3rd level colleges debating competition (in Irish). *Left to right*: Paul Drury, Maria Pepper, Dónal O Móráin (Gael Linn), me, Donal Foley (*Irish Times*) and Máire Crowe

The *Western Journal* years. At the Roscommon v Sligo Connacht Championship match in Roscommon with local TD Ray McSharry (left) and *Sligo Champion* reporter Leo Gray (centre)

Interviewing country and western singer Philomena Begley

Wedding day with Ceara – October 21st, 1983

Granny giving me her wedding ring outside Ransboro Church on our wedding day

Opening of RTÉ studio in Sligo, 1985. I'm interviewing RTÉ Head of News Wesley Boyd with cameraman Tony Cournane and sound recordist Tony Finnegan

Working with cameraman Ronald Verhoeven at L'Arc de Triomphe in Paris

With colleagues in Strasbourg. *Left to right*: Seán Flynn (*Irish Times*), John Downing (*Irish Independent*) and me

At the European Parliament in Strasbourg with MEPs Mark Killilea (left) and John Hume

from that plan. It made for boring television. We discovered that much more interesting material could be got by being in position immediately after the news conference concluded and throwing some unscheduled questions to the interviewee leaving the stage. The pictures were stronger and more personal. Sometimes, the adrenalin rush was over, the determination to deliver rehearsed answers was relaxed, and more newsworthy comments were made.

As the importance of some of the summits increased and technology advanced, RTÉ agreed to send its own satellite vans and crews to some of the events. It made sense on financial and news fronts. There was no limit to the amount of material that could be dispatched back to Dublin, at any time, with no extra cost implications. The satellite engineers, Jarlath Tierney, Tom Drury, Johnny Culloty and Derek McGuinness enjoyed the excitement of the international gatherings. Often, Ray Roantree, one of RTÉ's finest editors, took holidays and came to work as part of our RTÉ team. Once, at a Berlin summit, in a most un-Germanic way, the huge press centre was hit by a power failure. The RTÉ satellite van had a generator on board, and power cables from it kept our edit suite running in the otherwise dark building until the service was restored.

The ultimate validation of the satellite-vans policy came many years later in Paris. Jarlath and Tom had been working with Colm Murray at the annual Cheltenham horse-racing festival in England. Ed Mulhall approved the proposal that they would travel on to the Five Nations Rugby Championship in Paris, where Ireland were playing the host nation in the Stade de France. It was the famous day that a young Brian O'Driscoll scored three tries and David Humphreys nailed the penalty that clinched the victory. The coaches, Eddie O'Sullivan and

Warren Gatland, agreed to our request to run cables from the van into the Irish dressing room and to film the scenes there. It was the first time such permission had been given. Further unscheduled history was about to be made. Live into the *Six One* Sunday evening television news bulletin, as we interviewed the delighted try scorer, one of Brian O'Driscoll's tired team-mates, showered and exhausted, walked stark naked behind him through the camera shot. In our excitement we failed to spot the unscheduled appearance, but it was noticed by some of our more vigilant viewers, and, for a long time afterwards, an RTÉ colleague retained a screen-grab of the glitch.

We were on a high after the victory, and for the 9 p.m. television bulletin we relocated to the balcony of the Paris hotel where the two teams were having their post-match meal. Donal Lenihan, the team manager, was the live interviewee, but this time there was no surprise cameo appearance.

5

Power and loss

After Albert Reynolds succeeded Charlie Haughey as Fianna Fáil leader and Taoiseach in February 1992, he quickly began the purge. The previous year, when he challenged Haughey, the foreign-affairs minister, Gerard Collins, pleaded with him, live on the RTÉ *Six One News*, 'Albert, please don't burst up the party.' Collins was one of the first to go. One by one, the new boss called in senior cabinet ministers and told them they were being dropped from his team – the likes of Mary O'Rourke, Ray Burke, Rory O'Hanlon, Michael O'Kennedy and Noel Davern. Between senior and junior ministers, over a dozen were turfed out.

Those promoted included the beneficiary of Cathal Duffy's lobbying in my *Western Journal* days, Pádraig Flynn (justice), who had been sacked by Haughey, David Andrews (foreign affairs), Brian Cowen (labour), Joe Walsh (agriculture) and Charlie McCreevy (social welfare). Despite the regime change, Bertie Ahern retained his job as minister for finance.

P. J. Mara also moved on from the position of government press secretary. It was an obvious change as he had been close to Haughey for many years. Albert Reynolds hired Seán Duignan to work as his press secretary. Most of his colleagues knew him as Diggy. His new boss called him 'Die-gie'. He was aware that the public knew 'Die-gie' as RTÉ's political editor and then as an RTÉ newscaster and sensed he would be an asset. His media team also included journalist Mary Kerrigan and Tom Savage, who ran a media training and public-relations company with his wife, Terry Prone.

It was a challenge to get a sense of the new Taoiseach and to work out how he would perform on the European stage. He was from Rooskey in Co. Roscommon and won a scholarship to become a boarder in Summerhill College. During my time there, we were sometimes told how Albert Reynolds's business instincts surfaced when he ran the school tuck shop. His first job was in Ballymote station, working with CIÉ, and while based in the south Sligo town, he met his future wife, Kathleen. He started a sideline running dances. The string of ballrooms and other later ventures, including a successful pet-food business, helped him to become a self-made millionaire.

Soon after he became Taoiseach, Albert Reynolds made it clear that a priority for him was to make progress on Northern Ireland. While he was minister for finance, he struck up a relationship with his British counterpart, John Major. That link carried through to their Taoiseach and British prime minister phase. Invariably, when at EU events, they had their private bilateral meeting when the agenda always included what was happening in Northern Ireland. On their watch, the Downing Street Declaration was agreed, in December 1993. It created the circumstances for the August 1994 IRA ceasefire.

Once, during an off-the-record conversation with the Taoiseach, I shared a story, told to me by an influential Republican. It was about one of Mr Reynolds's constituents. As the result of his known political views and history, he was turned down as ineligible for a job in the Department of

Posts and Telegraphs. Albert Reynolds, the then minister with responsibility for the sector, intervened to have the ban lifted. But he made it known that if there was any breach of good faith, there would be consequences.

During his first months as Taoiseach, Reynolds's entrepreneur's instincts drew him towards the EU funding discussions that were gathering pace. Decisions about allocations of wealth transfers for a seven-year period were due to be taken at the Edinburgh summit in 1992. The businessman and former finance minister in Reynolds knew the significance of EU aid to Ireland's economy. With talk of EU expansion, and the possibility that poorer former Communist countries might be offered membership, this was likely to be Ireland's final opportunity to receive major wealth transfers from the Brussels coffers.

In October 1992, the Taoiseach headed for Spain on the government jet to support the Irish exhibitors at the Seville Expo. From there he planned to travel to Madrid for a bilateral meeting with the Spanish prime minister, Felipe González. It was part of the strategy to build up alliances in advance of the Edinburgh meeting of EU leaders. We followed him to Seville, but the bunged-up flight connections meant we wouldn't make it to Madrid to cover the political discussions there. Our request to cadge a lift in the exceptional circumstances was granted. We were going to be the first media team to travel on the government jet.

During a lunchtime Saturday check call from Seville to the RTÉ news desk, Barry Linnane explained how he had been trying to contact me. He apologized for what he was about to tell me. My father had died at Garden Hill hospital in Sligo. It was an earthquake I hadn't seen coming.

The kindness of strangers is an abiding memory from that time of numbing sadness. Seville airport offered no prospect of getting home. At Malaga airport, two hours down the coast, an Aer Lingus flight of JWT holidaymakers was scheduled to fly to Dublin, but it was full. An air hostess gave me her seat at the back of the plane. She used the jump seat, in the cockpit, during take-off and landing. When the food was being distributed, she gave me what I later discovered was her meal.

During that flight home, and many times since, I revisited the last time I saw my father. We had been home on holidays for the summer. I called to the house in Cairns Road to say goodbye, but I didn't hug him as I walked past him in the hallway towards the front door. It had been the scene of so many partings during our lives. The restrained emotions and suppressed tears of Daddy's brother Father Eamonn during his exits made an impression on a younger me. Daddy was entirely different. He never held back on showing love. That was always the way in our house. In whatever challenges life threw at us, unconditional love was the impregnable last line of defence. It would have been the most obvious and most natural thing to put my arms around Daddy that day and to tell him, one more time – in fact, a final time – that I loved him. But I didn't.

Earlier in the year he had been treated for lung cancer in Dublin. Mary lived in Harold's Cross, near the hospital, and was close to him during that time. Michael travelled up from Galway to visit him. I was in Brussels and didn't have a proper understanding of his disease, the prognosis and the possibility that he was dying. Ceara was early into her first pregnancy that final summer, and the optimist in me was looking forward to having a new grandchild for our parents. But sometimes life doesn't work out in that neat way.

Once, after Daddy's death, I came home, briefly, to visit Mammy as she was adjusting to a quiet house. Ceara stayed in Brussels with our baby, Moya. I walked the familiar route from Sligo town one evening but passed the turn for our road and called at the front door of Austin and Clare Jennings. Their son had been my school friend. They were surprised but glad to see me. The fire was burning in their large front room, the television was switched off, and Mrs Jennings served tea in china cups. I told them about Moya, and then I began to talk about Daddy. I cried and talked and cried for a long time. They sat there listening, saying nothing, letting me talk but understanding. It was a necessary revisiting of loss.

Years later, I returned to that grief. As with the most important stuff, like death and falling in and out of love, you can't plan for when loss intervenes in your life. It decides when to intrude. In this instance, it was a day when I was driving with our second child, near our home in Sligo. He is named after the grandfathers he never knew: John Roche and Joe Gorman. He is known as Joe. He brought back a sense of my father, without warning, that day. I wrote about it afterwards, probably as a form of therapy and self-understanding. What came out may have limited meaning for a wider audience. But it is an important part of me.

Joe
There seems to be a season when fathers slip away.
The day we buried you, I looked from the cemetery at Cleveragh
Over towards the Foxes Den
Smoke was rising in straight white lines from the chimneys of Tonaphubble

Through the crisp air
And disappearing into a clear blue sky.
It's a school morning.
A young boy sits in a van.
You rumble in your pockets.
From the jumble of yellow chalk for marking tyres,
The aspirins and cigarette butts,
you find a coin.
Slowly the hand is extended.
I wait and at the appropriate time
Grasp it with mock surprise.
Is it a bronze thruppence, with all the corners?
No, better.
It feels like a worn English sixpence.
You gently squeeze my leg and say, 'That's the good
     little boy.'
But I am already in Denis Feehily's shop,
Buying Macaroon Bars
And penny sweets.
One August day I slipped out past you.
As a child I'd seen too many sad farewells in that
     hallway on Cairns Road.
So there was no farewell
No clasping of your ailing body.
Five weeks later you were dead.
I have a boy now.
He carries your name and has your trusting, hazel eyes.
One recent day, with the same crisp autumn air, and a
     blue sky
I drove past Lisheen towards Strandhill.
Without warning, from his child seat,

He sang, in perfect pitch
'Postman Pat, Postman Pat and his black-and-white
* cat,*
Early in the morning, as the day is dawning,
Bringing all the letters in his van.'
When I heard that clear, happy voice, I knew,
I really knew
You are still alive.

*

In late 1992, Albert Reynolds found himself dealing with a crisis partly of his own making. After he took over as Taoiseach, he made it clear that he wasn't overkeen on the coalition arrangement with the Progressive Democrats, led by Des O'Malley. The tetchy relationship boiled over, leading to the collapse of the government. In the 25 November general election, Fianna Fáil, led by Reynolds, were punished. They lost nine seats, reducing their numbers to sixty-eight in the 166-member Dáil.

Fine Gael, under John Bruton in his first election as leader, dropped ten seats to forty-five. Dick Spring's Labour Party were seen as the big winners, increasing their seats by eighteen to thirty-three. The Progressive Democrats got a bounce from their row with Fianna Fáil, growing their numbers from four to ten. Democratic Left returned four TDs. Fianna Fáil was still the largest party, but many considered them 'damaged goods'. There was no obvious combination that would deliver the 84-plus seats required to form a government. One option being floated was a Fine Gael–Labour coalition, but, with a total of seventy-eight seats, it would have to be a minority administration.

Bruised by the general election, but still not officially out of his job as Taoiseach, Albert Reynolds headed off with his delegation – foreign-affairs minister David Andrews and finance minister Bertie Ahern included – to the summit of EU leaders in Edinburgh. The speculation in advance of the negotiations was that Ireland would seek to target £5 billion in EU transfers over the seven-year period up to 1999. It was an EU story that every Irish citizen could understand because it was about money.

Marian O'Neill was the production assistant who answered the phone when I rang to say we were ready to feed our television package for the Saturday night bulletin. 'Did we get our £5 or even £6 billion?' she asked.

'No,' I replied. 'According to Albert, we are in line to get £8 billion.'

At his news conference in the Irish delegation rooms, the outgoing Taoiseach looked towards the television camera and said, 'We have secured commitments of £8 billion. That's £3 million for every day of every week of every year for the seven years up to the end of 1999.'

After journalists filed their reports, they headed for the dinner hosted by the government press secretary, Seán Duignan. Because of the important funding discussions and the post-general-election uncertainty, the number of Dublin-based journalists covering the summit was higher than usual. Duignan had a deserved reputation as a raconteur as well as a journalist. Early in his life he had performed in Galway's Taibhdhearc Theatre. It was said that the actress Maureen O'Hara was once so taken by him that she encouraged him to pursue a career on the stage. His after-dinner remarks in Edinburgh that night had some of the defiance of Robert Emmett's speech from the dock.

Yet he gave the impression that he believed he was hosting the Last Supper.

The next morning, I spotted the Taoiseach in the hotel lobby where the Irish delegation was billeted. Our informal exchange was around the £8 billion windfall, as described by him the previous night. Martin Mansergh, his adviser on Northern Ireland matters, was in earshot of the conversation and briefly joined it. He was keen to know if there was any reaction to the news from the Labour Party.

Albert Reynolds returned to Ireland with what he considered was an £8 billion dowry, fit to tempt the Labour Party. The two groups had never before formed a coalition government. Dick Spring's Dáil speeches targeting the Fianna Fáil–Progressive Democrat administration had contributed to Labour's general-election success. But in the days immediately after the Edinburgh summit, significantly influenced by the potential offered by EU wealth transfers, Labour committed to take the plunge. The unlikely arrangement gave the partners 101 of the 166 Dáil seats – on paper, a very comfortable majority.

Some pressing housekeeping was required. Albert Reynolds and Pádraig Flynn were friends as well as colleagues. After their unsuccessful attempt to oust Charlie Haughey, they were both fired from his cabinet. When Haughey had to stand aside and Reynolds replaced him, he gave his pal, Flynn, the justice portfolio. Labour, nervous about the leap in the dark they were about to take, were very wary of the complications any tie-up with Flynn might bring. They remembered the impact of his comments about Mary Robinson in the presidential election campaign two years before. Flynn said, during an RTÉ radio debate, 'She had to have new clothes, a new look, a new hairdo', and had 'the new interest in family, being a mother and all that kind of thing. But none of us who knew Mary Robinson very well in previous incarnations ever heard her claiming to be a great wife and mother.'

Fortunately for Labour (and Fianna Fáil), there was a solution available that would take Pádraig Flynn far away from Dáil Éireann. Ray MacSharry had decided to not seek Irish government support for a second term as European commissioner (a move that Reynolds probably welcomed). Aged fifty-five, he was leaving political life and would follow a career in the private sector. The vacancy created an opportunity for Pádraig Flynn, and he was mustard-keen to take it.

At the first gathering of the new Jacques Delors-led Commission team in Brussels, the members quickly got a sense of the personality of their Irish colleague. The pronunciation of his first name – Pádraig – was causing difficulties for some. The national-school teacher in Flynn took over, and he gave them phonetical instructions. 'It's PAW-RICK . . . PAW-RICK. Say it after me, PAW-RICK.' Several volunteered for the trial and succeeded. Flynn went home to Castlebar for Christmas on 22 December, satisfied with the job offer of European commissioner for social affairs. He was in Brussels, familiarizing himself with his new responsibilities, when the Fianna Fáil–Labour government formally took office in Dublin on 12 January.

The £8 billion war chest came in for serious scrutiny soon into the life of the new administration. Bruce Millan, one of two British members of the European Commission and holder of the regional-policy portfolio, was among those taking issue with Dublin's calculations. One evening, at the entrance to the Breydel building in Brussels, I doorstepped Jacques Delors and put to him some of the arguments made by the Taoiseach and the Irish government. The Commission president didn't hold back. 'This is a liar,' he snapped. Despite his limited English, his exasperation was clear.

Dan Mulhall, a Department of Foreign Affairs official, was the Brussels-based press officer given responsibility to explain the Irish stance to international journalists. In the way that commercial travellers once had an array of samples to help market their wares, Dan carried around a selection of graphs and charts to explain the basis of the £8 billion calculation.

The disagreement between Dublin and the Commission intensified in June, culminating in the Irish government using its veto to prevent sign-off on the overall funding package. As tánaiste and minister for foreign affairs, Dick Spring was given responsibility to represent the government in what were now crisis discussions. His ally, interfacing with the Commission in a series of meetings at the Charlemagne building, would be Pádraig Flynn.

Greece, Portugal, Spain and Ireland had a special interest in the negotiations. As the four poorest member states, they were at the head of the queue for the structural and cohesion funds. But the wealthier countries were also determined to secure some return from their contributions to the Brussels coffers as they had disadvantaged regions in the running for EU grant aid.

Heading to a meeting on 2 July, Commissioner Flynn was asked what form might the discussions take. He responded, 'I'll tell you what they're going to talk about . . . Jingle, jangle. Did you ever have a cloth bag, with coins in it? You rattle the bag, hold it up to their ears, let them hear the sound, jingle jangle.' Flynn continued in his explanation. 'The way it is, you have four thirsty men, looking for drink. They've come into the company of eight others who are used to being well fed and well watered. And you have a bottle of whiskey in the press. So, what should you do? Keep the whiskey locked up, and start talking to them about the theory of thirst or the evils of drink? Not at all . . . you break open the bottle, you put four glasses on the table and you pour the four men a good drink, without measuring it. And when they are half-cut and in good humour, you have a check on what's left in the bottle, and that is the time you top up the glasses in whatever way suits you.'

Flynn and Spring were such unlikely partners. Spring, the barrister and former international rugby player but also the minister for foreign affairs, had never faced such a test on the international stage. Flynn, the commissioner, couldn't wait to commence what he expected would be a European version of the haggling he had practised at Mayo County Council. Back in Dublin, the businessman in Taoiseach Albert Reynolds knew that a result was needed to safeguard his political reputation.

The negotiations almost collapsed several times. Delors took the lead role for the Commission in the decisive stages. The 10 per cent devaluation of the Irish currency in January 1993 became an important presentational factor that helped to stretch the bottom line. Flynn used the grant aid attached to the European Social Fund he oversaw to help in his discussions with some of the member-state delegations.

Ireland's ambassador to the EU, Pádraig MacKernan, and Paddy Teahon, secretary at the Department of the Taoiseach, kept track of the wheeling and dealing. They knew the deal was done when Delors and Spring met on a corridor, away from the crowded negotiating room, spoke and shook hands.

In the agreed package, Ireland's share of the overall structural-funds package allocated to the four poorest countries fell from 13.5 per cent to 11.5 per cent. But the concessions, understandings and interpretations hammered out during the

negotiations allowed Spring to state at a late-night news conference on 21 July 1993 that the package for Ireland amounted to
£7.84 billion. The resolution of the funding row gave Albert
Reynolds the impetus to push on with other priorities.

Reynolds was a sharp dresser. Once, during an informal chat,
when I admired a tie he was wearing, he said something that
gave an insight beyond the immediate. 'If you wake up in bad
form, put on your best clothes. If you do that, the first person
you meet might say, "Jesus, you are looking well." By the time
a second or third person says it, you will start to believe it.'

Six months after the EU funding deal was nailed down, at
a media conference at the British prime minister's office in
London, Reynolds and his friend John Major announced what
became known as the Downing Street Declaration. It brought
momentum to Northern Ireland's peace process, and it created
the conditions for the IRA ceasefire in August 1994. The halting
of paramilitary killing and bombing was the most significant
achievement of Albert Reynolds's political career. But before
the year-end he was gone from office.

His problems started when a UTV journalist, Chris Moore,
revealed the shocking details of child sex abuse by a Co.
Cavan-based priest, Father Brendan Smyth. Seán Duignan, the
government press secretary, told me that when the story first
broke, the Taoiseach's question to him was, 'What's a pee-
dee-o-file?' Albert Reynolds was a practising Catholic, and,
like many of his generation, he struggled with the idea that a
priest would be systematically assaulting the large numbers of
children entrusted to his care.

The Taoiseach's inability to fully grasp the potential implications of the controversy was compounded when the office
of the attorney general became caught up in it. Questions

were raised about the efficiency of the office in processing
an application to extradite Father Smyth to face charges in
Northern Ireland. The debate was simmering at a time when
the Taoiseach was preparing to promote the attorney general,
Harry Whelehan, to the role of president of the High Court.
Trust between Fianna Fáil and Labour broke down, and, on
16 November, Dick Spring pulled his party out of the coalition government.

Three weeks later, Reynolds was still the Taoiseach, but in
name only. Finance minister Bertie Ahern had replaced him as
Fianna Fáil leader and was trying to form a new administration
with Spring's Labour Party. But all fell apart, chaotically, on 5
December. An *Irish Times* article that morning by Geraldine
Kennedy raised new doubts about Fianna Fáil's past dealings
with Labour.

Bertie Ahern was in Brussels, tied up at a meeting of EU ministers. Dick Spring was in Dublin, going cold on their planned
liaison. Albert Reynolds was in Budapest at a meeting of leaders
from the EU and the other members of an organization called
the Conference on Security and Cooperation in Europe. I was
in Hungary, stationed at the entrance of the meeting centre,
hoping to interview the Taoiseach. I watched the official car
with the Irish flag arrive at the set time, wait for ten minutes but
then move off, empty, to facilitate the exit of other delegations.
The same ritual happened a number of times.

Eventually the Taoiseach came down but was determined
to avoid any media questions. With his entourage, he sought
to exit the building by a different route. We followed him into
a huge kitchen, where uniformed chefs and other staff were
puzzled to see a group of men in suits, pursued by a cameraman,
rush through their place of work.

Ten days after Albert Reynolds's unorthodox retreat from Budapest, Labour formally changed partners to form a new administration with Fine Gael and Democratic Left. It became known as the Rainbow Coalition and was the first time that a new government, composed of different parties, was formed within the same Dáil term. It was also the first occasion since 1987 that Fine Gael was back in power.

The new administration was formed without elections and lasted two and a half years. One of its significant policy objectives was that it sought to reinforce Ireland's credentials for membership of the planned European single currency. The list of applicants for EU membership was increasing. Ireland and the UK were taking opposite views on the prospect of a more powerful Europe while they stepped up their efforts to make a breakthrough in Northern Ireland.

Dick Spring, the Labour Party leader, retained the role of tánaiste and minister for foreign affairs. But John Bruton, the Fine Gael leader, was now Taoiseach. Bruton had a visceral disdain for the IRA. Some of it was deeply personal. He had shared an office in Dáil Éireann with Senator Billy Fox, who was shot dead by IRA intruders in 1974, when they also burned down the home of his girlfriend, a Protestant, Marjorie Coulson, in Co. Monaghan. Bruton often found it difficult to hold back on his strongly held views in the company of Sinn Féin leaders.

When he partnered Albert Reynolds in government, Dick Spring usually took the lead role on outreach to Unionists. With John Bruton as his partner, Spring had to change roles and become the main interface with Republicans while the Fine Gael Taoiseach cultivated Unionism. On the EU stage, Spring acquired the status of 'a player' and part of a new generation. The name Dick Spring had a useful recognition factor. He presented well and was often in demand from international as well as Irish media after EU meetings. As well as his wry sense of humour, he had a tetchy side, influenced by the regular back pain he suffered as a result of injuries sustained in a car accident.

Dick Spring's father, Dan, was a Kerry TD from 1943 to 1981. He instilled in his son the need to remain mindful of the local base. The tánaiste once told me about a visit to Dáil Éireann when his TD father pointed out to him the political correspondent of the *Cork Examiner*, Liam O'Neill, and advised, 'Remember him: he is an important little man.' We saw some of the reasons for the Spring preoccupation with the home turf in the late summer of 1996. Ireland's six-month presidency of the EU was under way, giving the Rainbow ministers temporary international significance. Dick Spring decided to bring his fellow European foreign ministers to Tralee for their scheduled informal weekend gathering. It was a good opportunity to showcase his Kerry constituency. Even though Spring was the main government point of contact with Sinn Féin for the ongoing sensitive Northern Ireland peace-process manoeuvrings, local Republicans in Kerry staged protests that caused him embarrassment as he hosted his visitors.

Labour's Ruairí Quinn was another of those Rainbow Coalition principals who purred on the European stage. He was first elected to the Dáil in 1977 and never disguised his preference to be in government rather than opposition. As finance minister, he lapped up the responsibility of making the Irish case for inclusion in the planned EU single currency.

Fine Gael's Ivan Yates, the agriculture minister, was another able performer. He was younger than most of his Irish and European ministerial colleagues, but he was very comfortable on centre stage. He inherited a canny departmental press officer, Dermot Murphy, who had worked for the previous minister, Joe Walsh. Yates used to nickname him Archbishop Murphy or Monsignor Murphy.

They got more attention than planned for when they established Killarney in Murphy's native Co. Kerry as the centre for an informal meeting of EU agriculture ministers. The main farmers' lobbying group, the Irish Farmers' Association (IFA), had issues at the time, and it decided to stage a protest at the luxury hotel where the visitors were staying. The demonstrators broke through the garda security cordon, and dozens of them ran across the hotel lawns towards the conference centre. The scenes made for wonderful television pictures.

The Yates chain of betting outlets was expanding at the time. For a while, I was on the minister's Christmas-card list, and he sometimes added a line, 'Deirdre has purchased another shop.' He seemed to have at least some of the qualities and the ambition to be a future leader of his party. But, at the crossroads, he followed a different route. The business grew but got into difficulties. He left politics and became a sought-after talk-show host and after-dinner speaker.

Hugh Coveney, father of the future tánaiste and minister for foreign affairs Simon Coveney, was another minister in that short-lived Rainbow Coalition. He was from a business background, part of the 'merchant princes' tradition associated with Fine Gael in Cork. On his first visit to Brussels, we witnessed a very vivid example of his patrician instincts. He was minister for fisheries, and the annual December haggling over fish quotas often dragged beyond deadlines and continued dangerously close to Christmas Day. When he met the small group of Irish journalists and discovered that the *Cork Examiner* correspondent, Katherine Butler, was from Thurles, Minister Coveney spontaneously asked if she would like a lift home for Christmas in the government jet. One of the officials standing beside him almost choked with surprise. Katherine diplomatically explained that she had travel arrangements in place.

The Taoiseach in that coalition government, John Bruton, appointed the RTÉ journalist Shane Kenny as the government press secretary. In the role, Kenny had a very 'hands on' style. It was a beneficial arrangement for Bruton because Kenny acted as a defensive shield between his boss and the media. But it was a regular source of tension between the government press secretary and his former colleagues.

Bruton really enjoyed his short period on centre stage. Unlike the Fianna Fáil leaders, who dominated Dáil politics during Bruton's career, as a Fine Gael member he was linked into the Christian Democrat network that was the dominant force in EU politics. Connections as well as his track record on EU issues helped him to land the job of the EU ambassador to the United States from 2004 to 2009.

The summit of EU leaders held in Dublin in December 1996 was a significant achievement for that Rainbow Coalition. The administration and the British government were working productively on Northern Ireland issues. But there was growing divergence between Dublin and London on membership of the Brussels club. At the Dublin gathering, the design of banknotes for the proposed EU single currency was unveiled. Ireland was on track to become a member of the euro group; Britain would not be part of that project.

*

As journalism became a bigger, 24/7 industry during those years, and technology made the world a smaller place, there was an increase in the structures dealing with the flow and management of information. The unexpected continued to be the vital ingredient in news. Every once in a while, someone broke ranks from the predictable patterns, and that became a headline.

Pádraig Flynn did so on *The Late Late Show* in January 1999 in a classic example of car-crash television. He was in his second term as Ireland's member of the European Commission. His body clock was used to working Brussels time, and he was appearing live, with Gay Byrne, in the Donnybrook studios at the end of a long day. For his work as a commissioner, he had an able press officer, Barbara Nolan. He had a long-standing friendship with husband-and-wife communications advisers Tom Savage and Terry Prone. But he was flying solo in the Donnybrook studio, with a significant percentage of Ireland's population watching on.

There was a hint of what might be coming when the interviewer put it to him that he loved his role. Flynn was off, explaining how in politics there are two types of politicians: front runners and safe people. The front runners are motivators, they take terrible risks, they identify problems, and they try to put the solutions in place as against the ideological attitude.

'You are a front runner,' suggested Gay.

'You've said it . . . it's where the excitement is,' came the reply.

Next up, Gay moved to the Flood Tribunal that was investigating alleged payments to politicians, including fifty grand belonging to a Gilmartin man. Flynn responded, 'I want to tell you about that . . . I've said my piece about that. In fact, I've said too much because you can get yourself in the High Court for undermining the Tribunal so I ain't saying no more about this except to say just one thing and this is all I will say. I never asked or took money from anybody to do favours for anybody in my life.'

Gay continued, 'But you know Gilmartin? You know Tom Gilmartin?'

'Oh yes, yes, I haven't seen him now for some years. He is a Sligo man. Went to England. Made a lot of money. Came back. Wanted to do a lot of business in Ireland. Didn't work out for him. Didn't work out for him. He's not well. His wife isn't well. He is out of sorts.'

'But you are saying you never took money from anybody at any time for any reason?'

Flynn replied, 'I never took money from anybody to do a political favour as far as planning is concerned.'

Later in the conversation, Gay took a question from a member of the audience. A man raised the salaries of MEPs, and Commissioner Flynn responded by giving details of his own earnings. 'I get, give or take, it works out at about, with expenses, £140,000 a year, and I pay 30.3 per cent tax on that, so it is about a net £100,000, and out of that I run a home in Dublin, Castlebar and Brussels. I want to tell you something, try it sometime, when you have a couple of cars, and three houses, three homes and a few housekeepers, but remember, it is a well-paid job, a well-paid job, about 100,000 a year net.'

At the time, Tara Television service was offering repeats of some RTÉ programming, including *The Late Late Show*, in parts of the UK. The developer Tom Gilmartin learned about the comments and was annoyed by them. The controversy reignited.

The following Monday afternoon, Commissioner Flynn was back in Brussels, with the fallout continuing to make headlines. With a cameraman filming, I sought his response to fresh suggestions from Mr Gilmartin that money had been paid over. The commissioner wouldn't comment on the allegations. With one of his cabinet members, he entered a lift. The cameraman kept filming until the steel doors closed tight.

The Late Late Show appearance was a turning point in Flynn's career. In 2012, the Mahon Tribunal decided he had corruptly sought and received a payment from Mr Gilmartin in 1989. He rejected the findings. He subsequently resigned from the Fianna Fáil party as it was moving to expel him. His role as 'a front runner', revisiting the disputed £8 billion structural-funds negotiations, is unlikely to figure in official accounts of those proceedings. He was also the advocate of Ireland's proposed 12.5 per cent corporation tax scheme when it came before the European Commission. But he is most likely to be remembered for the 'I want to tell you something, try it sometime' *Late Late Show* remark about the 'couple of cars and three houses'.

Charlie McCreevy, then the minister for finance, was the provider of another spectacular example of the unexpected in June 2001. A summit of EU leaders was taking place in the Swedish city of Gothenburg. Ireland had caused a major surprise by voting no to the Nice Treaty. Bertie Ahern was Taoiseach at the time, and Brian Cowan was the minister for foreign affairs. Sometimes finance ministers from the member states were invited to summits, but their gatherings usually had sideshow status to the major political discussions.

Mandy Johnston was press officer for the finance minister at the time and diligent at her job. His business was over, and McCreevy would shortly be heading to the airport, but Mandy phoned to say he was available for interview, if required. I explained to her that the chances of him making airtime were slim to none unless he had something newsworthy on his mind. Mandy explained how the minister was keen to acknowledge 'the remarkably healthy development' of the rejection of the Nice Treaty by the people of Ireland.

I waited for the 'but' or the clarification from Mandy. There was none. I quickly scrambled a cameraman, and, within minutes, Charlie McCreevy turned up, as arranged, for interview about the referendum result. Immediately after my first question, he explained how all the main political parties, employers, unions, farming groups and the media had been in favour of a yes vote, but in their wisdom the plain people of Ireland decided to vote no. He told how politicians do not like it when people vote against them, but, 'speaking as an old-fashioned sixties liberal', he thought it was 'a very healthy sign'.

Back at RTÉ headquarters in Dublin, programme editor Mary Butler was busy, less than an hour away from the start of the hour-long *Six One* television news. I phoned her to alert her about the McCreevy Nice Referendum interview we had just recorded. 'What did he say?' she asked.

'Mary, he said the plain people of Ireland have spoken and it is a very healthy development.'

'Tommie, stop messing. Did he say anything interesting?'

'I swear, Mary, he said that and lots more.'

Mary Butler quickly revamped her programme running order, and we dispatched the McCreevy interview by satellite circuits from Sweden to Dublin. Charlie McCreevy, Mandy Johnston and their colleagues were in the air when the interview featured on the bulletin. When they landed in Dublin and switched on their mobile phones, they nearly melted.

Michael Noonan was leader of the main opposition party, Fine Gael, at the time. He was one of the first to react. He called on the Taoiseach, Bertie Ahern, to 'deal with' his finance minister and described the McCreevy remarks as reckless beyond belief, saying they turned him, the Taoiseach and their cabinet colleagues into figures of fun.

Ireland subsequently secured a number of 'clarifications' in relation to its policy on military neutrality, including a provision not binding Ireland to any future EU common defence policy. Turnout was 34.7 per cent in the June referendum, and almost 54 per cent voted against the treaty. With its clarifications gathered, the government held a second referendum. Turnout was up to almost 50 per cent, and the previous result was reversed with a 60 per cent yes vote.

That Gothenburg gathering, where Charlie McCreevy provided his unexpected interview, was my final time to work at an EU summit. Four years after he created international headlines, Charlie McCreevy was nominated as Ireland's representative on the European Commission and secured the internal market and services portfolio.

*

In the Europe editor role, most of my time was spent tracking EU issues and following major political events in European countries. But there were other adventures too. I made a series of low-budget half-hour programmes under the banner *Eurofocus*. One told the story of Needlepark, a public park in the Swiss city of Zurich, where free needles and medical advice were made available to heroin users in an effort to confine the activity to a single area. As the evening light faded, a man with a gun advised us to stop filming and told the cameraman, Hans Deforce, that if he didn't leave, he would throw him and his camera into the river.

Another programme told the story of Irish fans at an international soccer match in Denmark. We came upon Dermot Morgan from the *Father Ted* television series, with his young sons, among the supporters having breakfast in a Copenhagen hotel. Anne Cassin, a colleague from Dublin, made a fine programme for the series about the Erasmus scheme and how it encouraged third-level students to spend a period attending university in another member state.

The editing of the *Eurofocus* programmes usually concluded two days before the transmission deadline. The half-hour circuit cost for sending the material back to Dublin from Brussels would have run to several hundred pounds. I used to go to the Aer Lingus desk at Zaventem airport in Brussels in search of passengers heading to Dublin. Sometimes I'd recognize a would-be traveller. On many occasions I struck up a new friendship. The deal offered was £20 to send the tape by taxi from Dublin Airport to RTÉ or to compensate for the inconvenience of hand-delivering it. And £20 for spending in the airport duty-free. The unusual arrangement never failed – a programme tape never went astray.

One of the happiest memories involved the successful search for a missing Nobel Prize winner. Sometimes, when performing live, the singer-songwriter Christy Moore tells of turning on the BBC Home Service in the middle of the night and hearing of 'a British winner of the Nobel Prize for Literature, Seamus Heaney of Londonderry'. RTÉ's head of news, Joe Mulholland, had some of Christy Moore's instincts when the winner of the award was announced on 5 October 1995. He was determined that the national broadcasting service, not the BBC, would get the first Heaney interview. He phoned me in Brussels. Seamus and Marie Heaney were on holidays in Greece. Everybody was looking for them, but nobody could make contact with them.

It was a dream assignment: head to Greece and find the Nobel Prize winner before someone else gets to him.

My first mentor, John Healy, used to say, 'Kid, in our business you need a guardian angel.' Some helpful presence went into overdrive during the next twenty-four hours. On the flight from Brussels to Greece with cameraman Joseph Backes, in the Olympic Airlines magazine we spotted an ad for helicopter-hire services at Athens airport. The information was torn from the page and slipped into a jacket pocket.

Our call to the Athens hotel where the Heaneys were staying drew a blank. Yes, they had been there and were due to return the following week. But they had left with friends to visit a number of historic sites, and there was no forwarding address. The option to wait until the travellers returned risked failure. It was time to gamble. Personnel at Athens airport confirmed a helicopter was available for hire at 9 a.m. the following morning at a cost of $3,000. The details of my credit card were requested and given. If the planned business fell through, there would be a significant cancellation charge.

The next call was to the Heaney home in Ireland, using the number provided by Joe Mulholland. The message was simple: if the parents called and received the wonderful news about the Nobel Prize, please let them know we had a helicopter on standby to get them back to Athens so that they could make tracks to return home. All we wanted in return for the lift was an interview for RTÉ.

Then, as often happens when one is in a tight corner, the praying started. The hotel room was dark when the mobile phone started to ring, interrupting sleep. It was Seamus Heaney, phoning from Kalamata. The guardian angel was delivering. The Saturday morning helicopter flight brought us beyond Sparta to a small runway, 150 miles from Athens. Seamus and Marie, and their friends Dimitri and Cynthia Hadzi, were waiting in the bar-café part of the tiny airport building. They had learned about the Nobel Prize award from their son Christopher, when they phoned home the previous day. We had a copy of the *International Herald Tribune*, and, when Marie read the front-page story, she jumped up and down like a teenager.

A taxi brought us to a scenic location nearby, and Joseph began filming. Seamus gave his reaction to the news, told of his phone calls to their three children and to his siblings and then began reciting what would later be chosen as Ireland's favourite poem of the century: 'When all the others were away at Mass / I was all hers as we peeled potatoes.'

The interview done, we were ready to make tracks for Athens. But back in the airport café, trouble surfaced. Someone had tipped off a local crew. A cameraman and sound recordist were in our path as we headed for the helicopter. 'Please, sir, just say something. Just something, please.'

Seamus Heaney looked at me. He knew the details of our arrangement, but he also probably guessed the response. 'Maybe just one comment and then we'll head off.' Seamus switched to formal mode, said he was honoured with the award and was on his way back to Ireland. While the pilot fired up the engine, and we fastened our seat belts, I assured myself Joe Mulholland wouldn't start firing hatchets over one sentence. Then the local cameraman ran towards the helicopter, ducked under the rotating blades and began banging on the closed door. 'Please, sir, please, sir, do again, microphone no work.' The take-off process was under way and it wasn't going to be changed. With a clear conscience, we headed skywards.

During the flight back, I made calls to Irish embassy staff

in Athens and to Bride Rosney, special adviser to President
Robinson, and the planning began for a homecoming in Ireland.
Seamus provided the phone numbers of his publishers, Faber,
in England and his great friend Brian Friel, and asked that they
would be told about the arrangements. He wrote a postcard,
bought in the airport café, to Mary Lappin, a loyal friend in
Sligo where he had a bond with the Yeats Summer School from
early in his working life.

At Athens airport, a Greek journalist pal, Eleni Bourkaouris,
was waiting, and she manoeuvred like a getaway driver through
the city streets to television editing and transmission facilities.
The material featured on extended RTÉ television bulletins
that evening.

Stockholm was covered in snow two months later, the night
Seamus Heaney received the Nobel Prize. He told me that his
son Michael had warned him to avoid blubbering during the
ceremony at the city's national concert hall. But he said he did
make eye contact with his family as he formally bowed and it
was one of the happiest eye contacts ever.

He remembered our exertions in Greece and returned the
effort many years later. It was a Sunday evening in Glenties,
Co. Donegal, where the work of his friend Brian Friel was being
celebrated at the MacGill Summer School. Brian wasn't available to talk about himself, and the deadline for the 6 p.m. TV
bulletin was approaching. Seamus Heaney arrived on the main
street after the long drive from Dublin. I directed him towards a
parking spot, and, as soon as he got out of the car, I explained
my predicament. True to his nature, he delivered, a second time.

Seamus sent me a letter, dated June 2011. He enclosed a copy
of the long 'bit of a note' he wrote to himself on the flight home
to Dublin from Athens on Saturday 7 October 1995. It included

a description of our helicopter adventure earlier that day: 'a dream journey, up and over mountains and valleys, olives and vines, oranges and lemons, swaying along the hillsides, over the ridges, a little anxiety-inducing, but absolutely magical, a once-in-a-lifetime strangeness.'

His notes recalled the captain on the Dublin-bound flight coming down from the cockpit to congratulate him and Seamus wrote, 'Ahead of us the sky's a geyser – once again', a reference to a line from one of his early poems, 'Honeymoon Flight'.

He included in the envelope some thoughts on the back of a postcard featuring Paul Cezanne's painting, The Card Players. He signed off with the advice 'Keep Going – Seamus'.

When walking a stage of the Camino with Adrian O'Neill on 30 August 2013, he received a message to his phone that Seamus had died in a Dublin hospital. We sat without saying a word for a long time in a wood in northern Spain, remembering a wonderful man.

*

If tracking down Seamus Heaney ended successfully, the pursuit of his friend, another giant, Brian Friel was a long and more complex saga. In 1980, with the actor Stephen Rea, Friel established Field Day as a cultural and intellectual response to 'the political crisis in Northern Ireland'. From a base in Derry's Guildhall, they began staging productions, starting with Friel's Translations, that would afterwards tour Ireland and then travel on the international circuit. I was beginning my RTÉ career, based in Derry, during those early times of Field Day. Getting access to the in-demand, busy playwright Friel proved impossible. The administrators instead set up an interview with Stephen Rea.

Many years later, when I was based in Brussels, Ireland were playing the Netherlands in an important soccer match. We went to Amsterdam to film the scenes in an Irish pub. There, in the middle of the Irish expats, we found Stephen Rea. I couldn't believe our good fortune – the star of Neil Jordan's wonderful film *Angel* was taking time off from another movie project to indulge his passion for football. We had a great evening together.

A number of times afterwards I tried to persuade Brian Friel to do an interview. On two separate occasions, the McGill Summer School in Glenties, Co. Donegal celebrated his work. I was in there on the magical summer's night in 1991 when the members of the Abbey Theatre staged a production of his masterpiece *Dancing at Lughnasa* in the packed hall of Glenties Comprehensive School. The play is based around the lives of Friel's relatives who lived in the area. The audience had many locals who recognized the versions of their former neighbours on the stage and several times they whispered their names. Friel and his wife, Anne, sat in the front row with their friends Gay Byrne and Kathleen Watkins, watching the production. The occasion was so perfect that an RTÉ interview with the playwright would probably have taken from it.

In February 2009, Queen's University Belfast opened a studio theatre on its campus, named after Friel. I wrote to him at the time but again the opportunity to interview him eluded me. He wrote to me afterwards from his home in Greencastle. I still have the letter.

Dear Tommie,

Thank you for your note – and your patience. But I'm afraid, I'm as 'elusive' (your word) as ever. Others would say churlish. Others plain odd. But there it is. I do know I'm a nuisance but I also know you'll have some understanding of my position/attitude.

Warmest good wishes to yourself.

Brian

Shortly before he died in October 2015, out of the blue, his wife Anne rang. Brian was close by and Anne passed the phone to him. We spoke for a few moments. It was a conversation and a kindness I didn't expect and will never forget.

6

Living with cancer

I was thirty-seven when cancer came knocking unexpectedly. We were living in Belgium. I usually had breakfast at the same time most mornings, but eating patterns afterwards varied and were linked to work. I was travelling a lot, sometimes taking two flights or more in a week. The occasional stomach upset or diarrhoea was put down to irregular eating or dodgy food, consumed on the run.

But when we were home for Christmas in 1993, the level of discomfort from stomach cramps was sufficient to send me to a Sligo GP, Frank Hayes. We were due to take a local flight to Dublin that afternoon and from there head back to Brussels. Dr Hayes treated me in his Wine Street surgery but asked me to call him from Dublin Airport. When I reported that the pain was still active, he advised that we travel on to Belgium but seek help there if the problem hadn't eased.

The Belgian GP who called to our home that night in Rixensart dispatched me by ambulance with a letter to a hospital in Ottignies, eight kilometres away. I was brought to theatre with a suspected appendix problem. In the recovery room, as I emerged from sedation, a nurse from Burundi mentioned the word 'cancer' for the first time. Back in the surgical ward, a young surgeon, Bernard Majerus, came to my bedside. He explained that I hadn't an appendix issue, but he had discovered a blockage in my small bowel, caused by a tumour, and had removed it. He also said that he found other lesions further up, in my mesentery area (the scaffolding for the small bowel), and there were more small lumps on my liver. He was awaiting the results of tests, but he suspected I had a rare form of cancer, carcinoids or neuroendocrine tumours (NETs), that grow slowly and secrete hormones. They probably had been in my body for a long time. It was the first time I heard the word 'metastases', the term used to describe the collection of tumours that had spread from the primary site to my liver, gathering like fallen leaves at a drain.

Dr Majerus assured me that with the tumour in my small bowel gone, my digestive system would recover and function as normal again. He said that my condition would be regularly monitored, I should be able to live and work normally, and, with luck, I could live for many years. I began processing what he told me. I wasn't frightened by the idea of having cancer or ashamed of it. I didn't feel that I was terminally ill. The low moment came when Ceara swept into the ward with our nine-month-old daughter, Moya, keen to hear how the appendix problem had been tackled. That exchange, sharing unexpected news, was the only time that I struggled to keep things together.

There was a small oratory on the ground floor of the hospital. I will never forget the sense of peace I got while sitting there, reflecting, with nobody else around. It dawned on me that at some stage everybody dies. That's a truth we spend most of our lives avoiding or not acknowledging. I thought of my mother, losing her father before she was born. And Ceara, whose father died when she was a baby of less than a year. I prayed and hoped that the same would not happen to Moya and that I would live long enough to give her a sense of how much I loved her. Several times since, when trouble came knocking, I've searched for and found the sense of the inner peace I first experienced in the prayer room of that Belgian hospital. At its core is a phrase I heard my father use many times, 'We're all just passing through.'

One morning, soon after the surgery, an RTÉ colleague phoned, looking for a quick contribution to a radio programme. Rather than explain I was in hospital, recuperating, I participated in the short live radio interview. Afterwards I explained to a manager at base that I was recovering from a small operation and would be back at work shortly. The news found its way to Fintan Ryan, RTÉ's head of facilities, because he rang me. I told him about the small lump that was removed. 'And that will be benign and you'll be grand,' said Fintan quickly and then followed up, 'Did they find anything else?'

'Well, I have a few other spots . . . and some of them are on my liver,' I replied.

'Oh, Jesus, you're fucked,' Fintan blurted out. My great friend, hundreds of miles away, was so concerned for me that he couldn't restrain his worry.

'No, I'm not. I'll be grand. This is manageable,' I assured him. And I believed it.

During the days after surgery, while I recuperated at our home outside Brussels, Commissioner Pádraig Flynn made a lunchtime visit. His driver struggled to get the official car down the narrow path to our house. I was wearing a dressing gown as we sat drinking coffee. He asked about the nature of my illness and when I mentioned the Belgies had diagnosed a cancer condition, the shock registered on his face. I could see him scanning the room – thin man in his late thirties, wife with a young baby sitting opposite. After a telling silence, it was his turn to surprise. 'Make sure you get the best advice and the best treatment. And don't worry about the money side. Because while Flynn has it, you are welcome to it. Make sure you get the best treatment.' I thanked him for his kindness and quickly changed the subject. Ceara and I would never have entertained such an offer but we both recognized the sincerity behind the spontaneous response.

In the years immediately afterwards, I compartmentalized my health issue and got on with living. The policy of Dr Majerus and his colleagues was to monitor the condition, using a combination of scans, urine and blood tests, carried out every six months. An additional procedure was provided at the nuclear medicine unit of a large Brussels hospital, Saint-Luc. This involved injecting a marker into my body, so-called octreotide. The substance locked onto the special receptors in the tumour deposits so that during a scan they lit up like the lights on a Christmas tree.

The disease seemed to be stable. I carried on working and living at full tilt. Ceara and I discussed the hope of bringing new life into the world, a sibling for Moya. The possibility that she could find herself raising two small children alone seemed melodramatic to her, and she quickly dismissed it. Our son, Joe, arrived into the world on 4 July 1996, US Independence Day, the same birthday as my sister, Paula. I brought Moya to visit her new baby brother in the same Ottignies hospital where I was having my other adventures.

In the movie *Casablanca*, Humphrey Bogart has those great lines, 'Of all the gin joints in all the towns in all the world, she walks into mine.' My *Casablanca* moment happened in an almost empty Kempinski Hotel bar in Budapest. I was in Hungary with John Downing of the *Irish Independent*, covering a visit of President Mary Robinson. During downtime, we found ourselves sitting at a bar counter beside the Irish scientist Frank Gannon. He was based in University College Galway but was soon to take charge of the European Molecular Biology Organization in Heidelberg. He looked like the actor Donald Sutherland. Even though he came from my hometown, Sligo, and I was familiar with his parents' newsagent's, gift shop and bar, Broderick's, I had never met him. I knew his wife, Mary Murray, because she was a neighbour during our school years.

A friendship began that night. It deepened when we'd meet during Frank's occasional trips to Brussels for meetings of EU research groups. The scientist in him took an interest in my cancer condition. In time, his intervention would help to prolong my life. Other factors played a role too. At crucial times, unexpected good fortune helped me. Without such luck I would not be around to provide this account. The radiologist who carried out my ultrasound tests in Ottignies had a daughter working up her master's thesis about the preparations for the EU's single currency. He knew that my reporting work included tracking those plans. He would sound out my views and gather information for his daughter as he moved the scanning tool along my exposed stomach and viewed the images of my diseased liver on a monitor. At the end of one session, when I had shared my predictions about which member states might qualify for entry to the euro club, he said to me that it might be an idea to get a second opinion about my condition.

Two fascinating cases I was following in the Court of Justice of the European Union at the time involved Luxembourg citizens Raymond Kohll and Nicolas Decker. Kohll wanted

Luxembourg's health system to reimburse him for his young daughter's orthodontic treatment that he had paid for in nearby Germany. Decker was also pursuing the Luxembourg authorities, in his case for repayment for the prescription glasses he bought, over the border, in the Belgian town of Arlon. The Court of Justice – the EU's highest authority – ruled in their favour. It established the principle of an EU citizen having the right to access health care or services in a neighbouring member state, in certain circumstances. I sensed, at the time, that the court decision was significant, but I didn't fully grasp how important it would become for me.

In early 1998, Frank Gannon asked that we would set aside time for a chat when he was on a work trip to Brussels. During the conversation, he told me how he researched my health condition, and all the information gathered suggested an aggressive policy should be used against my disease. He said he was worried that if something wasn't done to deal with the tumours inside my body, the cancer would kill me. Sobered by Frank's forthright advice, I sought information from what was then a young internet system. It threw up details of a Carcinoid Cancer Foundation, based in New York, established by an authority on the disease, Dr Richard Warner.

Late one night, when I found the courage to call the foundation, Richard's wife, Monica, answered the phone. From the other side of the Atlantic, her empathy to a total stranger came through. Yes, I could come for a consultation in New York, but it might be a better option to seek help in her native country, Sweden. She had just returned from visiting there, and a doctor based in the city of Uppsala, Kjell Öberg, was an expert on the condition. Prompted by Monica Warner's suggestion, I made contact with the Swedes. They quickly confirmed by email that they would see me. It seemed that a new, more serious phase of life as a patient with a cancer condition was about to begin.

A practical issue required attention. How could it be funded? Surgeon Peter Morrison agreed to meet me in Sligo. As we sat down at the end of his working day in rooms at Sligo's Garden Hill hospital, he said that each time he spotted my reports on RTÉ he remembered fixing a hernia problem in my groin area in 1987. When I began explaining the reason for my visit and mentioned 'carcinoids', his face changed. His concern for me was obvious. As he listened to my account of what was found during the surgery in Belgium, I wondered was he revisiting the hernia operation and questioning if a hidden tumour might have caused that problem.

I told him how I was hoping to go to Sweden for expert help, using the EU judgments from the Kohll and Decker cases in the Court of Justice. Eligibility for financial support from my native country would require the recommendation of an Irish consultant and the authorization of my local health board. I showed Dr Morrison the documentation about it. He had never before received such a request. He instantly said he would support it because it offered me the possibility of treatment that he could not provide. It was also new territory for the North Western Health Board, whose chief executive, Pat Harvey, signed for me what is called an E112 form. Thanks to their backing, I became the first Irish patient to travel to Sweden, using my rights as an EU citizen, established in a Court of Justice judgment, to access care abroad.

The instinct that journalism encourages to pursue information had a role in setting me on course for my travels to Uppsala. I decided that I would treat the trip to Sweden as a news story. I was about to begin acquiring knowledge that might, in time, be of interest to others. There probably was another truth that I wasn't admitting to myself: a busy news assignment creates a constant flow of logistical demands, and it limits the space to indulge in worry or fear. I arranged a rendezvous with a Swedish cameraman and prepared to go travelling behind enemy lines.

That April 1998 trip introduced me to Sweden's oldest university hospital, Uppsala, where a team of experts had established an internationally recognized centre for the treatment of NETs. The unit was run by Professor Kjell Öberg. His work history suggested he was in his fifties, but he had the face of a young man. As he provided a quick tour of the facilities, his gait did justice to his penchant for cross-country skiing. After studying my files and recent set of test results, Öberg sat me down and explained the future I might face without intervention. It would likely involve tumour growth, with symptoms including flushing and diarrhoea and more liver metastases. The disease might then spread to the bones and the brain. He agreed to take over the management of my treatment. It would involve twice-yearly visits to Uppsala to track the development of the disease.

Professor Öberg recommended that I immediately begin taking an injection of a drug called interferon, three times a week. For over twenty years his team had been using it to treat patients at the centre. When interferon was discovered in the 1970s, some US clinicians hailed it as the silver bullet for many cancers. It actually featured on the front cover of *Time* magazine in March 1980. The hope quickly dissipated, and, in some cases, the side effects of the drug became more challenging than the original illness. But Öberg and a handful of others persisted with prescribing low doses of interferon for carcinoid patients. They recorded consistent patterns of positive results.

Those days in the Swedish hospital were the first times spent among patients with the same condition. We gathered for meals in a common room on the ward. It had facilities to make tea and coffee and space to watch television and chat. The majority of the group were Swedes, from other areas of the country as well as the immediate region. A lot of them spoke English. Without prompting, Darwinian 'survival of the fittest' instincts kicked in. I found myself looking at the others, checking whether they too were thin and had a tell-tale patch of blotchy skin under the cheekbone. In conversations punctuated by pauses, we shared details of our lives, including frequency of diarrhoea and flushing episodes, date of first diagnosis and history of coping with the disease. All the time the mind was quietly doing the sums, working out one's at-risk status in the subset of the chronically ill.

A young doctor, Staffan Welin, was my main contact in Uppsala during that first visit. He introduced me to a surgeon colleague, Per Hellman, who agreed to have a role in supervising my care. He was younger than Öberg and, like all the staff at the centre, was comfortable communicating in English. He explained to me it was not possible to get rid of the disease. It is a chronic condition, and I would have to live with it. His objective would be to contain it. The interferon injections were the first weapon in the fight, but he was keen to begin planning for the removal of the diseased lymph nodes in the mesentery area. They were likely to spread the cancer and cause further complications. Even though they were close to a main blood artery, the aorta, he was confident he could carry out the procedure without causing damage.

The freelance Swedish cameraman was filming the exchanges between Per Hellman and me.

'It sounds like I am not going to die from this thing for a long time.'

'You seem to be very fit right now. If we can keep the liver as it is, or maybe make it a little bit better, you are not going to die from this for a long time.'

'How long?'

'Hmm. That's a very difficult question . . . Maybe twenty, thirty years, but no one really knows the answer.' It was a gunk to discover that the disease was active. But the realization was balanced by the relief that I had found the Swedes, and, in the range of cancer challenges, a NETs condition might be at the manageable end.

The interferon injections had side effects: flu-like symptoms and fatigue. The drug could also dampen the mood. It became important to not lie in bed in the mornings, shadowboxing with vulnerability. Surgeon Per Hellman kept track of the six-monthly test results. Two years after we first met, he advised that it was time to return to Uppsala for surgery. Once more I was on a story, using journalism as a shield. As I regained consciousness after the operation, a cameraman filmed Per Hellman explaining the outcome. 'You did not have any tumour in the small intestine, but you had the lymph node that we talked about and that's taken away now. We had to take part of the small bowel too, otherwise it would have been impossible to take out the lymph node, but you have plenty of small bowel left.'

'How is the prognosis, Per?'

'It's good. You have this type of tumour that grows very slowly. We have taken away the risky part . . . now, the treatment in the future will be for your liver.'

Our two children were very young at the time, and I had

insisted that Ceara remain with them in Ireland while I travelled to Sweden. I had miscalculated the debilitating effects of the surgery. Stupidly, the offer of company from family members and close friends was declined. But RTÉ colleague Joe Mulholland made his unilateral decision, and he was a welcome sight when he arrived in Uppsala to help me on the journey home.

*

Eighteen months passed before the circumstances coalesced to make public the story of the cancer journey. The twice-yearly checks in Sweden indicated the disease was stable. I was back in Belfast, working in Ireland, and decided that it was time to share the information about the E112 system and the opportunities it offered to Irish patients. My mother as well as my father had passed so there was no risk of offending her reservations about sharing personal matters. Ceara agreed to set aside her own misgivings.

RTÉ assigned a talented producer, Julian Vignoles, to oversee the *True Lives* television documentary. 'Europe, Cancer and Me' was screened on Tuesday, 8 January 2002. Unusually, because of the viewer reaction to it, the programme was repeated the following weekend. But it also drew significant criticism from some of the country's leading doctors. Some of them took offence even before the programme aired.

As part of its advance publicity campaign, RTÉ provided *Irish Times* journalist Kathy Sheridan with a copy of the programme, and she interviewed me about it. Her article was flagged on the *Irish Times* front page on Monday, 31 December: 'Form E112 Probably Saved Tommie Gorman's Life'. Kathy's feature on page 12 faithfully reflected our conversation. As well as telling how the E112 form had secured access to life-saving treatment in another EU member state, it included my views about the 'desperately degrading two-tier system we already have and which is insulting to us as a race'.

The day after the documentary was aired, the RTÉ programme *Liveline* called, keen to discuss it. As the live radio interview began, I wasn't aware that oncologist Dr John Crown was already lined up to participate. I hadn't seen his article in that morning's *Irish Times*, under the headline 'Factual Inaccuracies in Gorman's Portrayal of Irish Cancer Services'. He had submitted it in response to Kathy Sheridan's feature. There was no merit in participating in a Punch and Judy-like row on the national airwaves. The exchanges were civilized. I was familiar with Dr Crown's work as one of the country's leading clinicians in his field. In later years our paths crossed a number of times, and the interactions were always respectful.

Several other medics took issue with my views, and one suggested I could have 'all the treatment modalities somewhere in Dublin'. Peter Morrison, the Sligo surgeon, was criticized by some of his colleagues for supporting my application to access treatment abroad. In reference to his decision, one of his fellow medics wrote, 'Sligo is nearer Dublin 4 than Uppsala. Why was Tommie Gorman sent to Sweden?'

It was unfortunate that the programme drew me into a public spat with some of the country's most accomplished consultants. But it resulted in thousands of letters, cards, emails and phone calls. The expressions of empathy and support were humbling, and the scale of the response was unexpected. The documentary had found resonance with a sector of society that was challenged by illness and fearful it was not being adequately served by the country's health service. It shared important information with patients who had the same form of rare cancer and were in danger of falling into the cracks in the Irish health service. They became part of the next set of Irish citizens who availed of their right to travel to Uppsala for treatment and care.

Catherine Cheattle in Tramore, Co. Waterford, was one of the first to write. She had been told she had a terminal condition and she was sent home to die. Her son and his partner brought forward their wedding date so that Catherine would be present for it. Her husband, Frank, was wary of going to sleep in case she slipped away during the night. When Catherine went on her first trip to Sweden, a young consultant, Dan Granberg, assured her that her disease could be stabilized, and, with luck, she would survive for many years. That's what happened.

John Fallon from Ballina in Co. Mayo was another who made contact. During his surgery in Castlebar, Co. Mayo, an NET was discovered and removed. As John recovered in the hospital, a doctor told him about the Uppsala centre that had featured in the RTÉ documentary and advised him to follow up on it. Aidan Hennessey from Ballybofey, Co. Donegal, had been receiving treatment in Ireland for carcinoid disease since 1994. He too contacted me for advice on how to access care in Sweden. Patrick McAndrew, a young father from Bonniconlon in Co. Mayo, was another with NET secondaries on his liver. He was resigned to accepting that he was in the final stages of his life. He and his family had given up hope until he travelled to Uppsala where the team took over the management of his disease.

From 2002 onwards, the pattern developed of Irish people with NETs cancer using the E112 system to access care abroad. Patients from Israel, Argentina, as well as some other European countries were also availing of the Swedish expertise. Many of the larger EU member states had their own dedicated centres. For the citizens of a small country like Ireland, where there was no established treatment path for patients with our rare form of cancer, the Uppsala unit was a godsend. In the different specialist areas, including radiology, gastroenterology, endocrinology, surgery and oncology, it had a team of experts able to identify and treat the disease.

Tom O'Donoghue, a school principal from Co. Tipperary, Dublin-based HR manager Carmel Connellan, Terry O'Neill from Dublin and Margaret Browne from Galway were among the first group of fellow travellers. Our standard itinerary involved a direct flight from Dublin to Stockholm, or sometimes an extra leg taking in Copenhagen, then a bus or taxi from the airport to Uppsala and three days or more for tests or treatment in building 78B, the endocrine oncology unit. Sometimes we felt we were like the wide-eyed participants of a school tour or a package holiday, absorbing the details of the unfamiliar. But in this instance it involved the facilities that might keep us alive.

We learned how a particular diet had to be followed in advance of twenty-four-hour urine collection, avoiding tomatoes, chocolate, bananas and coffee. The CT, MRI and ultrasound scans took place a distance away from our ward on the vast complex, so a porter would arrive driving a battery-powered vehicle like a golf buggy to transport us, via the network of tunnels underneath the buildings and the public road, to the radiology department.

The hospital is within walking distance of the town. Because of its university links and the Fyris river running through it, Uppsala has a feel of Galway in the 1970s. Often, in between tests, to reassure myself that I was alive and healthy, I'd go for long walks along the river into the countryside. The cinema close to the hospital shows films in English, and it too proved a welcome source of distraction. Inevitably, Uppsala has an Irish pub, O'Connor's, and some nights I arranged to meet surgeon Per Hellman there, minus his white coat.

Two years after the major bout of surgery, one of Uppsala's senior consultants, Barbro Eriksson, spotted me doing an interview about Northern Ireland on Swedish television and noticed that I was flushing during it. When I travelled to Uppsala for my six-monthly check, Barbro's suspicions were confirmed. The levels of hormones secreted from the tumours were up and these resulted in dilation of the veins in the face. A condition called carcinoid syndrome was confirmed. In response to the problem, my treatment regime changed. As well as the interferon jab I was now giving myself once a week, a new drug, octreotide (Sandostatin), was prescribed, and it had to be injected into the muscle every twenty-eight days by a doctor or nurse. Depending on when the due date fell, I'd get the monthly Sandostatin jab at the practice of Belfast GP Domhnall MacAuley, or from my sister-in-law in Sligo, Yvonne Barrett, a nurse.

By the Swedes' calculations, I had thirty tumours, dotted like pepper and salt on my liver. They explained that surgery was not feasible as it would turn the organ into a Swiss cheese. The purpose of the monthly injections was to restrict the spread of the disease and to counteract the effects of the harmful hormones secreted by the tumours. If problems arose, other treatments would be considered. Liver replacement wasn't an option as even with a successfully functioning new organ the disease would remain elsewhere in my body. The likelihood was the disease and the new liver could not coexist and I would be in deep trouble within two years.

Four years of stable health followed. Like earlier adventures, what happened in 2006 was unexpected. A cameraman colleague, Donal Wylde, was in Belfast, giving refresher training to the three office crews. At the end of his day's work, we were going for something to eat when I became ill. Donal brought me to the emergency department of Belfast's Royal Victoria Hospital. It was busy to the point of bedlam. Well after midnight, a kind nurse, Evelyn Harden, found a quiet space on a corridor to park my bed. My liver function indicators were highly abnormal, but a series of tests identified that the problem was an inflamed gall bladder, blocked by gallstones, not my cancer condition.

Weeks later, after the gall-bladder infection had settled, I was called back to the Royal Victoria Hospital to have it removed. The night before the operation, a young anaesthetist came to the ward to discuss the plans. I explained to her about my NETs condition and asked if arrangements were in place to provide a drip supply of a product called octreotide (similar to the Sandostatin I was receiving) during the surgery. The Swedes were always advising us to ask that the drug be made available during any significant operation, to act as a safety net in case a surge of harmful hormones was released while on the operating table. The anaesthetist was unfamiliar with the practice so I phoned Dr Dan Granberg in Uppsala. Thankfully, he answered the call immediately and explained the rationale behind the policy to the anaesthetist.

The following morning, a gowned surgeon arrived into the ward, ready for action, and I was first on his list. He was surprised when I asked about the octreotide drip that I had brought to the attention of his colleague the previous night. He then leafed through his paperwork and found the new page of information. My place in the operating queue changed while a search was organized to get hold of the product. Once that was done, the troublesome gall bladder was expertly removed without a hitch. It was reinforcement of two truths I learned many times during my life as a patient: (1) you need luck, and (2) ultimately you have to take some responsibility for managing your own condition.

The drama in the Royal Victoria Hospital was not over. The final act happened during recovery after the operation. I was confined to bed, hooked up to a number of machines, when a patient from the opposite side of the ward wandered over late one night. He began tinkering at the tubes and connections, telling me how he wanted to put on the kettle to make a cup of tea. The Co. Tipperary-born sister in charge of the ward heard my shouts, arrived at the speed of light and restored order.

Several years passed before I discovered that a side effect of the Sandostatin injections I began taking in 2002 is that they sometimes create gallstones.

*

The year 2008 marked the tenth anniversary of my first trip to Uppsala. But a decade after the Swedes took over management of my care, eight years after Per Hellman's intricate surgery work, the 'stable' status of the disease changed and the description changed to 'progression'. The dogs had awoken from their slumber. The Swedes assured me they had a plan to send them back to sleep again. They would reach into their armoury for new weaponry. Their proposed response involved a new form of therapy (known as radionuclide therapy), using a product called lutetium-177. This product latches itself to the tumour cells and goes to work by releasing radioactive emissions and nuking the nearby tumour cells, or so it's hoped. The Swedes were accessing it from a nuclear medicine plant in Holland. The same treatment was being provided at another internationally recognized centre, the Erasmus hospital in Rotterdam.

Consistent with its history, Uppsala was among the first places in the world to offer the option. It would be a further ten years before the US regulatory authority, the Food and Drug Administration, approved the use of the drug on patients in the United States. Good luck again had me in the right place to access the treatment I needed. I was the very first of what would become a long line of Irish patients to receive the new lutetium therapy.

The plan involved spending several days in Sweden, preparing for the first infusion, getting it and then remaining in the hospital while the impact was closely monitored. One factor requiring attention was the possible danger of the treatment causing kidney damage. The team hoped I would be able to tolerate four rounds, spaced by gaps of six to eight weeks.

I was excited when I was wheeled in to the treatment room in the nuclear medicine unit for the first dose. I remained conscious throughout the procedure, over several hours. The radioactive substance arrived in a sealed metal container, and a team in protective suits began feeding it into my body by a drip. It was like a scene from *Star Wars*. Afterwards, I was brought back to a single isolation room and remained there for twenty-four hours while the radioactivity calmed and slowly exited my body. When I was heading for Ireland at the end of each cycle, the hospital authorities provided a formal explanatory letter in case the radioactive residue set off an alarm at the airport security scanners.

Work provided great distraction during that phase of new treatment. Once the Stockholm flight arrived in Dublin Airport, journalism took over. There was a lot going on. The DUP changed its leader, with Peter Robinson replacing Ian Paisley. Brian Cowen took over from Bertie Ahern as Taoiseach and Fianna Fáil leader. RTÉ opened a swish new Belfast office on the ninth floor of the Centrepoint building, opposite the BBC. When I needed to slip away to Sweden, without fuss my back was covered by one of my RTÉ colleagues – Michael Fisher, Brendan Wright or Áine Ní Ghallchóir – or by two enthusiastic reporters on attachment from Dublin: Laura Whelan and Sharon Gaffney.

After the lutetium treatment, the Swedes told me I could stop the weekly interferon injections. The associated side effects – flu-like symptoms and fatigue – disappeared when the injections ceased. But a year after the final round of the lutetium, Dan Granberg in Uppsala was concerned by the results of tests. He told me that I required further intervention because the disease was still active. This time he was recommending a procedure called radioembolization. It involves using tiny beads of radium, made by an Australian company, Sirtex, to scour the cancerous areas of the liver.

So in February 2010 I was back in Sweden once more. In the procedure room, an incision was made in my groin area and a catheter was inserted into the large artery of the leg. I was fully conscious, listening to the account of it being advanced to the hepatic artery, which supplies the liver tumours with blood. I was chatting away to the team as they then began to direct the millions of microspheres through the catheter towards the problem areas.

But all of a sudden I couldn't talk. Dan Granberg quickly realized that some of the liver tumours were reacting to the disturbance by secreting hormones. He immediately took corrective action by upping my infusion doses of octreotide to stop me arresting on the table. The alert lasted no more than two minutes as Dan's prompt action cancelled out the danger.

There was a second part to the saga. In the endocrine oncology unit, activity levels were scaled back at the weekends and the small number of patients left there were usually transferred to another area of the hospital. That's how I ended up in an unfamiliar part of the hospital on the weekend after the radioembolization procedure. On a Saturday afternoon, I was in a single room, alone. Lying in bed, weak, I was drifting in and out of consciousness. I said to myself, *This is how people die.* I also thought, *I've had a good life.* I was in no way angry, and I was actually ready to go. Suddenly there was another person in the room. It was a doctor I knew, a Serbian woman, Gordana Kozlovacki. From meetings over the years, we had become friends, helped by long discussions about politics in Northern Ireland and her accounts of her experiences in the Balkans.

That weekend, Gordana was at home, on call for emergencies only. But she decided to come to the hospital to check on me. When I described how I felt, she immediately examined the area of my groin where an incision had been made. A nurse called Madde came to help her. From below the skin at the wound site they extracted a sizeable lump of pus. Gordana afterwards told me sepsis was the issue.

Four months later, when Dan Granberg and his colleagues assessed the impact of the radioembolization work, they were pleased with the results. But one tumour was still causing trouble. Once more they reached into their weapons locker. Because of where the problem was located on my liver, surgery wasn't an option. This time, Dan recommended a procedure called radiofrequency ablation.

His colleague who took charge of the work was an interventionist radiologist. Using the images on a screen to guide her, she directed a needle-like probe towards the trouble spot. Once it locked onto the tumour, an electrical current was generated through the probe to zap it. The laparoscopy method was used – only a small hole was made in the skin when inserting the probe. The necessary work was done in less than an hour. Immediately afterwards the liver area was sore, but following a few days' rest I was ready to go back to Ireland and keen to resume work.

*

The procedure was a complete success. The troublesome tumour has not reappeared since. That radiofrequency ablation work was carried out in June 2010. It was the final time that I travelled to Uppsala to avail of the Swedish expertise to keep me alive. The next decade involved a radical change of emphasis when I became involved in the efforts to establish our own Irish version of the Swedish model. The Dublin-based endocrinologist Donal O'Shea made the first approach about improving the structures and facilities for NETs patients in Ireland.

In recent years, Donal became widely known for his contributions to the RTÉ television series *Operation Transformation*. He has two brothers, Diarmuid, a Dublin-based consultant geriatrician, and Conor, a former Irish rugby international and coach. Their late father, Jerome, was a legendary GAA player who won three All-Ireland titles with Kerry in the 1950s.

In his work at St Vincent's Hospital in Dublin, Donal was regularly meeting people with NETs disease. He became one of the first Irish doctors to sign the E112 applications of patients who needed a consultant's support to access care in Sweden.

Donal was aware of my health situation and the growing number of fellow patients travelling abroad. He phoned me and asked that we meet to discuss what sort of improvements could be made.

In our first discussions, he was honest about Ireland's absence of proper services for people with our disease. Donal talks in a calm, deliberate way and usually makes eye contact with you when speaking. What he proposed that day surprised me. He suggested that we campaign for the establishment of a national centre in Ireland where NETs patients could receive the appropriate level of care. He said that some of his colleagues at St Vincent's Hospital, including pancreatic surgeon Justin Geoghegan and liver surgeon Donal Maguire, had experience in treating NETs patients and were keen to improve services. He suggested Vincent's was the place best for a national centre.

Donal was very frank about his own situation. He was keen to help people with NETs disease, but he was busy with his specialist areas, which included diabetes and obesity. He said there were others, better than himself, who could lead the project once a centre was established. The minister for health and children, Mary Harney, was one of the people we lobbied. Dr Susan O'Reilly was next on our list. She had taken over as director of the National Cancer Control Programme to oversee the implementation of Ireland's cancer strategy. She and her successor, Dr Jerome Coffey, both became important supporters of our plan.

During one of our meetings, Donal O'Shea became animated. He had discovered who he believed would be the ideal person to take charge of the project: Carlow-born gastroenterologist Dermot O'Toole. He had worked for a number of years in France and was acquiring an international reputation for his work on neuroendocrine tumours. Donal believed he would be a great asset if he could be tempted back to Ireland.

The whole project moved up a gear in the autumn of 2011. Many doctors within the Irish health system who were caring for patients with NETs disease were themselves trying to improve the treatment pathways. On 15 October, two Cork-based consultants, surgeon Críostóir Ó Súilleabháin and oncologist Derek Power, organized a one-day meeting of their colleagues at UCC. It was their third such symposium on foregut cancers, but this event was dedicated to the management of NETs. The speakers included experts from the United States, Italy, Denmark and the UK. Dan Granberg arrived from Uppsala in Sweden, and Dermot O'Toole was invited from France. Donal O'Shea came down from Dublin.

It really was a major gathering of international experts. For the organizers, the venue was ideal: Cork, the real capital of Ireland. Unusually, the gathering of medics included a public session for 'patient information discussions'. As someone known to have the condition, I was asked to address it. The large room was full. It was the first such major engagement between Irish NETs patients and their family members with doctors who were trying to keep them alive and healthy.

After the formal discussions ended that night, during a dinner I was honoured to sit beside Professor Gerry O'Sullivan. I had never met him before, but he had extraordinary charisma. He had a strong West Cork accent and was very proud of his farming background. He was a brilliant surgeon and a major figure in cancer research. He was also known for the down-to-earth way he related to his patients. I talked to him about our campaign to establish a national centre for NETs disease and mentioned the positive energy during that earlier meeting

of patients and doctors. Gerry O'Sullivan passed away four
months later from a multiple myeloma cancer condition. He
was sixty-five and a heroic figure of Irish medicine.

He wasn't to know it, but at that symposium he attended
in his UCC alma mater, the seeds were sown for what become
a unique version of *meitheal* or cooperation in the Irish health
service. Encouraged by that UCC conference, the following
year at Trinity College in Dublin we held our first meeting
of NETs patients and their families and decided to set up
a support group. We called it the Netpatient Network and
elected a committee of volunteers and a number of officers.
Mark McDonnell from Lucan, Co. Dublin, agreed to become
chairman. He had been recently diagnosed with the disease.
Parisch Browne from Galway, whose mother, Margaret, was
receiving treatment in Uppsala, volunteered for the role of secretary. A young Co. Wexford accountant, Colm O'Callaghan,
with a NETs condition, accepted the job of treasurer. I was
appointed president.

By 2012, Dermot O'Toole was back in Ireland from France,
working as a gastroenterologist in Dublin's St James's Hospital
and lecturing at Trinity College. The potential 'big-name
signing' was now on the island. The national centre for NETs
care was getting closer. But to achieve the desired result deci-
sion-makers had to think beyond established structures and act
imaginatively. St James's Hospital, Professor O'Toole's workplace, is linked to Trinity College. But St Vincent's Hospital, the
proposed NETs centre location, has academic ties to UCD. A
hybrid work arrangement, involving someone having a foot in
both blocs, is unusual. Thus, 26 June 2014 was an important
day when Susan O'Reilly, the director of Ireland's National
Cancer Control programme, announced the appointment of

Professor O'Toole as national lead, committed to working out of St Vincent's for a number of days each week.

The experts in Sweden had kept me alive and healthy for over a decade. The care they offered was better than what was available in Belgium or in Ireland. But Dermot O'Toole, Donal O'Shea and their colleagues were now committed to building an Irish centre for patients like me. I put my trust in their hands on the understanding that if I needed a procedure to stay alive that they could not provide, they would support me accessing it in Uppsala or elsewhere.

The main value of having a designated place for treating patients with a rare disease is, if run properly, it produces better outcomes. When the different specialists are regularly dealing with the same patterns of symptoms and illness, they become more competent and more fulfilled. Dermot O'Toole and his colleagues began to introduce the changes. One good example was the small but important tweak that happened in the pathology department. During a standard six-month or annual NETs patient review, the level of the chromogranin hormone in the blood is checked. Each day, the hospital processes hundreds of blood samples. With a NETs case, the correct procedure is to have an ice pack on standby, ready to attach to the blood-collection tube. If this practice is not followed, unreliable analysis may result. Lisa Cullen, a nurse administrator, quickly became the centre's main contact point for patients. She works part-time and is paid part-time, but, in practice, she was under pressure to provide a full-time service. Her colleague, Geri Daly, also became proficient in multitasking.

Our support group decided to set aside a day each year, a Saturday in November, when all the different parties come together and seek to pool their energy, expertise and experience.

From the very first gathering, we realized we had discovered a powerful formula: patients, their families and friends, doctors and other health professionals, the pharmaceutical companies and the health-service administrators – all together, committed to improving services.

The question-and-answer session is always the most important part of the day. As well as the Irish consultants, the guest speakers at the gatherings have included the Swedish doctors Kjell Öberg, Per Hellman, Barbro Eriksson, Dan Granberg and Gordana Kozlovacki. For patients and their loved ones, it is an opportunity to have open, face-to-face engagement with experts who are committed to helping them. Many of them have liver secondaries. Some may have a NETs primary tumour on the pancreas. Often they are afraid that they are dying. It is a deeply emotional experience to be among a group with a similar challenge and with doctors who offer hope of prolonging life.

Catherine Donohoe is an important contributor to the annual patient-day events. She is the Health Service Executive (HSE) manager who oversees the issuing of the E112 forms that allow patients to access treatment abroad. The unit she manages is based in Kilkenny. The consistent experience of our patients' organization is that the HSE seeks to help rather than hinder requests for assistance.

An estimated 3,000 Irish people are living with the condition. Sometimes it seems like a lot more. In the way that when you change a car you suddenly spot lots of people driving a similar model, I'm regularly surprised by who is sharing the NETs journey. Andrew Doyle was a Fine Gael government minister for agriculture when he first turned up at our annual patient day. As a journalist, I had many dealings with media lawyer Andrea Martin before coming to know we shared a health challenge.

In 2017, St Vincent's was awarded accreditation as a European centre of excellence for NETs care. It is the thirty-ninth European hospital to get the status, and it is a significant achievement just three years after it formally began to provide specialized care. But it is, at best, a work in progress, and weaknesses in the structure regularly arise. For years, other European centres like Uppsala have been routinely using a product called gallium during scans to identify NETs cancer sites. In Ireland, just two hospitals – both in Dublin: St Vincent's and St James's – offer the facility. In practice, many of our patients struggle to get access to the service. The Irish situation is inferior to the norm elsewhere in Europe.

As the volume of NETs patients coming to the centre increased, the St Vincent's Hospital management struggled to provide the extra staff required. One consistent source of frustration is how sometimes patients with the condition are not referred to the centre of excellence. As a patients' support group, we have raised this problem with senior health-service administrators a number of times.

NETs is often a difficult condition to diagnose, and it is not uncommon in Ireland to come across examples of patients who are receiving inappropriate treatment in an inappropriate place. St Vincent's best but far-from-perfect working relationships are with colleagues in Cork, Waterford and Galway, with the three regional hospitals acting like satellites to the main centre of excellence.

Most of the procedures I received more than a decade ago in Sweden are now available in Dublin. Lutetium treatment is the last highly important missing piece of the jigsaw. Since 2008, the HSE has continued to fund hundreds of Irish patients to receive it in Uppsala and, in more recent times, in Rotterdam and London. Dermot O'Toole is introducing the first lutetium treatment at St Vincent's in late 2022. It will be several years before the Dublin facility has the capacity to serve every Irish NETs patient who requires the procedure. Until that happens, the HSE will continue to fund the costs of patients availing of the service overseas. But for those who, for illness or age reasons, are not able to go abroad, the new Dublin option should improve and prolong their lives. In the longer term, it will provide Ireland with a genuine centre of excellence.

It's ten years since the inaugural meeting of our support group. The current Director of the Cancer Control Programme, radiologist Prof. Risteárd Ó Laoide, has been a supportive presence during that decade. The facilities are dramatically better now, and the direction of travel is positive.

Our support group has a website and a Facebook presence. The social-media traffic is overseen by two of our Cork-based committee members: Mary O'Brien, who has a NETs condition, and her carer, Eoin O'Leary. Often they are the first point of contact for patients and their families who are seeking advice. It is an important service because it is sometimes the place where worries and fears are expressed.

NETs is sometimes called the hedgehog cancer because of its slow growth pattern. But it's a sad truth that sometimes the disease is aggressive and ruthless, that it cannot be stopped or beaten. Steve Jobs, the founder of Apple, one of the world's richest and brightest entrepreneurs, had a NETs diagnosis. Even though he fought to stay alive and had access to expert treatment, he died from the illness.

Among the first committee members of our support group, our secretary, Parisch Browne, lost his mother, Margaret. Our treasurer, Colm O'Callaghan, tried so hard to stay alive for his wife, Majella, and their two boys, but he died in 2017. Mick Fallon, from Templeogue in Dublin, was an energetic building contractor in his forties, very active in his community, when he was diagnosed in 2016. He travelled to Uppsala for several bouts of lutetium treatment and was determined to stay alive for his wife, Sinéad, and their two daughters. We lost Mick in January 2021. Gary Westby, from Skerries in Co. Dublin, lived with the disease for several years. He and his wife, Maura, often took charge of welcoming newcomers to the annual patient day. Gary died in October 2020.

Gerardine Hayes, based in Clonakilty, Co. Cork, was a medical representative for the Novartis pharmaceutical company which manufactures the Sandostatin injection product that many of us receive every twenty-eight days. She was a regular attendee at our annual gatherings and a great practical friend for patients. One afternoon, when I called her with a query, she was unusually subdued. She reluctantly explained how she had been diagnosed with Motor Neurone Disease. She had been for checks after noticing she was sometimes dragging a leg during her busy workdays visiting doctors in hospitals. Gerardine died in July 2020, survived by her husband, Francis, and their daughter, Maedhbh. One of the medics who helps our patients' group lost a sibling to the disease. It is a tribute to his humanity that he quietly rejoices each time he gives a patient good news.

For part of their lives, in Ireland there was no version of a service for people with NETs disease. In some way they had a part in improving that situation and it is part of their legacy. A small but telling indication of the transformation is that Dermot O'Toole, who pioneered treatment of the condition in Ireland, has served as the president of the European NETs treatment consultants network, and Mark McDonnell, the first chairman of the Netpatient Network, is the current chairman of the international patients' support group.

It's twelve years since my last cancer procedure in Sweden. Since then, my treatment has been a case of monthly injections and tests every six months. The scans on the second floor of St Vincent's are carried out by radiographers. It's always a busy place. We chat during the preparations. Finding a site to insert a catheter is often a problem because, as a Swedish nurse once said, my arms are made back to front. Once that's done, I'm ready to slide inside the scanner and hear the familiar instructions, 'Breathe in, hold your breath, breathe out again.'

Invariably the radiographers are younger than me. They are trained to not discuss what they have seen. That function is the responsibility of the consultant radiologist when the results of all the tests are presented for discussion at the multidisciplinary team meeting with all the other experts. But sometimes I sense from the radiographers' silence that the number of liver tumours spotted during the examination is a shock. In such situations, I usually say, 'Don't be spooked. They were first noticed in 1994 and have probably been there since before then.' On a number of occasions, Dermot O'Toole's delight, even surprise, when conveying my stable results is obvious. We both know that I'm on the extreme end of fortunate. Once or twice he has come up with the explanation, 'It must be something in the tumour biology.'

In 2020, for the first time, a scan picked up evidence of a small NETs tumour on my lung. It's highly likely that the chronic disease will mount another stage of active challenge. I'm a positive factor for the Swedes' survivor statistics, and I know it. A steep slope connects the second beach in Rosses

Point to the public car park. I call it 'stress-test hill'. When I found myself struggling for breath after it, I knew I was in need of repair. In 2018, cardiologist Niall Mulvihill fitted a stent in one of my arteries and that problem was fixed.

In that Belgian hospital oratory in 1994, circumstances encouraged me to think about my own mortality. The pleadings and hopes made then have all been answered and more. Awareness of my good fortune and acceptance that I'm owed nothing regularly provided ballast and perspective in the years since my cancer diagnosis. In a very real way it has helped me to understand who and what matters.

7

Love, sport and the
Roy Keane interview

Fred Nérac shared with me something profound that his father had said. It was summarized in the phrase, 'What is life but love and sport.' Fred was one of the first new friends I made in Brussels. He was a tall, handsome freelance editor-cameraman from Chambéry in the French Alps. Often during an edit he would rhythmically tap his fingers along the bench, following his instincts as a jazz drummer. He was fun company when having a beer or a coffee at the end of a long day, as, invariably, he would want to dance. When swimmer Michelle Smith was first breaking records, we travelled to the Netherlands to interview her and her husband Erik de Bruin. Afterwards, we rushed back down the road to Belgium to see Fred's young boy, Alex, in the water at a local gala.

When Fred applied for a freelance contract with my colleague from ITN, Bill Neely, I was honoured to provide a reference for him. He worked with Bill on major international stories and reported from war zones in Kosovo and Afghanistan. In March 2003, Fred was part of an ITN team that travelled to Iraq, following the Coalition invasion. They were caught in a battle between US and Iraqi forces. Correspondent Terry Lloyd was shot dead. An interpreter hired in Kuwait was also killed. Cameraman Daniel Demoustier survived the firefight.

Although Fred is presumed dead, his body was never found. His widow, Fabienne, and their children, Alex and Camille, live in Belgium. Their pain was deepened by the lack of information about how Fred had died and their inability to have a proper funeral for him. One of my many cherished memories is how Fred and I struggled to understand each other during our early casual conversations. He told me a number of times that his mother was 'a Miss'. It took a while for me to realize that he was attempting to explain that she was a beauty queen when his father first fell in love with her.

In the months before I finished working in Brussels, Fred was in the middle of an ongoing row and stand-off with his father. When he confided in me about it, I advised him to patch it up. I told him about the void left by the passing of both my father and mother and what I'd do to have thirty seconds in their company. He brought his father to my going-away party. It was the last time I saw him.

The indoor football matches we played at the rented facility of the British School in Tervuren lit up those Brussels years, suspending truth and allowing us to be boys. We had a core Irish group: Seán Flynn from the *Irish Times*, Conor Leeson from the Irish Business and Employers Confederation, Michael Treacy from the IFA, Gerry Murphy from Enterprise Ireland and a Department of Foreign Affairs contingent that included John Boyd, David Cooney, Ciaran Grace and Dan Mulhall. Dan had several brothers, but we regularly told him that he played like an only child because he rarely passed the ball.

We mostly played against German colleagues and always had a beer with them afterwards. My off-centre nose is the

result of international teamwork. It is the work of a junior
South African doctor in a Brussels hospital after an accidental
elbow by a Swedish colleague during one of those games. Tribal
instincts took over when we occasionally played against some
of an English group who used the pitches.

In 1997, when Belgium were hosting Ireland in a European
qualifier play-off, RTÉ's soccer correspondent Tony
O'Donoghue came with his colleagues for a kickabout. The
visiting party including analyst and former Ireland, Manchester
United, UCD defender and Dublin GAA centre half-back Kevin
Moran. That was the only time I played alongside greatness.

But work regularly provided access to another section of
dreamworld, none better than northern Italy in 1994. Ireland
had been drawn in the same USA World Cup group as Italy.
Our mission was to deliver a series of television packages from
the training camp of our opponents. The Italians were using
Milanello, the facilities of AC Milan, the club then owned by the
billionaire Silvio Berlusconi. Suggesting that it was like walking
onto a movie set doesn't come near to describing the experience.
It was more like entering through the open gates of Heaven.

Roberto Baggio – *Il Divin Codino* (The Divine Ponytail) – was
sitting with his legs crossed on the lush grass, talking to several
journalists. Three of the AC Milan contingent, Maldini, Baresi
and Costacurta, were together. Signori and Zola were practising
crosses and frees. They were using a prop in the training session –
wooden figures on a frame with wheels, creating the challenge of
a defensive wall. Suddenly there was great excitement. A visitor
arrived to the camp, and the players converged around him
like a popular cousin. It was one of the team sponsors, Giorgio
Armani, the famous designer, dressed like a model. In the midst
of such exuberance, there was one sad sight. In the distance, the

wonderful twenty-nine-year-old Dutch striker Marco van Basten was jogging alone, testing the ankle injury that would end his international and his AC Milan career.

I would love to revisit and change one part of that magical time. Coming to the end of the session, the players were taking penalties against the giant goalkeeper, Inter's Gianluca Pagliuca. There were no stewards and no barriers interrupting our view or access. It was as relaxed as being close to a kickabout among friends. Pagliuca smiled and acknowledged us a number of times as he collected a stray ball. After the final penalty, in a space of no more than fifteen or twenty seconds, I could have, should have, seized my chance. It would have involved jumping the barrier, grabbing a ball and challenging the Italian first-team keeper. And then, like I saw Danny Blanchflower do on a black-and-white television in the 1962 Cup Final against Burnley's Adam Blacklaw, I could look to one corner, put the ball in the other. My cameraman could have filmed me scoring a penalty against the Italian keeper. But, stupid me, I missed my chance to take evidence of the visit to dreamland, and it will never come again.

*

Work also provided the chance to observe the workings of Manchester United and their manager, Alex Ferguson, on their European travels. The Irish angle was our way in. When United defeated Barcelona 2–1 in the 1991 Cup Winners' Cup Final, Cork-born Denis Irwin lined out at right full. He had signed from Oldham Athletic the previous year. The match took place at the Feijenoord stadium in Rotterdam, less than a two-hour drive from Brussels.

Media access was a doddle. Seán Flynn of the *Irish Times* came in the crew van with us as a makeshift sound recordist. Tom Mulhall, over from Waterford on a visit to his diplomat son, Dan, in Brussels, was delighted with the opportunity to act as 'fixer'. We picked up television interviews in the stadium lounge after the presentation ceremony. Following four barren years at Old Trafford, Alex Ferguson was accumulating silverware – the FA Cup the previous year now followed by the European trophy. His relief was palpable. There had been times when his position was in doubt, and he now had grounds to believe he had turned a corner.

After he won his first league title in 1993, Ferguson brought a second Cork native to Old Trafford. Roy Keane's combative midfield presence was one of many factors that would make United the dominant power in domestic competitions. The constant presence of Irwin and Keane in Ferguson's first eleven increased Irish interest in the club's fortunes. They hadn't won the major European trophy since 1968 – Matt Busby's side that included two Irish full backs, Shay Brennan and Tony Dunne, as well as Northern Ireland's George Best. Speculation grew about whether Ferguson could crack the challenge.

Rebranded the Champions' League in 1992, the main European club competition became slicker. It was more lucrative, too, thanks to additional sponsorship. The television audiences grew as did the media numbers, tracking every twist and turn. When following United to stadiums in places like Milan, Dortmund and Porto, the pressure increased to make some connection with Ferguson, a central figure. It turned out his brother, Martin, had once managed Waterford in the League of Ireland, and that became a useful starting point in conversation.

When the Manchester United boss discovered I was from Sligo, another ball bounced. Decades before, as a young manager trying to learn the trade, he had often received helpful guidance from Sean Fallon, who was then assistant manager to Jock Stein at Celtic, the kingpins of Scottish football. As well as being a Celtic legend from his playing days, Sean Fallon was a native of Sligo. I now had another factor to help make a connection when seeking a soundbite on the margins of a press conference.

RTÉ journalist Richard Crowley was our makeshift sound recordist the night Roy Keane tore into Juventus to deliver a 3–2 Champions League semi-final victory at the Stadio delle Alpi in Turin. The two Corkmen played in what was such an awesome performance it was applauded by many of the Italian fans. Afterwards we took our place behind the crash barriers, the RTÉ branding prominently displayed, in the hope of catching the eye-line of the departing pair.

Keane's yellow card from his heroics in Turin meant he was suspended for the final against Bayern Munich at the Camp Nou stadium in Barcelona. Ferguson kept faith with his ever-reliable Denis Irwin. Richard Crowley was waylaid by his day job, waiting many miles away for an interview with Burmese leader Aung San Suu Kyi that never happened. Another RTÉ colleague, Gerald Barry, gleefully filled the vacancy of fixer cum sound recordist. He witnessed the miraculous comeback when injury-time goals from Teddy Sheringham and Ole Gunnar Solskjær gave Ferguson and United a 2–1 victory. Afterwards, we took our place in the line for the soundbite reflections. Denis Irwin was his usual helpful self. On the night he was entitled to conflicting emotions, Roy Keane went past us but returned.

I saw him in action one final time on the European mainland. In September 2000, Ireland were due to play against the

Netherlands in a World Cup qualifier. Keane had turned twenty-nine the previous month. Under manager Mick McCarthy they had come up short in the qualifiers for the 1998 World Cup Finals in France and the 2000 Euros co-hosted by Belgium and the Netherlands. Their tough qualifying group for the 2002 World Cup in Japan and South Korea included Portugal and the Netherlands.

In the Amsterdam Arena, Robbie Keane headed Ireland into a shock lead after twenty-one minutes. Twenty minutes into the second half, Jason McAteer arrowed a second, low into the corner. The Dutch pulled one back in the seventy-first minute, and Giovanni Van Bronckhorst broke Irish hearts with a spectacular long-range equalizer in the eighty-fourth. We were at the pitchside when the final whistle sounded. Mick McCarthy seemed caught between relief and disappointment. Keane's body language was different. Years of playing with Ferguson's United had taught him when you have the chance you must draw blood. Otherwise the chance is lost.

The following September the Dutch came to Dublin for what turned out to be the decisive clash. Keane whacked Marc Overmars in the opening minute and continued in gladiatorial mode, similar to Turin two years before. Again, Jason McAteer scored with style. It turned out to be the only goal. Missing Gary Kelly after his red card, ten-man Ireland had put out the Dutch and would seal qualification in a two-match play-off against Iran.

Lorraine O'Sullivan's Inpho agency photograph of the limp McCarthy–Keane handshake after the defeat of the Dutch at Lansdowne Road suggested all was not well between manager and captain. The pot boiled over in Saipan.

I became involved in covering one of the biggest Irish sports stories of the decade by default. In May 2002, Ireland's World

Cup squad were in Saipan, preparing for the World Cup finals in Japan and South Korea. A row between Keane and McCarthy erupted and Keane was ready to leave the camp – but the storm passed. The trouble broke out again after McCarthy read the *Irish Times* account of an interview Keane had given to two journalists, Tom Humphries and Paul Kimmage. A raw verbal confrontation between the pair took place at a squad meeting, and McCarthy instructed his team captain to leave the camp.

RTÉ's London correspondent Brian O'Connell was the obvious person to head for Manchester in advance of the arrival of the exiled Keane. But Brian was on leave. Our head of news, Ed Mulhall, knew of my interest in sport. He phoned Belfast and asked me to cover the story. Conor O'Brien gathered camera kit and a mobile edit pack in jig time, and we headed to the airport, with a hire car ordered for the other side.

Once we arrived in Manchester, the priority was to get a handle on the logistics. The RTÉ news desk in Dublin helped with details of a possible contact: Roy Keane's London-based adviser cum lawyer, Michael Kennedy. We then made our way to Hale, fifteen kilometres from Old Trafford. The media huddle outside the closed gates of a large house on South Downs Drive confirmed we had found the right address. We assembled a short television report for the evening bulletins to fly the RTÉ flag and then set in for the arrival of the main man.

Conor had his camera on his shoulder the following morning when the vehicle with Roy Keane in the back seat arrived and then disappeared behind the electronic gates. The excitement moved up several gears shortly afterwards when he re-emerged with his dog and headed towards what was probably a familiar woodland trail. One of the reporters asked, 'What's the dog's name, Roy?' but he ignored all questions. It was the same pattern of silence when he returned with Triggs and went back into his home. The pictures were vivid and the subject a portrait of defiance. The consensus among colleagues was that was our lot. The word from their news desks was that Keane and his agent, Michael Kennedy, had a deal done with the *Mail on Sunday* and that's where he would provide his version of events. All the other media organizations left, and we found ourselves alone.

Our reason for staying was that we had lodged a request for an interview the previous day and that was still in play. My good fortune was that Michael Kennedy took my call when I rang his workplace, Herbert Reeves & Co., in Hackney. I had never before met him or spoken to him. While in the past I had taken my place in the media line, gathering comments from Roy Keane before and after a number of Champions League games, it was unlikely I had registered on his consciousness.

The strong part of the pitch to Michael Kennedy was the RTÉ brand – guaranteed access to the nation's audience. I had explained that Roy Keane was a very popular captain of our national team, and that the whole country was talking about what had happened and would like to hear his account of why he would not be taking part in the World Cup in Japan.

Foolishly, during that first telephone conversation I didn't ask Michael Kennedy for his mobile number, but when I called his London office landline number on the Saturday, my heart lifted. He answered it. For many years afterwards, the pattern continued. Michael or his right hand, Kerri Blake, weren't just available on that office line from Monday to Friday. They would usually answer it after hours, weekends included.

During that second discussion, I told him how Ireland was at fever pitch and that many supporters were still hoping that the row could be resolved. I also suggested to Michael that if the British newspaper the *Mail on Sunday* was set to have an exclusive interview about the crisis in Ireland's World Cup camp, wouldn't it make sense to bring the story to an Irish audience through RTÉ?

Back in Dublin, Ed Mulhall was tracking every twist and turn. He was 100 per cent supportive of the approach that if RTÉ secured an exclusive interview it would get a prime-time slot and would be transmitted in its original form, without edits. The offer was now with Michael Kennedy. All we could do was wait.

In Hale, locals shared their stories about one of their celebrity neighbours. A coffee-shop owner told how Roy Keane sometimes brought his father there when he was visiting from Ireland. A newsagent near Keane's house said the Manchester United player regularly bought his papers there and was 'a nice man'. While we were having a sandwich in a bar, a customer with Irish relations joined us and told how Hale was a good place for totty.

Sunday's newspapers on both sides of the Irish Sea had extensive coverage of the feud. The *Mail*'s exclusive Roy Keane interview included details of him dismissing the possibility of a return to the World Cup. It quoted him saying, 'There is absolutely no chance of that happening, never in a million years. I have been hurt too much by what has happened, let down by so many people within the Irish camp. People are saying it is up to me to apologize. That's very funny. I think it should be the other way round. I won't be going back to Japan. Maybe, just maybe, there is a slight chance I could play for Ireland again, once Mick McCarthy is no longer the manager.' The language suggested an irretrievable breakdown had taken place.

In our dash from Belfast to Manchester the previous Friday, we came prepared for a forty-eight-hour shift at most. But we were still there on Sunday evening and the chances of getting the interview were increasing. The journalist Eamon Dunphy subsequently said that Roy Keane sought his views about it. I have no reason to doubt that. Keane knew Dunphy through working on Keane's autobiography. It was Michael Kennedy who confirmed the interview would happen on Monday afternoon. We immediately called a local hotel and booked an interview space in a function room. Conor hired a local freelance cameraman and asked him to bring lighting. In Ireland, RTÉ confirmed it planned to broadcast an interview with Roy Keane that evening.

As news of RTÉ's interview agreement spread, some media outlets speculated that 'Keane may apologize'. That grew legs to 'Keane expected to apologize'. I didn't imagine that would happen. Nor did I think it appropriate. My priority was to tease out if there was any chance the mess could be resolved so that Ireland could be represented by its best available team in the World Cup tournament.

There were five us in the function room of the Moat Hotel: the two cameramen, Michael Kennedy, Roy Keane and me. As Conor and his colleague adjusted the lights and checked their sound levels, there was time to chat with the interviewee. I mentioned how, early on the Saturday morning, before he got home from the airport, we spotted some of his children at the upstairs windows. 'Looking forward to their daddy coming home,' I said. He had a half smile as he delivered the self-deprecating reply: 'Thinking about the presents.'

As soon as the interview began, in his first response he made clear what most angered him: his view that, in front of his teammates, he had been accused of disloyalty to the team by faking injury (prior to the final qualifying match against Iran).

We discussed the background to his disagreement with Mick McCarthy, the inadequate training conditions in Saipan and his reservations about the preparations. A number of times he returned to what was said in front of the players during the final row, when Mick McCarthy confronted him about the *Irish Times* interview. Keane's position was that his loyalty to his country had been questioned in the accusation that he faked an injury.

I tried to convey the scale of disappointment among fans in Ireland: their team was going to take part in the World Cup without its captain and most important player. My second-last question sought to establish if there was any chance of a reconciliation. 'But if the other parties in this come to you – the FAI, Mick McCarthy (a proud man), the players . . . if they come to you and say, for the good of the country, we want to find a solution to this, we'd like you to be playing for Ireland, are you willing to meet them halfway?'

'I want to play for Ireland . . . We'll have to see . . . Possibly yes . . . There's nobody wants to play for Ireland as much as me . . . I've been involved since I was fifteen, fourteen, going for trials up in Dublin . . . and this is what it's all about, playing in world cups . . . so, hopefully, you never know . . . you just never know . . . but . . . you know, we'll see.'

Immediately after the interview I thanked Michael Kennedy for his help. On his way through the hotel reception, Roy Keane was asked for an autograph and signed it. We walked with him to the hotel car park, and he drove off.

The next challenge, against the clock, was to transfer the material to a master tape, synchronizing the sound and pictures from the two-camera shoot. We paused that work to send back a short extract from the interview for the *Six One*

television bulletin. Two hours later, we were so pressed for
time that the full interview was transmitted live as it was being
received in Donnybrook.

Twenty years on, my view from that day has not changed.
I felt Roy Keane was open to returning to the World Cup and
had said enough to make that possible. But it would have
required enlightened leadership by the FAI to intervene and
resolve the row. Most of its executive members had left for
the World Cup. A young John Delaney, the honorary treasurer, was holding the fort back in Ireland. Mick McCarthy,
his squad and the senior FAI figures were in a different time
zone in Saipan, getting second-hand accounts of what was
happening. Roy Keane was back at his home in Hale, monitoring the reaction, Sky News included.

Even before the full interview was transmitted, John Delaney
gave his verdict, based on what he had seen on the *Six One
News*. He said, 'It doesn't seem we can achieve a resolution
here, to be fair.' Pressed about it, told how the row had taken
place a week ago, tempers should have cooled, maybe wiser
counsel should prevail, John Delaney reiterated his view: 'I
don't think that is achievable at this stage to be fair. The tran-
script of what Roy has said in full – we will hear it in full at half
eight, it will go to the team hotel, but I don't see any change in
the attitude, to be straight.' It was the very essence of tragedy.
No single person or issue to blame, the worst possible outcome
that nobody wanted but could not prevent.

In the immediate aftermath, I kept up contact with Michael
Kennedy. In February 2003, he phoned me with the story of
Roy Keane's retirement from international football to concen-
trate on his club career. By then, Brian Kerr had replaced Mick
McCarthy as the Ireland manager, and he had spoken to Keane

about playing for the team again. Medical advice was a factor in his decision to retire. He did return to play for Kerr in 2004, but, after Ireland failed to qualify for the World Cup finals, he brought down the curtain for a final time in 2005.

I interviewed him in Dublin in April 2003. There was a connection to the 'Triggs episodes' outside his home in Hale after he returned from Saipan. My old friend from the telethon days, Maria Mulcahy, was doing public-relations work for Irish Guide Dogs for the Blind, and Roy Keane came to Ireland to promote a fundraising event.

One poignant reminder of Keane's character happened in January 2004. Sinn Féin's Martin McGuinness phoned me with an unexpected request. An eighteen-year-old Derry man, Gerard Logue, was travelling with his family to the Manchester United and Southampton game at Old Trafford. Gerard was seriously ill with cancer. Was there any chance of him getting to meet his favourite player, Roy Keane, after the match?

I phoned Michael Kennedy at his London office, apologized for the late request for what was a lunchtime game the following day and explained the circumstances. Immediately after Manchester United beat Southampton, Roy Keane sought out Gerard Logue and his father, Paddy, and brought them into the players' lounge. He introduced them to Ruud van Nistelrooy and Louis Saha, who had scored during the 3–2 victory, and several other players.

Keane joked with Gerard that one of the reasons he was delighted with the victory was that Danny Higginbotham, a former United teammate, was playing for Southampton. He said that he had never before presented a jersey to someone immediately after wearing it during a game. He signed the jersey and handed it and the pen to Gerard. He then helped him to get

autographs of the different United players, including the signa-
ture of a young Cristiano Ronaldo, on a paper napkin.

Gerard was the only son of Paddy and Teresa Logue. He
had three younger sisters. To this day, his parents remember
how the word Gerard kept saying that night in England and
during the journey home to Derry was 'unbelievable'. He was
so worried that his Roy Keane jersey might be stolen from the
Manchester hotel that he asked his mother if he should store it
in the bedroom safe.

After Gerard died later that year, Martin McGuinness told
me of seeing all the mementos of Old Trafford when he called
to the wake house. In Gerard's memory, his family and friends
in Derry started a fundraising walk. During the years since they
have raised over £100,000 for cancer charities.

The Logues saw a side of a football star that lifted their son's
journey in the final year of his life.

Two decades on, Keane remains a mesmerizing character, now
in a different phase. As a pundit, or as a guest in television studios,
he has box-office qualities. Knowledge, mischief, humour, edge,
confidence, good looks, timing, delivery . . . British as well as
Irish audiences are drawn to him in huge numbers.

In the years after the Saipan saga, practicalities kicked in, and
some of the animosity was parked. When Keane was managing
Sunderland and Mick McCarthy was in charge of Wolves, they
met and shook hands prior to the clubs meeting in 2006. Keane
felt let down by Niall Quinn and other senior players at the time
of the World Cup row. But they worked closely together when
Quinn and a group of Irish businessmen owned Sunderland
and Keane managed the club. As assistant manager to Martin
O'Neill with the national team, he worked with the FAI for five
years when John Delaney was its chief executive.

While he is likely to continue dividing opinion, nobody can ever doubt he was one of Ireland's few world-class footballers. Togged out, he became an enforcer, resolved to do all that was necessary to win. From the very beginning, throughout his career, he had constantly pushed himself to become exceptional. He was the Cork outsider who was deemed 'too small' and didn't make the cut for the Irish schoolboys squad when he first travelled to Dublin for trials. From his days with Rockmount in Cork to his first break, signing with League of Ireland First Division side Cobh Ramblers, he always showed the required enormous self-belief and drive.

He was still a teenager when he left Cork and moved to England after Nottingham Forest bought him. Over a three-year period he adjusted and rose to the top in the environment created by one of the most unique partnership management teams in the history of British football, Brian Clough and Peter Taylor. When Nottingham Forest were relegated, he turned down the advances of Blackburn Rovers, managed by Kenny Dalglish, and instead signed for Alex Ferguson's Manchester United. At the time of that £3.75 million British club record deal, he was a month shy of his twenty-second birthday.

Keane became the powerhouse in the most successful British club of the 1990s. In the tunnel at Highbury he squared up to Arsenal's Patrick Vieira, a lynchpin of the 1998 French World Cup-winning team. In the Champions League semi-final, he outshone another French World Cup star, Zinedine Zidane of Juventus. Alex Ferguson saw him as his mirror image on the field. Towards the end of Keane's career, they fell out, and the parting was far from perfect.

If television revenue and sponsorship deals have brought huge wealth to the game, it is a brutally tough place. I saw an example of that in Belgium with Jean-Marc Bosman. In a landmark 1995 European Court of Justice ruling, he had won the right of soccer players to move without hindrance to another club once their contract had expired. It transformed the earning potential of generations of his fellow players. But by the time the ruling was made, Bosman's best playing days and earning potential were behind him. When we interviewed him, in his modest home, he asked for a payment for the interview. Unused to such requests, we paid him the equivalent of €100.

At the time of the 2002 World Cup, Roy Keane had fought his way to the top of that heap. He was captain of Manchester United, used to its standards, and he knew what it took to win. He had overcome serious injury, and he realized it was probably his last outside chance of success with the national team. A handful of his Irish teammates were well placed in the trade. Others were operating at a lower level. A few younger ones were intent on making progress. The FAI did not have the structures, the mindset or the necessary complement of talented personnel to manage that complex matrix. In the two decades afterwards, the scale of the shortcomings became clear.

Managing elite athletes, in any sport, requires leadership skills. I saw it, at a distance, with Manchester United under Ferguson. I had a close-up view of the working methods of John O'Mahony, who managed Galway to All-Ireland Senior Football Championship victories in 1999 and 2001. In 1989, his Mayo team were beaten by Cork in an All-Ireland final. In 1994, he managed Leitrim to what was their second Connacht Senior Football Championship title – the previous one was in 1927.

O'Mahony was a schoolteacher by day and involved in what is an amateur sport in his free time. It was a completely different world to professional football. But in his approach to coaching and his treatment of players O'Mahony was guided by the principle 'Five-star treatment for a five-star performance'. On issues like nutrition and the use of a sports psychologist, he was ahead of many of his contemporaries. He took an interest in small but important details, such as the food players received after each training session and making sure they and their partners were the important people during after-match meals.

Eddie O'Sullivan, who later managed the Irish rugby team, was the fitness adviser in O'Mahony's Galway back-room team. Based on a friendship from my first days in journalism, I was delighted to help with his video analysis during those times.

I doubt that Roy Keane will ever have managerial success on a par with his playing career. His gifts and his determination came from within, and it is impossible to fully pass on or recreate those instincts in a team situation. One of his most important legacies is that he highlighted the standards that are required in a team setting to optimize the chances of success.

The best part of the Saipan story for me was meeting Michael Kennedy. He was one of six children, raised in working-class England. His father and mother were from Kerry – members of what his brother John said, 'were not the Windrush generation but the Dublin–Holyhead generation' that settled in North London. Michael traced his interest in the law to when his carpenter father fell off a building site and suffered serious injuries. His trade union represented him, and the action was settled on the steps of the court.

Michael didn't go to university but instead trained in a legal office for five years. After hours, he continued working at the brown desk and old typewriter in the bedroom he shared with his brother, Jim, in the family home. According to his brother

John, Michael became the go-to man for the Irish community, including a man called Frank, who ran the Archway Tavern and doubled up as a mechanic. One day, a young Irish footballer mentioned to Frank that he was looking for legal advice. Frank had Michael Kennedy's number on a pad beside the phone behind the bar, and that's how Michael Kennedy became David O'Leary's lawyer.

At one stage, Michael represented several members of Arsenal, Manchester United and Ireland. Alex Ferguson trusted him. When he moved out of the family home, he left the brown desk behind in the bedroom. In the drawers his family found many uncashed cheques from neighbours and friends that he had represented. Over the years, every once in a while I would call the office number, and he always seemed to be there. In 2008, I was awarded an honorary degree by the National University of Ireland, Galway. Sometime afterwards, one of the Galway academics told me that during their preparatory checks they had contacted Michael Kennedy as well as Ian and Eileen Paisley.

In June 2020, a distraught Kerri Blake phoned me from the Herbert Reeves office in London. Michael had taken ill at work on the previous Friday evening and had died in hospital from heart issues. Due to COVID-19, his funeral remembrance service in North London was postponed. The rescheduled gathering was held at St Joseph's Church, on Highgate Hill, on 4 September 2021, with a reception afterwards in the pavilion of St Aloysius' College. Two landmarks in Michael's life. Pandemic-related travel restrictions prevented me from joining the formal farewells. Michael's brother John told the gathering, 'In the end, he was like one of his football clients, leaving the field at the top of his game.'

He was a special man.

8

Belfast

My wife, Ceara, and our two children relocated to Sligo in the summer of 1997. Ceara's mother, Chris, had contracted cancer soon after she retired. It was an aggressive form of the disease. She had moved to Sligo to be closer to her daughters, Mary, Yvonne and Frances, and Ceara also wanted to spend more time with her.

Our four-year-old daughter, Moya, was ready to start school, and our son, Joe, had just turned one. One day, when Moya was with me in the supermarket, close to our rented home in Rixensart, she wandered off down one of the aisles. At the time, Belgium was traumatized by the crimes of Mark Dutroux, who kidnapped and murdered children. In those brief seconds when Moya was missing, I was terrified. It seemed as if circumstances were telling us that it was time to relocate the family to where we considered 'home'.

We agreed that I would try to commute between Belgium and Ireland, working long stretches and then taking breaks with the family. The job was still a great adventure. Some important EU stories were in mid-cycle, like the move to a single currency and the admission of new member states. In Ireland, Eileen Magnier was thriving as RTÉ's north-western correspondent so there was no vacancy in my old job. Another reason for remaining in Brussels was that I had my health issues to address. If I was going to become a more regular presence in the secure nest that Ceara was creating with our little ones in Ireland, I was keen to maximize the odds of staying alive for them.

One winter's night, two police officers called to the door in Rixensart. While I was in Ireland, visiting Ceara and the children, a gang had used our rented house as a base to monitor and then to abduct and rob a neighbour who had a jewellery business. They left behind cigarette butts. Awareness that dangerous criminals had found a way into the house was unnerving. I moved into an apartment on Avenue des Cerisiers, in walking distance of the RTÉ office in Brussels.

The children have happy memories of return visits to Belgium, where they were born, and their adventures on the Brussels trams and Metro system. My heart jumped with excitement each time Ceara emerged with them through the sliding doors of Zaventem airport. Aer Lingus had great fly-drive deals to Ireland at the time, and sometimes, when I'd arrive home in a hired car to Sligo, the pair would rush out to inspect it. Sligo Airport was five minutes from our house and it had daily links to Dublin. If I was at risk of missing a flight, the airport manager, Joe Corcoran, would phone to say the Fokker 50 will be leaving shortly.

I was just in the door from Belgium one July afternoon in 2000 when word came through of the Concorde crash in Paris. I consulted with the trio and got their permission to immediately return. The Aer Lingus flight to Dublin and an instant connection to Paris Charles de Gaulle Airport had me in place for a live contribution to the evening news.

In 2001, the role of RTÉ's northern editor became vacant when David Davin-Power was keen to return south. Sean

Whelan had been my partner in Brussels and was well able to put his stamp on the job. In time, Paul Cunningham arrived from Dublin to work with him.

There was a strong personal reason for wanting to go to Belfast. In their teens, Mammy was separated from her only sister when Peggy left to join the Cross and Passion order. Peggy once told me how she had danced with just one man, her sister's boyfriend – my father. And, she added, he was a very poor dancer. Her life as a nun brought her to Argentina, Sweden, England and Scotland. But she was now based in a community house on the Glen Road in Belfast. Sometimes she would borrow the car and drive down to stay a few days with Mammy in Sligo. During those visits they were young girls again. It was as if they were making up for the loss of contact in their earlier lives. My hope was that if we had a base in Belfast it would facilitate more happy times together for the sisters.

In February 2001, Peggy died suddenly in Belfast, sitting in a chair, while watching the RTÉ religious-affairs programme *Would You Believe* with several of her fellow nuns close by. Minutes before, she had returned from the kitchen with ice cream for the group. The following month, in a Sligo hospital, Daddy's sister, my godmother, Mary Creed, passed away. Two months later, in May, Mammy died suddenly in Sligo. The following month, June, in Pleasanton, Texas, Father Tommie O'Brien, a benevolent presence during our formative years, was found dead in his chair.

It was 'a scattering', the loss of four oak trees. All were gone before I moved back to Ireland in September 2001. Ceara found a perfect house for me on Belfast's North Parade, requiring little maintenance. Apart from when the family came visiting, I lived there alone, but I always associated it with Mammy and

Peggy. One upstairs bedroom had a big bay window with space for a table, a computer and a microphone. Many late-night and early-morning radio contributions were made from that makeshift studio over the next two decades.

The main work-related attraction of switching from Brussels to Belfast was that it offered a ringside seat to observe and report on the peace process. The Good Friday Agreement had been signed three years before so a story of international significance was happening in Northern Ireland. After twelve years reporting change in Europe and the role EU values had in that transformation, it would be fascinating to see if the patterns were repeated on our island. In Brussels, I had observed how membership of the EU was a positive force in British–Irish relations. The changed status brought Ireland out from behind the shadow of its nearest neighbour. But, as participants in the big club, the two countries discovered how much they had in common. This was an unexpected bonus after centuries of rancour.

I had advance knowledge of the 1994 IRA ceasefire. We were home from Brussels on holidays, and a contact, dating back to my days in the north-west, gave me accurate details of what was coming. At a planning meeting in RTÉ's Dublin headquarters, I shared the confidential information with senior newsroom management. The IRA was keen to have a contact person in RTÉ. As I was going to be returning to Brussels, I suggested my colleague Charlie Bird for the role.

On 31 August, the day the IRA ceasefire was formally announced, the European Commission president, Jacques Delors, was quick to welcome it. He committed then that the EU would provide financial support to help underpin peace in a practical way. The promise was consistent with the philosophy, championed by Delors throughout his Brussels years, to share the resources of the wealthier member states and regions with poorer and marginalized communities.

On many Strasbourg nights, I had been in John Hume's company in his favourite restaurant, Maison des Tanneurs. Afterwards, he'd walk along the bridge that links France to Germany and absorb the images that inspired what became known as 'Hume's Single Transferrable Speech' about peace and reconciliation. The Social Democratic and Labour Party (SDLP) leader brought the principles of Europe's reconciliation to the crafting of the Good Friday Agreement. Could those EU values, involving compromise, respecting difference and shunning violence, find expression in Ireland's peace process? That was a question that intrigued me as I returned to become RTÉ's northern editor.

The RTÉ office was on the ninth floor of a drab box of a building that looked like an apartment block from Eastern Europe. The team included two veterans of the Troubles, reporters Michael Fisher and Brendan Wright; a young energetic journalist from Co. Monaghan, Declan McBennett; Máire Killoran of TG4; engineer, Gerry McCann; secretary, Arlene Williamson, and cameraman, Johnny Coughlan, and sound recordist, Gerry O'Brien, who had been there for most of the Troubles. Some of those Belfast colleagues had worked for RTÉ during the most violent years in Northern Ireland. They routinely went without fear to the scenes of horrendous crimes, aware the RTÉ association sometimes brought additional risk.

The 'war' was effectively over, but the structures to underpin a functioning democratic society were not set up. The Good Friday Agreement was an enlightened master plan, but there were no delivery mechanisms in place to ensure that it would be implemented. Northern Ireland's politicians, including those who had worked in Westminster and Brussels, had no experience of forming and running a devolved government. A mandatory coalition, involving all the major parties, was the model proposed for Northern Ireland's unique circumstances. But this was completely different to the government–opposition model of Westminster, Dublin and all other Western democracies. Because the envisaged Stormont structure was unique, there was no neighbouring jurisdiction with a template that could be used as a reference point.

I spent the first years in the new posting observing and reporting on dysfunction. For most of the time, Stormont was closed. Every few months, the British and Irish governments would arrange talks with the main parties. One by one, the different groups would emerge from the discussions, explain to the assembled media why agreement was not possible and then leave. It was a ritual with a built-in acceptance of procrastination.

The Ulster Unionist Party (UUP) and the SDLP had played the prominent roles in the Good Friday Agreement negotiations. Their representatives, David Trimble and Seamus Mallon, took the first minister and deputy first minister positions in the first power-sharing Executive. But the administration couldn't work effectively without the participation of the more extreme wings of nationalism and Unionism: Sinn Féin and the DUP. The challenge that dogged efforts to form a power-sharing Executive was how to ensure that Sinn Féin was committed to exclusively peaceful means and that the IRA's violent campaign was over.

Significant events happened at Hillsborough, Co. Down, on 21 October 2003. The British and Irish governments were keen to create the circumstances that would see Northern Ireland Assembly elections take place the following month. After that contest was held, the revival of power-sharing at Stormont could follow. But first, decommissioning of IRA weapons would have to take place and be verified by the Canadian general appointed to oversee that process, General John de Chastelain. The UUP leader, David Trimble, would not commit to entering an administration with Sinn Féin until Republicans had put their weapons beyond use.

Early that Monday morning, the British government kicked off the choreography with its contribution. Downing Street released a statement confirming that Northern Ireland elections to revive the suspended power-sharing Assembly would take place on 25 November. The next element of the agreed sequence saw Gerry Adams, the Sinn Féin president, host a media conference, telling of his wishes to reach out to Unionists and to understand their hopes and fears. In relation to the IRA, he said it wanted 'full and irreversible implementation of the Good Friday Agreement in all its aspects' which would 'provide a full and final closure of the conflict'.

All seemed to be on track. The British prime minister, Tony Blair, was on a London flight to Northern Ireland. The Taoiseach, Bertie Ahern, foreign-affairs minister, Brian Cowen, and their officials boarded the government jet in Baldonnell. They had a lightning scare during a difficult flight north but didn't see it as a portent of trouble ahead.

Soon after the two delegations convened at Hillsborough Castle, it was clear the schedule was slipping. General de Chastelain was running well behind his expected arrival time. Months before, after a period when the relationship was suspended, he had renewed contact with the IRA. He and a colleague were now overdue at a news conference in Hillsborough to give an account of the IRA weapons-decommissioning they had witnessed. When de Chastelain arrived, more than an hour late, he looked tired. For someone known for his neat dress sense, he appeared dishevelled.

The function room in Hillsborough was packed with journalists, photographers and camera crews. In a side room, I caught sight of a strained-looking Tony Blair attempting to have a conversation with the general about what he might say in his public remarks. The prime minister asked, 'But John, couldn't you say—' The general was listening but making no commitments.

Soon after the news conference began, the slow public slide into car-crash territory was under way. De Chastelain confirmed that compared to the previous two decommissioning acts, this was the most substantial. The IRA had put beyond use automatic weapons, including machine guns and explosives and explosives materials. But, crucially, he was not prepared to go into specifics. Eamonn Mallie of Downtown Radio was among the first journalists given an opportunity to question de Chastelain. Mallie swiftly found the pressure points and squeezed. He made dramatic use of the word 'ordnance'. But the general was not forthcoming.

Back at the headquarters of the UUP in East Belfast, David Trimble and his colleagues were watching the live pictures of the news conference. They had spent several hours waiting. When Trimble saw de Chastelain struggle to convince, he flipped. The Hillsborough event was barely over when, thirty miles away, the Ulster Unionists held their own news conference. In one withering appraisal, Trimble said, 'We probably have less confidence in the process than we had an hour ago.' An obvious conclusion about those October days is that the IRA came up short in the secret dealings they had with General de Chastelain.

One highly sensitive element of that saga has never been publicly dissected. As part of the preparations for that sequence of events, Sinn Féin's leadership sought a major and hugely problematic concession from the Irish government. In return for IRA weapons-decommissioning, the Republican movement wanted the men convicted in relation to the murder of Garda Jerry McCabe in Co. Limerick in 1996 to be released on licence. Sinn Féin pushed for Michael McDowell, the minister for justice, to make the commitment in a letter. Guided by one of his close advisers, he refused to do so. But he, along with the Taoiseach, Bertie Ahern, and the minister for foreign affairs, Brian Cowen, on behalf of the government, gave an undertaking that the release would happen, provided the promised weapons-decommissioning took place. Provisional arrangements were made for the release of the prisoners from Castlerea Prison. But they were not triggered because of the press conference debacle at Hillsborough. When the de Chastelain media conference ended in disaster and David Trimble rejected the decommissioning accounts, the release of the IRA prisoners was stopped.

Sinn Féin and the IRA may or may not have planned it, but the net effect of the unconvincing decommissioning episode was that it drove the UUP leader, David Trimble, away from the negotiating table. For several weeks before Hillsborough, against his instincts and his pattern of behaviour since the 1998 Good Friday Agreement, Trimble had sought to explore developing some sort of relationship with Sinn Féin, Gerry Adams included. That was now over.

During the heated Assembly election campaign that followed, the DUP dogged the UUP for the way they had been fooled by Sinn Féin. They sought to portray Trimble and his colleagues as weak. The message gained traction with some Unionist voters. In the 25 November Assembly elections, for the first time, the DUP became the largest party. It returned with thirty members, an increase of ten. The UUP, with twenty-seven, were down one member. The change represented a significant shift within Unionism. It has remained that way since, with the DUP the dominant voice.

The very same pattern happened within nationalism. Sinn Féin gained six seats, electing twenty-four members. The SDLP dropped six and went from twenty-four down to eighteen. Five years after the Good Friday Agreement, the two parties on the extremes had moved towards centre stage.

Mo Mowlam was gone from Northern Ireland when I moved to the Belfast job. True to her reputation, when I went to see her at her home in London, she didn't hold back on what she believed was an important truth. She had been the Northern Ireland secretary from May 1997 until October 1999. Traditionally, it is a difficult job. The holder is the on-the-ground representative of the British government and the main point of contact for the local political parties. Another important responsibility involves maintaining relations with the Irish government via the minister for foreign affairs.

Mo had the role for the year before the Good Friday Agreement was signed and for eighteen months after it. Her reputation as a straight talker who disliked formality and enjoyed the occasional drink and swear word made her popular. That celebrity status was confirmed by the standing ovation she received at the 1998 Labour Party conference. It may have been a factor in Tony Blair's decision to shift her to a lower-profile role in Westminster.

When we met in London, she was blunt about what she believed was the major weakness of the Good Friday Agreement. She told me she regretted that the DUP were not involved in the negotiations and had not signed up to it. She felt that was a vital missing link. For the first time in its forty-two-year history, the

DUP was the leading party in Northern Ireland after the 2003 Assembly elections, with almost 26 per cent of the total vote. The question created by its success was if it had the ability to switch from a party of protest to a party of power.

Early in 2004 it began to lay the foundations for change. On Thursday, 4 January, a bagpiper led three defectors from the UUP into a cheering hall of DUP members in Lisburn. All of them had been elected in the November Assembly contest two months before. Jeffrey Donaldson was by far the best known. In the early 1980s he was the constituency agent for the UUP MP Enoch Powell. He later worked as the personal assistant to the UUP leader, James Molyneaux, and succeeded him as the MP for the Lagan Valley constituency in 1997. The following year, Donaldson distanced himself from the UUP negotiating team as it prepared to commit to the Good Friday Agreement. He then became the most prominent in-house critic of David Trimble in the four years of confidence-sapping reviews of Trimble's leadership that followed.

During the November 2003 Assembly election campaign, the DUP sought to deliberately goad the Ulster Unionists by unveiling a DUP mobile billboard outside their rivals' head-quarters. When David Trimble confronted them on the street, the DUP's deputy leader, Peter Robinson, his wife, Iris, and another of the DUP MPs, Willie McCrea, taunted him, asking 'Where is Jeffrey? Where is Jeffrey?'

Trimble replied, 'Jeffrey agrees with our manifesto – he issued a statement to that effect today.' What Robinson knew and Trimble feared was formally confirmed by Donaldson's change of sides two months later.

Arlene Foster was another significant capture by the DUP. A Co. Fermanagh-based solicitor, she worked in Enniskillen for the legal firm of the UUP chairman, James Cooper. She aligned herself with the Donaldson faction of critics during the UUP discussions of Trimble's stewardship. Less than two months after her election as an Assembly member, she too was jumping ship.

Like Foster, the third defector, Norah Beare, was also a new UUP Assembly member. She had worked as Jeffrey Donaldson's personal assistant for fifteen years. Transfers from Donaldson's 34.2 per cent share of the first-preference votes were crucial in getting her elected in the six-seat constituency as she herself received just 3.7 per cent in the first count.

As well as providing a very public morale boost, the three new members increased the DUP Assembly numbers to thirty-three and cut the UUP total to twenty-four. It gave Ian Paisley and his party the confidence to begin taking deliberate small steps towards centre stage and power. My first chance to interview Ian Paisley, one to one, was on the DUP's 'battle bus' one cold November evening during the 2003 Assembly election campaign. Our paths had crossed briefly, years before, in Brussels and Strasbourg. I knew that in Northern Ireland Paisley was a major force. Gaining an understanding of him was essential in order to have any chance of doing my job properly.

He was seventy-seven and had a bible with him on the bus. As cameraman Conor O'Brien squeezed into the bright polyester seat to set for the best interview angle, I told the DUP leader how my late grand-aunt Dora had worked for many years as a nun in a Cross and Passion school, at Willowfield in Loyalist East Belfast. She had once surprised us by saying that some of Paisley's Catholic constituents found Paisley a useful MP.

That journey along the roads of south Fermanagh provided an instructive lesson in how to engage with Ian Paisley. He was like certain old Fiat models. Smooth on the road, but, if revved up to very high speeds, all changed. If you wanted a row, it didn't take much prodding to work him into a rant. But, if given respect and probed about what he hoped to achieve during what remained of his life, Paisley opened up more and said more.

Conor and I ended the night filming at a DUP fundraising dinner and auction in the Valley Hotel in Fivemiletown, where the party leader was the guest of honour. With the RTÉ branding on our equipment and my Southern accent, we were obviously different – two Catholics getting a close-up view of Ian Paisley among the DUP's grass roots.

On 29 January 2004, I watched Ian Paisley walk in the front doors of 17 Grosvenor Place, London, the Irish embassy in Britain, close to Buckingham Palace, with the Irish and EU flags flying from the balcony overhead. The venue had been deliberately chosen for the first meeting between the DUP leader and Taoiseach Bertie Ahern. The Irish ambassador, Daithí Ó Ceallaigh, was delighted when Paisley agreed to sign the visitors book. In an anecdote that would reassure his supporters, Paisley told how he insisted he would be served a boiled egg so he could personally remove the shell top and guard against any attempt to poison him.

Before they started their formal discussions, the two men prayed. Ahern was comfortable in the evangelical space. Every year he would have black ashes on his forehead on the Catholic feast day Ash Wednesday. Every November, he gave up alcohol and attended Mass each day for the souls of the dead – another Catholic tradition.

To help assess the import of the occasion, the Taoiseach had with him the minister for foreign affairs, Brian Cowen, the minister for justice, Michael McDowell, and minister of state Tom Kitt. Paisley set out the minimum terms under which his party would consider entering a power-sharing administration with Sinn Féin. The IRA had to leave the stage, and he expected the Irish government to assist in achieving that change.

Ian Paisley was accompanied to the delegation by Peter Robinson and Nigel Dodds. Jeffrey Donaldson was there, too, even though he had been a member of the party for less than a month. As the founder of the DUP, Ian Paisley was the party's undisputed front-of-house presence. But Peter Robinson, his deputy, was the chief strategist. He didn't have his leader's charisma or profile. Both were content with the division of responsibilities because it played to their strengths. Robinson enjoyed the mechanics of shaping the party's philosophy and profile. He hired young professionals to work in the DUP's back-room team.

One of these was Timothy Johnston, an accountant from Portadown, Co. Armagh. In a past phase, as a twenty-one-year-old member of a television audience during a live UTV programme, Johnston caused Tony Blair acute discomfort when he accused the British prime minister of being soft to Republicans. Johnston had been affiliated to the UUP in Queen's University. Richard Bullick, another of Robinson's advisers, was a Conservative then. Over the next two decades, when the DUP had five different leaders, Johnston and Bullick remained the spine of the DUP machine.

In February 2004, John Hume announced he wouldn't be seeking re-election to the European Parliament. In the June elections, the SDLP candidate, Martin Morgan, failed to retain the seat held by Hume since 1979. It was taken by Sinn Féin's Bairbre de Brún, confirming the pattern of the Assembly elections the previous year. Like John Hume, Ian Paisley had clocked up twenty-five years' service as an MEP, and he, too, decided to retire. There was a debate within the DUP about its candidate. Maurice Morrow, the party chairman, lost out, and Jim Allister, who was supported by Peter Robinson, got the nomination. He retained the seat, but three years later Allister quarrelled with the DUP over its power-sharing relationship with Sinn Féin and left to found his Traditional Unionist Voice (TUV) party.

We filmed Ian Paisley, campaigning for Jim Allister, before those European elections. He had turned seventy-eight the previous month. Space for an afternoon rest was built into his itinerary. At the time I didn't twig the significance of the nap.

On 22 July, Jeffrey Donaldson and Martin McGuinness, as well as UUP Assembly member Dermot Nesbitt, addressed a session of the MacGill Summer School in Glenties, Co. Donegal. For the audience in the packed hall, it was an opportunity to evaluate if there was any prospect of the DUP and Sinn Féin reaching an accommodation to become partners in power-sharing. Although Donaldson was less than a year in the DUP, he was the person nominated to make the trip south.

In the Highlands Hotel, he was introduced to a special adviser of Martin McGuinness, Aidan McAteer, and his wife, Teresa. The following month, Donaldson was given the responsibility to state the DUP case to an overwhelmingly nationalist audience at the West Belfast Festival. As he arrived at the Falls Road venue, he was greeted by the chief executive of the West Belfast Partnership Board with a greeting that put him back on his heels. A smiling Geraldine McAteer said to him, 'I believe you met Aidan McAteer and his wife, Teresa, in Glenties last month. I was Aidan's first wife.'

The British and Irish governments set aside three days at the start of September 2004 for talks with Northern Ireland's political parties. The venue chosen was the conference centre at Leeds Castle in the Kent countryside, eighty kilometres south of London. Tony Blair and Bertie Ahern were keen to gauge the odds of the DUP and Sinn Féin working towards an agreement.

Brief excitement came early from an unexpected quarter. The UUP leader, David Trimble, turned up in a soft-top sports car with fellow MPs, chief whip Roy Beggs and Lady Sylvia Hermon. The greater impact was caused by the arrival of the DUP leader, Ian Paisley. He had spent several days in hospital with heart issues. On medical advice, rather than travel by plane he came to the south of England by ferry and car. Camera crews swarmed around him at the conference-centre entrance. He had lost weight, the skin was hanging from his pale face, and he looked many years older than his seventy-eight years.

For its coverage from RTÉ's Dublin studios, *Prime Time* presenter Miriam O'Callaghan sought my help in arranging two down-the-line live guests. Sinn Féin provided the party's vice-president and West Tyrone MP Pat Doherty. After much cajoling, the DUP eventually offered its South Fermanagh Assembly member, Arlene Foster. As they waited, under the camera lights, on grass opposite the castle, to be called in to the programme, Foster refused to face or look at Pat Doherty. 'Would our guests like a glass of water or a drink?' I asked. 'I'll have a brandy,' said Foster. Minutes later, after I arrived with her order, she downed the brandy in one gulp and maintained a confrontational stance during her programme contribution.

The discussions failed to make progress. The significance of that Leeds Castle event occurred in the journey from it. After he crossed the border on the journey to the ferry in Stranraer, Ian Paisley diverted to see an eminent clinician in Glasgow. The advice he received during that visit helped to transform his ailing health. For several weeks, it had seemed the DUP leader was nearing the end of his life. But now he had energy again and with it the sense that he might have a chance to make an unexpected contribution to history.

Before September ended, the DUP made a significant gesture. Ian Paisley crossed the border for the party's first discussions at Government Buildings in Dublin. The host team was Taoiseach Bertie Ahern, minister for foreign affairs Dermot Ahern, and three civil servants who figured prominently during the peace process: Michael Collins, Brendan Scannell and Adrian O'Neill. The DUP delegation comprised Ian Paisley, his deputy, Peter Robinson, and their two key advisers: Timothy Johnston and Richard Bullick. (In some of the subsequent turbulent episodes within the DUP, Robinson wondered if the omission of Nigel Dodds from that Dublin delegation was a costly mistake.)

The terms under which the DUP would enter power-sharing with Sinn Féin continued to be the sticking point in the negotiations conducted by the two governments. One inconclusive session took place at the Irish embassy in London in November. Sinn Féin set up base camp in the huge office, to the left-hand side of the entrance. Gerry Kelly, one of its negotiating team, was a leading figure in the IRA breakout from the Maze prison in 1981 and afterwards spent years on the run in mainland Europe until he was apprehended in Amsterdam. During breaks in the embassy discussions, Kelly reverted to a habit developed during his past life. He stretched out on the office floor and catnapped.

The DUP were determined that their support base would be assuaged by how the IRA weapons-decommissioning issue was addressed. Photographic or video evidence was one format frequently raised. In their systematic and ultimately successful campaign to undermine David Trimble, Paisley and Robinson had labelled him and his party as pushovers and weak. They were determined to not leave the DUP vulnerable to the same accusation.

On Saturday, 27 November, Paisley left no room for ambiguity when he spoke at the annual DUP dinner in his North Antrim constituency. On decommissioning, he said, 'Unionists will not settle for another disingenuous and valueless decommissioning event. They are going to see before they believe. Seeing is believing.' He went on to say, 'Sinn Féin's leader, Gerry Adams, says we want to humiliate the IRA. There's nothing wrong with that. I think it is a very noble thing. The IRA needs to be humiliated. And they need to wear their sackcloth and ashes not in a back room but openly. And we have no apology to make for the stand we are taking.'

Later in his speech, Dr Paisley said, 'I am willing to consider urgently the right deal at any time. I would like to be in a position to say yes to a fair deal, and I hope I will be able to say that but have the resolve and the integrity to say no to another bad deal for the Ulster people.' BBC Northern Ireland had a camera crew recording the Paisley speech. The headline picked itself: Paisley demands the IRA are humiliated and must wear sackcloth and ashes. His statement that he was ready and willing to strike the right deal got lost in the noise and the backlash.

On the weekend before Christmas, a major news story broke without warning. An armed gang had stolen £26.5 million from the vaults of the Northern Bank in Belfast, immediately opposite City Hall. Members of the families of two bank officials were taken hostage and severely traumatized, but no shots were fired. It was the largest such robbery on the island of Ireland. Sinn Féin's Martin McGuinness insisted that the IRA were not involved, but few believed him.

Many theories about the motivation for the robbery were aired. Had the Paisley assertion that the IRA needed to be humiliated cleared the way for a two-fingered response? Was the IRA gathering a retirement fund as it prepared to leave the stage? Had Adams and McGuinness been given a message in the ongoing debate within the Republican movement?

The chief constable of the Police Service of Northern Ireland (PSNI), Hugh Orde, took dramatic action to reduce the impact of the raid. On his encouragement, the bank's Danish parent company swiftly issued £10, £20, £50 and £100 notes with a new design. The intervention made a lot of the stolen money worthless, and it provoked a response. To embarrass the police, £50,000 taken from the Northern Bank was planted in the toilets of the PSNI club in South Belfast.

The Northern Bank Robbery placed Sinn Féin under the spotlight. The events in Magennis's bar in Belfast city centre at the end of January 2005 escalated that pressure to crisis point. A thirty-three-year-old father of two, Robert McCartney, tried to act as peacemaker in a row between a neighbour, Brendan Devine, and a group of local Republicans. He was attacked with a broken bottle, dragged outside, beaten with metal bars and stabbed. His throat was cut, and he died from his wounds.

After the violence, the crime scene was cleaned, CCTV footage was removed, clothes of the attackers were burned, and no ambulance was called. A passing police patrol car found Robert McCartney fatally wounded on a traffic island. The victim lived in the nearby Short Strand nationalist area. He was completely innocent and died because he tried to intervene in a row. Known IRA members were involved in his murder and in the subsequent destruction of evidence.

Robert's five sisters – Paula, Catherine, Gemma, Donna and Claire – and his partner, Bridgeen Hagans, began a public campaign to have those responsible for the crime brought before the courts. The Republican movement was under severe pressure in its own heartlands. The IRA issued a statement, claiming two of its members were involved in the killing and saying 'it was prepared to shoot the people directly involved'. The McCartney family immediately declined the offer.

Gerry Adams and Martin McGuinness travelled to Government Buildings in Dublin for confidential talks with Taoiseach Bertie Ahern, foreign-affairs minister Brian Cowen, and justice minister Michael McDowell. Irish government officials Michael Collins and Adrian O'Neill were also present. The exchanges became very heated and broke up when Bertie Ahern conveyed to the Sinn Féin leadership that he was suspending contact with them.

The pressure then acquired an international dimension in a very public way. The US travel visa granted to the Sinn Féin president, Gerry Adams, against the advice of the British government in the summer of 1994 was an important backdrop to what was a historic IRA ceasefire. Access to its US support base and funds as well as to the White House and Capitol Hill in Washington was an important asset for Sinn Féin.

In March 2005, Gerry Adams found himself and his party frozen out of US power circles. Instead, Robert McCartney's family were the guests, given access to all areas. Hillary Clinton met them and publicly acknowledged their courage and bravery. Senator Edward Kennedy stood beside them at a news conference and, in a message to the IRA, said there is a time to hold them and to fold them and it was their time to leave the stage. When Gerry Adams attended an Ireland Funds dinner, the guest speaker, Senator John McCain, singled him out from the podium and criticized the IRA.

Robert McCartney's sisters were staying in Jury's Hotel on Washington's Dupont Circle. They had limited funds and were taking turns sleeping in the bed and on the floor, sometimes eating Mars bars to cut the hunger. But more than any pressure exerted by the Irish and British governments, the DUP and other political parties, the campaign by Robert McCartney's family brought home to the IRA that it was an obstacle, blocking the development of the peace process and the prospects of Sinn Féin.

Martin McAleese, the husband of President Mary McAleese, was the person who revived the contacts between the Irish government and Sinn Féin. One Saturday night he invited Taoiseach Bertie Ahern and Sinn Féin president Gerry Adams to a private meeting at Áras an Uachtaráin. No official function was scheduled so the catering staff were off duty. The first tentative exchanges didn't produce a row, and, as the discussions continued, Dr McAleese asked if any of the guests were hungry. His son, Justin, was dispatched to collect an order from McDonald's.

The restoration of contacts between the Irish government and Sinn Féin was one of many significant McAleese interventions. Throughout her fourteen years as president, Mary McAleese and her husband sought to honour her election campaign promise to be a bridge-builder. At times, the work involved stretching beyond their comfort zone. They were both Northern Catholics with attitudes influenced by their experiences growing up during the Troubles. President McAleese set new records for visits made to Northern Ireland. She also welcomed cross-community groups to afternoon and evening functions at her Dublin residence.

Denis Moloney, a Belfast solicitor, and his sister, Maria, did important on-the-ground work for them. Moloney's client base included Loyalists as well as nationalists. Dr Ian Adamson, a Unionist lord mayor of Belfast, historian and personal physician of Ian Paisley, set up the meeting with the McAleeses at the Somme Museum in Co. Down in July 2008. The president and Dr Paisley shook hands. It was one occasion when the exchanges struggled to get beyond the formal.

The president also worked to develop a relationship with Britain's royal family, building on the work of her predecessor, Mary Robinson. It culminated in the state visit to Ireland by Queen Elizabeth in 2011, just months before Mary McAleese left office in her fourteenth year as president.

Martin McAleese took on a freelance role that was unique in the history of North–South relations. He developed a relationship with representatives of Loyalist communities, including former paramilitaries. His regular contacts included Jackie McDonald, once a leading figure in the Ulster Defence Association. Dr McAleese was assisted by Áine de Baróid, a Co. Cork-born Department of Finance official on secondment. Dr McAleese regularly travelled to hard-line Loyalist areas for private discussions. He also brought down groups to golf outings at the K Club in Kildare and to functions at Áras an Uachtaráin. He provided some of them with tickets for major sporting occasions. Early into his practice of bringing groups of former paramilitaries to Áras an Uachtaráin, he learned an important culinary lesson: tomato ketchup, chips and steak was the menu of choice.

Efforts to agree the terms of a political breakthrough were put on hold to allow for Westminster elections in May 2005. The electorate gave the Paisley–Robinson and Adams–McGuinness teams a mandate to resume their work. The DUP routed the UUP, taking four new seats, bringing their House of Commons representation to nine. David Trimble failed to retain Upper Bann, leading to his resignation as UUP leader and his replacement by Reg Empey. Lady Sylvia Hermon was the only UUP representative to retain her seat, in North Down. Sinn Féin took an extra seat, returning five MPs. The SDLP held three seats: party leader Mark Durkan regained the Foyle (Derry) seat from Sinn Féin, compensating for Sinn Féin's Conor Murphy's victory in Newry and Armagh, where the SDLP's Seamus Mallon was retiring.

Two months later, on 25 July, the IRA announced a formal end to its campaign. It stated, 'All IRA units have been ordered to dump arms. All volunteers have been instructed to assist the development of purely political and democratic programmes through exclusively peaceful means. Volunteers must not engage in any other activities whatsoever.' Traditionally, the IRA delivered information through statements issued in the name of 'P. O'Neill'.

As the DUP and others noted, this historic news was communicated in a video message, delivered by Séanna Walsh, who once served a prison sentence with Bobby Sands. It was the first time since 1972 that an individual had represented the IRA while not wearing a mask. (Walsh is also a fluent Irish speaker and, fourteen years later, became the manager of the James Connolly Visitor Centre in Belfast.)

In a Belfast news conference, scheduled to complement the IRA statement, the Sinn Féin president, Gerry Adams, said,

'There's a time to resist, to stand up and to confront the enemy by arms if necessary. In other words, unfortunately, there's a time for war. There's also a time to engage, to reach out and put war behind us all. This is that time. This is a time for peace.'

On Sunday, 25 September, Tyrone defeated Kerry in the All-Ireland Senior Football Championship final. The phone call with the tip-off came as I walked from the match at Croke Park along the Drumcondra Road. Michelle McCaughran was the programme editor preparing RTÉ's 6 p.m. news bulletin. She instantly understood the significance of my information and knew she had a lead story. Using a mobile phone, I found a quiet spot on the footpath to break the news that IRA decommissioning had taken place and that details would be confirmed at a news conference in Belfast the following day.

Twenty-three months after his unconvincing engagement with the IRA, General John de Chastelain had inspected significant decommissioning of IRA weapons and explosives. There were no videos or photographs to support his account, but this time there were two convincing witnesses chosen by Sinn Féin to back up the de Chastelain testimony: Father Alex Reid and Revd Harold Good.

9

Compromise and power

From the IRA ceasefire in 1994, followed by the Good Friday Agreement in 1998, a dramatic reduction continued in the levels of death and destruction from the three previous decades. But the efforts to create the political structures that would underpin the peace continued at snail's pace. Ian Paisley had built his DUP support base around his animosity to a Sinn Féin party that believed in a united Ireland. He and Peter Robinson recognized that their only route to government was in partnership with their traditional enemies. Their challenge was to enter into an arrangement that could be sold as a victory to their supporters.

The British and Irish governments pressed on with their role of matchmakers, accepting that the unlikely couple wouldn't meet across a table to agree their future. In October 2006, they set aside three days for talks with all the Northern Ireland parties at St Andrews in Scotland in an effort to address some of the unresolved issues. It proved to be a highly significant staging post.

Ian Paisley and his wife, Eileen, were due to return from Scotland to Northern Ireland on Friday, 13 October, to celebrate their fiftieth wedding anniversary. The political discussions had to be structured to suit that deadline. On the Thursday night, Bertie Ahern and Tony Blair were reviewing the talks. There had been no breakthrough. As they teased out how they might package the stalemate the following day, in the chit-chat, the issue of a present for the departing Paisleys came up.

Bertie Ahern had a smile on his face. His officials had put some thought into the Irish offering. They had commissioned Liam O'Neill, a Co. Galway-based wood sculptor, to carve a bowl from a fallen walnut tree, several thousand years old. President Mary Robinson had once presented Queen Elizabeth with a piece of work by the same artist. The Paisley gift had extra significance because the tree had grown at the site of the Battle of the Boyne.

Tony Blair was silent. Then he asked one of his officials about the British offering. It was a photo album. An expensive one. The British floated the idea of a joint offering, but Bertie Ahern didn't engage.

The British and Irish delegations went to bed that night convinced they were facing into one more version of putting a brave face on failure. While they slept, the magic happened. The following morning, Blair was the first to sense that the two main protagonists might be in a mood for cutting a deal. He quickly marshalled his forces to prepare a media event to announce the St Andrews Agreement.

As happens in negotiations, the drafting of texts flows with pace when resistance is not an issue. The eighteen-page document was printed and shared by mid-morning when the participants gathered in the main meeting room. Bertie Ahern presented Ian and Eileen Paisley with the bowl. The gift would be given a special place in the Paisley home on Cypress Avenue in Belfast. Tony Blair handed over the photo album.

The slow political mating game now had momentum. The advances at St Andrews created a road map that could lead the DUP into power-sharing with Sinn Féin. Gerry Adams and Martin McGuinness persuaded their party to hold a special *árd fheis* (conference) in January where its long-standing policy of not supporting Northern Ireland's policing and justice structures would be reviewed. Assembly elections were due in March, and that could clear the way for the formation of a power-sharing administration.

But some of Ian Paisley's colleagues and supporters were deeply unhappy. They feared they were shaping up to commit to an offence that is unacceptable in the DUP rule-book: a sell-out. On 24 November, with Peter Robinson's backing, Dr Paisley was in Stormont, preparing to read a text that would confirm his party was on the journey to commit itself to power-sharing. But their party was in turmoil. Twelve of its representatives, including Nigel Dodds, Jim Allister, Gregory Campbell, Maurice Morrow and William McCrea, were demanding that their leader apply the brakes. Journalists called them the Twelve Apostles.

As the clocked ticked towards Paisley's scheduled speaking time in the Stormont chamber, the bizarre intervened. A security officer began grappling with a man who was attempting to make a forced entry through the swing doors of the main Stormont building. Cameramen assembled in the Great Hall, awaiting the fallout from the Paisley speech, quickly switched to filming the mêlée.

The intruder was Michael Stone, a Loyalist who was convicted of three counts of murder following his attack on mourners at an IRA funeral in West Belfast in 1988. Now out under licence, he had come with home-made weapons and explosives to seek out Gerry Adams and Martin McGuinness. He daubed graffiti on the exterior wall of the parliament building before attempting his dramatic entrance. As Stone was taken away by the police, the chamber was evacuated. It wasn't Stone's intention, but he had prevented the public undermining of Ian Paisley by a dozen of his colleagues in the Stormont chamber.

That afternoon, I interviewed the DUP leader in a small upstairs room in Stormont. He had an open bible on the table. I had never seen him so tired and so low. But in the days afterwards, Peter Robinson and his supporters managed to reconcile the different factions within the DUP. It was one of Robinson's most significant achievements, even if the dissension was parked but not defeated.

On the last weekend of January 2007, Sinn Féin decided that the party could give its support to the PSNI and it would nominate members to the Northern Ireland Policing Board. Almost 1,000 members attended the special conference in Dublin's Royal Dublin Society Hall. An overwhelming majority supported the motion – there were no walkouts. McGuinness, Adams and their supporters had done all the necessary homework.

In the March 2007 Assembly elections, the DUP and Sinn Féin increased their seat numbers from the 2003 contest: the DUP to thirty-six (from thirty), and Sinn Féin to twenty-eight (from twenty-four). The UUP returned eighteen representatives, the SDLP sixteen and the Alliance Party of Northern Ireland (Alliance) seven.

Years of rows, setbacks and stalemate had created the view that Northern Ireland was addicted to missed deadlines. RTÉ colleagues in Dublin were among those prepared for a repeat of that pattern on Monday, 26 March, as Northern Ireland's parties gathered at Stormont. Conor O'Brien was the cameraman requested to come alone to a room on the first floor. Over the phone, he gave me a sense of what was to come. Colleagues at base were put on standby for pictures of unexpected history.

Conor's shots showed Ian Paisley, Gerry Adams and their DUP and Sinn Féin colleagues seated around a table, agreeing the modalities to form a government.

Singer-songwriter Luka Bloom was on a flight to Australia when the pictures appeared on a news feed. He cried with surprise.

Stormont couldn't accommodate the numbers seeking entry to Devolution Day on 8 May 2007. The new power-sharing Executive that would restore devolved government in Northern Ireland included one SDLP and two UUP members. But it was unique because, for the first time, it was led by a DUP and Sinn Féin partnership.

Peter Hain had served as Northern Ireland secretary for two years. He was at the centre of two incidents that gave a sense of the dramatic changes under way. In the days before the set-piece event, he had to vacate his offices at Stormont Castle to make way for Ian Paisley and Martin McGuinness. The representative of the British government had no choice but to find accommodation elsewhere. In Hain's case, he welcomed the discommoding as proof of success.

Hain's parents were veterans of the anti-apartheid campaign in South Africa. They were proud of their son's work and were keen to come over to Belfast for the celebrations. But entry tickets to the ceremonies in Stormont Parliament Buildings were in demand. A former leading member of the IRA, Martin McGuinness, provided the required two passes for the family of the Northern Ireland secretary.

Flanked by Tony Blair and Bertie Ahern, the two principals in the new administration descended the marble staircase into the Stormont Great Hall. In his address, Ian Paisley couldn't resist drawing from the Book of Ecclesiastes. In his controversial past, his booming made famous phrases like 'Never, Never, Never'

and 'No Surrender'. The audience before him and viewers of
the live television pictures now watched him read from his King
James bible: 'To every thing there is a season, and a time to
every purpose under the heaven: a time to be born, and a time
to die; a time to plant, and a time to pluck up that which is
planted.' After the formalities concluded, Martin McGuinness
introduced his new partner in government to his mother, Peggy,
and his wife, Bernie.

For Tony Blair, the restoration of power-sharing, involving
two unlikely partners, represented the final chapter of what
was one of the genuine successes of his political career. From
his first days as British prime minister in 1997, he had given
priority to achieving peace in Northern Ireland. His reputation
would be stained by his decision to align with the United States
in the so-called War Against Terror and the invasion of Iraq, a
gamble that backfired. With the Northern Ireland peace process
he also bet the house. But in this instance he hit the jackpot.
A month after the Stormont celebrations, he stepped aside as
prime minister and made way for Gordon Brown.

Blair's partner, Taoiseach Bertie Ahern, had longer to bask
in the afterglow of their historic success. During a decade of
negotiations, the Irish government took primary responsibility
for delivering nationalism; the British government dealt with
Unionism. There were low points in Bertie Ahern's dealings
with Sinn Féin. During the final days of the Good Friday negotiations in 1998, his mother, Julia, was dying. He sacrificed time
with her waiting for overdue Sinn Féin members to arrive for
a meeting in Dublin. The IRA's decommissioning-lite ruse in
October 2003 was another flashpoint. Contacts were suspended
for several weeks in 2005 after the Northern Bank Robbery and
the murder of Robert McCartney. Ahern knew that the growth

of Sinn Féin as an all-island political party could have negative long-term implications for Fianna Fáil. Yet he persevered.

His lap of honour began a week after the Stormont event when he became the first Taoiseach to address a joint sitting of the House of Commons and the House of Lords in Westminster. In July 2007, he welcomed Ian Paisley to Farmleigh House in Dublin's Phoenix Park. On the journey south, the DUP leader remembered preparing for their first meeting at the Irish embassy in London, three years before. He said that day he would not shake hands with the Taoiseach until a political settlement was reached, but when an agreement was in place he would give such a grip that it would leave an impression on Bertie Ahern's hand. As he bounded from his official car at Farmleigh, Dr Paisley shouted, 'I better shake hands with this man, I'm going to give you a good grip.'

A year later, Bertie Ahern stepped aside as Taoiseach and made way for Brian Cowen. In March 2012, he would resign from Fianna Fáil after his reputation was damaged by bruising encounters around his financial affairs during a public inquiry.

Ian Paisley revelled in the positive reaction to his unexpected transformation. For decades, Irish America had consistently classed him a negative force. I reported on the four-day trip he and Martin McGuinness made to the United States in December 2007. It was probably one of the happiest times in their lives. The DUP leader was the bigger draw. They rang the bell to signal the start of a trading day in the New York Stock Exchange. Niall Burgess and his wife, Marie, hosted a party for them at the Irish consulate in New York. Paisley had no reservations playing the role of 'star turn'. He laughed and joked with the high-achievers from a top slice of Irish America who waited for their chance to engage with him. In casual conversation, when the DUP leader referred to his partner in government as 'my deputy', McGuinness smiled. When Paisley mounted the staircase in the consulate to get a night view of the city, McGuinness linked him up the steps.

At a function in the New York home of the chairperson of the Ireland Funds, Loretta Brennan Glucksman, the actor and movie star Liam Neeson was among the VIPs. As a young Catholic growing up in Ballymena, Co. Antrim, he sneaked in to Paisley rallies to observe the controversial performer in full flow. In the Big Apple, the two met as equals.

Dr Paisley was also accompanied by his son, Ian Junior. The US trip was a high point in their political and family life. At the Oval Office in the White House, alongside Martin McGuinness, they chatted and joked with the US president, George Bush.

On the very day that the leaders of the power-sharing administration were feted in Washington, in Northern Ireland Jim Allister moved to formally register his opposition to Ian Paisley's new persona. In Belfast, he announced the formation of a new party, TUV. In 2004, the DUP had backed him as Paisley's successor in the European Parliament. But he resigned from the party on 27 March 2007, twenty-four hours after it met with Sinn Féin at Stormont.

Allister was opposed to power-sharing with Republicans and the Good Friday Agreement that gave them the right to partici-pate in a mandatory coalition government. He was conscious of the tag 'The Chuckle Brothers' used by Gerry Moriarty of the *Irish Times* to describe Paisley and McGuinness. He knew that the description unnerved a section of the DUP support base, including members of the Free Presbyterian Church founded by Paisley. Allister committed himself to an approach that portrayed the DUP strategy as a form of betrayal or defeat.

Others who backed the party's decision to enter government with Republicans had misgivings about Ian Paisley for a different reason. He would turn eighty-two in April 2008. He was revelling in the limelight, but they had concerns about his ability to do the complex, demanding job of first minister.

In February 2008, the DUP lost a by-election in the Dromore Council when its candidate was defeated by the UUP candidate, who benefitted from TUV transfers. The following month, Ian Paisley announced his decision to resign as first minister and DUP leader. The party quickly rubber-stamped Peter Robinson, without a contest, as his replacement for both roles. Four hundred Paisley supporters attended the formal farewell event for him at Belfast's King's Hall on 30 May. If his dramatic conversion from troublemaker to peacemaker surprised many, he himself was ill prepared for his hasty exit from centre stage.

The depth of his hurt was laid bare in two television programmes made by Eamonn Mallie and his son, Michael, and screened by the BBC in January 2014. In the two-part *Genesis to Revelation* series, Dr Paisley claimed he had been ousted from the party he founded by colleagues including Peter Robinson and Nigel Dodds. His wife, Eileen, told of the pain caused when he had to resign as moderator of the Free Presbyterian Church and when he lost the role of preacher at the huge Martyr's Memorial Church on Belfast's Ravenhill Road. She described his treatment as 'iniquitous, nasty, ungodly and un-Christian'.

Nine months after those BBC programmes were aired, following a long illness, eighty-eight-year-old Ian Paisley died. He had a private funeral, attended by only his family members. He is buried in the cemetery alongside Ballygowan Free Presbyterian Church, seven miles from his Belfast home. A tent was erected around the plot to provide privacy for the mourners as his remains were lowered into the grave. A month after the funeral, the Paisley family organized a memorial service at the Ulster Hall in Belfast. The 830 invited guests included Peter Robinson and the deputy first minister, Martin McGuinness. But there was no public farewell for the person who throughout his controversial life could attract tens of thousands to his rallies. Seven years later, Ian Paisley Junior said, 'My father went to the grave with a broken heart because of what happened in his church and in his party.'

In contrast to the falling out with the party and the church he founded, in the final years of his life Ian Paisley was reconciled with the neighbouring jurisdiction. During his last days as first minister and DUP leader, with his wife, Eileen, he made a second visit to the Battle of the Boyne site in Co. Louth where they were welcomed by Taoiseach Bertie Ahern and a number of his cabinet colleagues.

That afternoon, Mrs Paisley made the most significant speech. During unscripted remarks, she recalled her feelings when returning from the United States and looking out the plane window at the Emerald Isle below. She said, 'I wished I could swim for I would jump out and swim the rest of the way home to Ireland. It was so precious and so green and so fresh and so welcoming. It was home, and that is the thing about here.'

In retirement, Dr Paisley made several trips across the border. During a visit to Cobh, Co. Cork, a member of the public presented him with a Celtic cross, and it was given a place in the family home. In Banada, Co. Sligo, he was invited to unveil a work marking his contribution to reconciliation. It is installed in a peace park officially opened by John Hume several years before. I spent time with him during those days.

The hosts arranged accommodation for the Paisley family in the Yeats County Inn in Curry, on the Sligo–Mayo border. Three generations of the Paisley family came. In the local-authority building in Tubbercurry, Ian Paisley was like Santa Claus, with locals queuing to be photographed with him. Dr Paisley told me he felt 'at home' among them.

He made a number of trips to Dublin and signed the visitors book at Government Buildings in the presence of Taoiseach Enda Kenny. He stayed at Farmleigh House, the state guest-house in the Phoenix Park. His last public appearance was on 21 November 2013, at Belfast City Hall, when he and President Michael D. Higgins were the guests at a function to celebrate the legacy of St Columbanus. Like a once famous vaudeville figure, Ian Paisley chatted and chuckled with his visitor while the cameras clicked. He was the centre of attention for a final time.

The SDLP's Seamus Mallon once said, 'For many, the face of Paisley is the ugly face of threats and incitement and bigotry. For others, maybe a different generation, it will be that of an elderly man coming to terms with his mortality.' Mallon was the SDLP MP for Newry and Armagh during some of the most violent years of the Troubles. He attended the funerals of several constituents murdered by Loyalists, and he experienced incidents of partisan behaviour by sections of the security forces. He remembered the phase when Paisley actively encouraged the formation of a Loyalist militia, The Third Force, and the sense of foreboding caused in nationalist communities by images of large numbers, in paramilitary uniform, marching behind Dr Paisley and Peter Robinson.

Some Loyalist paramilitaries who served lengthy prison terms claim they were affected by the fiery rhetoric of Ian Paisley and others at influential periods in their lives. But, the Third

Force episode apart, the DUP kept its distance from Loyalist paramilitary organizations. The UUP (often said by Paisley to be the home of 'big house Unionism') was even more successful in avoiding such associations. Both parties also managed to prevent the paramilitaries developing into a competitive political presence, despite the best efforts of the likes of David Ervine, Billy Hutchinson and Gary McMichael.

Seamus Mallon's party colleague, the SDLP leader John Hume, was the first nationalist to develop a working relationship with Paisley. In their role as members of the European Parliament, with the UUP MEP Jim Nicholson, they lobbied the EU institutions for agricultural supports and structural funds. The unlikely coalition, working together in a pragmatic way on a specific issue, had an impact in Brussels. It ran counter to the widely held perception of Northern Ireland's divisive politics.

Paisley's preacher and politician roles made him unique. He had an impressive presence in his religious role. When photographer John Harrison died in 2010, Dr Paisley officiated at his funeral. John was only hours home from a US trip with a Stormont delegation when he suffered a heart attack. He was very popular, and a community hall was required to accommodate the overflow of mourners at the memorial service. There was complete silence in both crowded venues when Dr Paisley began reciting the lyrics of an American gospel song:

> We are going down the valley one by one
> With our faces tow'rd the setting of the sun;
> Down the valley where the mournful cypress grows,
> Where the stream of death in silence onward flows.

Paisley once called to the Co. Tyrone home of Catholic woman Vera McVeigh and prayed with her for the return of the remains of her missing son, Columba. He was seventeen when he was abducted by the IRA in 1975, killed and buried in a secret location. He was one of the group who became known as 'The Disappeared'. A number of the victims were found on foot of information provided by the IRA. But, despite several searches for Columba McVeigh in isolated border boglands, his remains were never located. Mrs McVeigh died in May 2007, six months after the Paisley visit and his appeal for information.

In his dealings with journalists, Paisley sometimes had an edge that bordered on menace, particularly in his early years. A colleague from Dublin was among a group of reporters quizzing him on a Belfast street one dark evening, with a crowd of Paisley supporters in attendance. He remarked on her Southern accent. On another occasion, when visiting RTÉ journalist Bill O'Herlihy was in the huddle of reporters, Dr Paisley asked him had he been drinking as there seemed to be a smell of alcohol in the air. Bill was always quick on his feet and reputedly answered, 'No, I'm an orange man, like yourself.'

In his role as RTÉ's northern editor, Jim Dougal, a Catholic and former clerical student, had a good working relationship with Paisley. The DUP leader, as well as John Hume and Jim Nicholson, supported Dougal when he successfully sought the role of European Commission representative in Belfast. The RTÉ Belfast base, opened in 2008, has a painting by one of the Paisleys' daughters, Rhonda, on display in the main office. Cathal Goan, the director general, an Irish-speaking native of Ardoyne, approved the purchase. It depicts a bunch of poppies in a vase and often generates conversation when strangers visit the office.

My years in Belfast coincided with the phase in Ian Paisley's life when he was conscious of his legacy and how history might view him. My most enjoyable engagements were the interviews I did with him for the RTÉ *This Week* Sunday radio programme when Gerald Barry was the editor in charge. He knew Paisley's backstory and gave time and space to what he recognized was dramatic change in one of the most important figures in recent Irish history. In some of those interviews, it was possible to get a sense of Paisley moving from his long history as an outsider. Mary McAleese told me she cried while listening to one of them.

There is a significant body of evidence to suggest that the DUP leader had a negative role in deepening and extending the Troubles. It can also be argued that Paisley's involvement was vital to unleash the potential of the peace process. Irony had its say in the end. He made his reputation as an outsider. He had a brief phase of almost universal popularity. But in his final days he felt that he had been abandoned by some of his own flock.

Peter Robinson took over as DUP leader and first minister in June 2008, believing devolution's honeymoon was over. He was fifty-nine, a year older than Martin McGuinness. He knew they could never become a new version of the Chuckle Brothers. Robinson's intention was to respect Sinn Féin's mandate but to keep the relationship businesslike. He was shy and cautious by nature. Ian Paisley had been the front-of-house presence of the DUP while Robinson was the producer-director in the wings. That would now have to change.

Martin McGuinness, in contrast, enjoyed making connections. Even those who despised what he stood for were often struck by his keenness to engage. It hadn't always been that way. A Sligo friend, Barney Bree, was a bank clerk in Derry in the late 1960s. He remembered a shy young McGuinness coming in with lodgements from the butcher's shop where he worked. Then came the phase, which features in black-and-white newsreels, when McGuinness had a mop of curly hair and a tweed jacket, and a likeness to Art Garfunkel, as he walked around Free Derry as a recognized IRA leader.

My dealings with him began in Derry in the early 1980s. Mitchel McLaughlin was the main Sinn Féin media contact at the time. In the early hours of St Patrick's Day 1984, a special sitting of the District Court in Letterkenny was held in relation to Patrick McIntyre, one of the IRA members who had escaped from the Maze prison and who was arrested in south Donegal. Two women from the Traveller community were also brought before District Justice Liam McMenamin. They had been arrested on charges of shoplifting ladies', gents' and children's clothes, valued at £131. Because there was nobody present at the late-night proceedings to provide bail of £500, they were going to be sent to prison on St Patrick's Day and would remain there until the next court hearing. I remembered the time from our childhood in Sligo when my parents brought a family from their sodden tent into our home. From the press box, I indicated I would act as guarantor. (The money was never required as the bail conditions were honoured.) In Derry, McGuinness read an account of those court proceedings in a local newspaper, and he often said he traced our relationship back to that time.

McGuinness served a six-month sentence in Portlaoise Prison for an IRA-membership conviction in 1974 and always said publicly that he left the organization afterwards. I don't believe the break came then. I've always felt there was a time in his life when he was involved in, sanctioned and had knowledge of killings and bombings. But then came the phase when he committed himself to exclusively to politics. He didn't want to return to the awfulness of that earlier period. Nor would he or many of those from the different factions involved in the

Troubles ever tell the full details about their past. One of the reasons he put so much of himself into the Stormont role was that he really wanted to make power-sharing work.

One night in Derry, in 2014, I was interviewing McGuinness live for the RTÉ 9 p.m. television bulletin. We were perched on the grass, below the city walls, overlooking the Bogside. McGuinness's home was close by, and he had come to us directly from there. Peter Doherty, his neighbour, was the cameraman, filming the interview and sending the signal through our small satellite van. Unusually, Paul, the Sinn Féin minder/driver who accompanied McGuinness everywhere, hadn't turned up.

Critics of McGuinness, who opposed Sinn Féin's partici-pating in power-sharing, spotted us under the camera lights. They began hurling stones in our direction. The missiles were whizzing down on us and past us in the dark. One struck the small dish on the van and interrupted our transmission. McGuinness was directly opposite me. He retained an icy calm. I remember looking at him, and his countenance, particularly his eyes, seemed to convey a knowledge of far worse times when he might have reacted differently. After his minder arrived, the stone-throwers on the walls jumped into a car and fled. The signal was re-established, and, following the commercial break in the news bulletin, we resumed our contribution.

McGuinness often said that the events he witnessed in Derry during the late 1960s shaped his life. Exposure to violence and loss did the same to Robinson. His former school friend, Harry Beggs, was a twenty-three-year-old killed by an IRA bomb attack on the Electricity Board's Belfast headquarters in August 1971. Robinson said, 'The murder made me angry, wanting retribu-tion, and very bitter.' He gave up his job as an estate agent and committed himself to a full-time political life with the DUP.

The pair, almost the same age but from completely different backgrounds, were given the responsibility to lead Northern Ireland through what Robinson rightly described as 'the hard yards' phase of the peace process. There was very little public appreciation of the magnitude of the challenge they faced.

After the 1994 IRA ceasefire, the 1998 Good Friday Agreement and the 2007 decision by the DUP and Sinn Féin to enter a power-sharing government, the outside world had a sense of 'that place is sorted, let them now get on with it'. But the participants themselves and the communities they served were ill prepared for it. The two main factions, Unionists and nationalists, distrusted each other and had completely different views about the past and the future. Their political leaders were required to participate in a mandatory grand coalition model of devolved government, where all were expected to cooperate. It was a unique construct, completely different to the government–opposition norm elsewhere. Those attempting to make it function were constantly interrupted by the cycle of local, Assembly, Westminster and European elections where they had to compete against each other for their very survival.

The members elected to the Assembly and those given ministerial responsibilities in the Executive had no experience in the role. Yet they were expected to make policy decisions in complex areas including health, education and infrastructure. They presided over a civil service used to the status of a branch office that received its instructions and funding from headquarters in London. They were monitored by a media whose main function for decades involved recording the taking of innocent life in the cycle of tit-for-tat killings and claim and counterclaim.

Unlike the devolved administrations in Edinburgh and Cardiff, and, indeed, the governments in London and Dublin,

Northern Ireland has the additional challenge of attempting to deal with its past. Nationalists and Unionists have completely different interpretations about who had primary responsibility for the mayhem of the Troubles. It was a society where what one community regarded as success was automatically viewed by the other as failure or sell-out.

Robinson and McGuinness each had an office in the Stormont Castle building on the Stormont Estate and on opposite sides of Stormont Parliament Buildings. They each formed a strong bond with a small team who helped maintain the link with the party and support base but who also carried day-to-day responsibilities for the first minister–deputy first minister relationship.

In Robinson's case, his tight circle included Timothy Johnston, Richard Bullick and John Robinson, who completed a placement in Washington after he graduated, with a group that included Justin McAleese, son of the president, and Noel Rock, a future Fine Gael TD. For a time, Simon Hamilton was part of that DUP team. He later became the economy minister, before leaving politics for a career in the private sector. Robinson also recruited a law graduate, Emma Little-Pengelly. Her husband, Richard, was a senior civil servant. Her father had served a prison sentence for Ulster Defence Association activities, and this was one of the rare examples of the DUP straying from its policy of maintaining an arm's-length relationship with Loyalist paramilitaries.

The two key advisers in the McGuinness team had an IRA past. As a nineteen-year-old in the 1970s, Aidan McAteer was convicted for his role in an attack on a British Army barracks. His father, Hugh McAteer, was a leading member of the Belfast IRA in the 1950s, and his uncle Eddie, an accountant, took the political route as a Derry-based representative of the Nationalist

Party. Leo Green spent seventeen years in prison for a convic-
tion related to the murder of an RUC officer, and he spent
fifty-three days on hunger strike in 1980. His brother, John
Francis Green, was an IRA member shot dead by the Ulster
Volunteer Force in a farmhouse near Castleblayney in 1975.
Other party members who worked closely with McGuinness
at different times included Vincent Parker, Ciarán Quinn
and Mark Mullan. The civil servants who worked alongside
McGuinness in his role as deputy first minister included Mark
McLoughlin, Anne Martin and Brian McAvoy (later the Ulster
secretary of the GAA).

Robinson's relationship with his small group helped him
retain tight control of the DUP. While he had some critics in the
party, they rarely surfaced to publicly criticize him. McGuinness
wasn't the boss of Sinn Féin, but his closeness to the party president, Gerry Adams, was extraordinary. Within political parties
or in coalitions, I never saw a political relationship like it. The
Belfast–Derry factor was one of their many differences. But in
almost two decades, in public and in private dealings, one never
uttered a sentence undermining or challenging the other.

The first major challenge that the Robinson–McGuinness
partnership faced was the transfer of responsibility for justice
and policing matters from Westminster to Stormont. Brian
Cowen had replaced Bertie Ahern as Taoiseach in July 2008,
and Gordon Brown was Tony Blair's successor as British prime
minister. The Northern Ireland secretary, Shaun Woodward,
and the Irish minister for foreign affairs, Micheál Martin, had
responsibility for attempting to make progress in what were
tortuously slow negotiations.

There was an obvious reason why the justice issue had not
been addressed. It was extraordinarily difficult. Nationalists and

Unionists had differing views about who was most culpable for the Troubles. Incidents that fuelled their disagreement about the past and the present kept occurring. In 2001, the first Northern Ireland police ombudsman, Nuala O'Loan, had produced a report into the 1998 Omagh bombing. She criticized how the RUC had handled information that some form of attack was being planned. She also took issue with the police follow-up investigation of the explosion that killed twenty-nine people and two unborn babies.

No suitable candidate from Northern Ireland was found to head up the rebranded RUC, the PSNI. The role went to Hugh Orde, who had a background in the London Metropolitan Police. (When his seven-year term ended, in April 2009, his replacement, Matt Baggott, was also English.) Paramilitaries were still active in some Republican and Loyalist communities. Because of its historical links with the IRA and the fact that some of its representatives in Stormont had an IRA past, Sinn Féin was regularly in the sights of Unionists on justice issues.

The murder of Paul Quinn from Cullyhanna, Co. Armagh, in October 2007, caused public outrage and added to tensions in the power-sharing Executive. The twenty-one-year-old was lured over the border to Oram in Co. Monaghan and beaten by several men, using pickaxe handles and iron bars. He died from his injuries in a Drogheda hospital that night. His parents claimed that known IRA members were behind the assault. They continued to highlight how nobody was prepared to come forward with information to help the inquiries of the gardaí and the PSNI.

The Orange Order, a powerful force within Unionism, had its priorities in the justice and policing debate. It took issue with how, each year, the Parades Commission exercised its authority to curtail some proposed Orange marches at interface areas. It wanted concessions on this issue to be part of any deal between the DUP and Sinn Féin.

McGuinness and Robinson were struggling to find common ground on very difficult issues when events intervened. On 7 March, dissident Republicans shot dead two British soldiers in Antrim. They were ambushed when they came to collect a pizza delivery at the entrance to their army base. Two days later, dissidents shot dead PSNI constable Stephen Carroll, after luring him to a distress call in a Portadown, Co. Armagh, housing estate. He was the first PSNI officer to be murdered. Martin McGuinness described those responsible as 'traitors to the island of Ireland'. I watched him make those comments at a news conference outside Stormont Castle. He was standing alongside Peter Robinson and the PSNI chief constable, Hugh Orde. I thought McGuinness was making a significant state-ment, at some personal risk.

I looked at Peter Robinson as he noted the initiative taken by McGuinness. But at that time I had no sense of the earthquake the DUP leader was dealing with in his own personal life. It didn't become public until nine months later. His wife, Iris, announced in December 2009 that for mental-health reasons she was resigning from public life, including her role as MP for Strangford. Two weeks later, I was sitting with three other journalists in Peter Robinson's home when he told us that his wife had tried to take her own life on 1 March over a brief extramarital affair.

The Robinsons had no choice about making public the inti-mate details. BBC Northern Ireland's *Spotlight* investigation team had got wind of the affair and was set to broadcast a programme about it the following night. Among the significant allegations the programme-makers would make was that Mrs Robinson had helped the man she was involved with to secure a £50,000 loan for his business. The question arose: had she, as an MP, created propriety issues for herself (and for her husband after he learned about it).

Four of us were invited to the Robinsons' house: Mark Devenport from the BBC, UTV's Ken Reid, Deric Henderson of the PA and myself. Of the many times I'd seen Peter Robinson close-up, this was his lowest moment. Afterwards, some comments were made suggesting that some of his aides had strategically placed a picture behind where he sat for the interview. It had a To Dad message: 'Even when I am taller than you, I will still look up to you.' What actually happened was that our cameraman, Joe Mawhinney, had only minutes to make his preparations when we were given access to what was a crisis zone. Joe spotted the piece and moved it to dress the camera shot. He gave no consideration to what the text said, and neither did we.

The acknowledgement of infidelity, followed by the *Spotlight* programme, put the Robinsons in the public glare like never before. In the weeks before the revelations, the strains over justice and policing deepened. During one news conference in Coleraine, an embarrassed Taoiseach Brian Cowen stood with Robinson on one side and McGuinness on the other, squabbling. On one of those January days when public interest in the affair simmered, in the privacy of a Stormont room, McGuinness sympathized with Robinson over his problems and extended his hand towards him. They had been joint leaders of the power-sharing administration for seventeen months. For the very first time, Robinson relented and shook hands with McGuinness.

The DUP leader actually stood aside from the first-minister role on 11 January to allow for scrutiny around the issue of the £50,000 loan. Arlene Foster, the enterprise minister, was

At a fundraising five-a-side football event for the Simon Community in Galway. *Left to right*: journalist Cathal Mac Coille, me, Ollie Jennings (manager of the Saw Doctors), journalist Michelle McCaughran and Michael D. Higgins

Interviewing the DUP leader, Revd Ian Paisley, during that important phase in the peace process when he was Northern Ireland's First Minister

Seamus Heaney in Bellaghy turf bog, wearing the clothes of his late father. The photo was taken by my friend Bobbie Hanvey

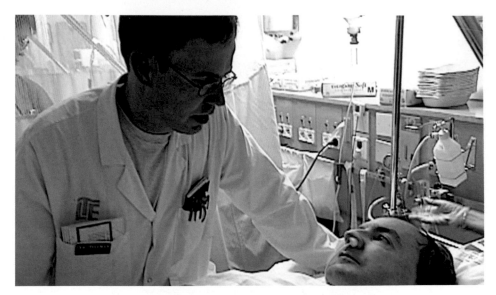

Professor Per Hellman with me after surgery at the University Hospital, Uppsala

St Vincent's Hospital, Dublin, June 2017 with fellow NETs patients, celebrating the hospital receiving recognition as a centre of excellence for NETs treatment. *Left to right*: me, Terry O'Neill, Andrea Martin, Mark McDonnell, Simon Harris TD (Minister for Health), Professor Dermot O'Toole, Colm O'Callaghan, Tom O'Donoghue and John Fallon

Interviewing former US President Bill Clinton in New York on the day he received his portrait by the artist Colin Davidson

Peter Robinson at his final meeting of the North-South Ministerial Council in Armagh, December 2015. *Left to right*: NI Deputy First Minister Martin McGuinness, me, NI First Minister Peter Robinson

14 days before Brexit: an RTÉ News bulletin discussion with newscaster Sharon Ní Bheoláin, Brussels editor Tony Connelly and London correspondent Sean Whelan

May 2018: showing the demarcation line of the Irish border to the then Belgian prime minister, Charles Michel (now President of the European Council) at Ravensdale, Co Louth, when he visited the area with Enterprise Minister Heather Humphreys

Courtesy of the Logue family

Roy Keane presenting his signed jersey to Gerard Logue at Old Trafford in January 2004

Lawyer Michael Kennedy who helped secure the Roy Keane interview in 2002

Courtesy of the Kennedy family

Prince Charles, meeting Noel 'Mousey' Jinks among the crowds at Mullaghmore in 2015

Our Westawake WhatsApp group at Salthill, Galway in June 2021. *Left to right*: Sean O'Rourke, me, Michael Lally, Ray Burke, Jim Fahy, Charlie Bird (and photographer Joe O'Brien)

With Boris Johnson at the DUP party conference in November 2018

Paula, walking with her dog, Cara, on Raughley beach in North Sligo

Our final photo together before Paula's death. *Left to right*: Michael, Paula, Mary and me

Moya, playing cello at a concert in Brussels

Joe's graduation day at Northeastern University, Boston, in May 2019

Ceara

nominated as his temporary replacement. The push to make a breakthrough on the devolution of justice and policing, the missing piece of the Good Friday Agreement jigsaw, then moved into a new phase. Those negotiations took place at Hillsborough Castle. They were very difficult.

Micheál Martin, as minister for foreign affairs, and Shaun Woodward, the Northern Ireland secretary, took responsibility for trying to keep the discussions on track. Prime Minister Gordon Brown came over from London; Taoiseach Brian Cowen travelled up from Dublin. They stayed beyond schedule as the haggling was now running longer than the negotiation of the Good Friday Agreement. Fiona McCoy, an official in the Northern Ireland Office, brought several Department of Foreign Affairs diplomats to the nearby Marks & Spencer for emergency supplies of socks, shirts and underwear. With a PSNI escort, the Taoiseach's private secretary, Nick Reddy, later made the trip to stock up for the politicians. On a number of nights, Arlene Foster was the only significant DUP figure who remained around to support her party leader. The bond between them strengthened during those times.

I was due to go to Sweden for surgery that couldn't be postponed. I was hoping to be around to report on the breakthrough. The night of my departure, the two sides were still at loggerheads. But before I left, something encouraging happened. Robinson, Foster, Adams and McGuinness all signed a card, wishing me well on my travels. It was brought out discreetly, in the snow, and handed over to me through the bars of the closed gates of Hillsborough Castle. An RTÉ colleague, Eimear Lowe, took over the shift.

I was in a hospital bed in Uppsala, recovering, when the news came through that the deal was done. Peter Robinson formally returned to his role as first minister on 4 February. The decisive breakthrough came the following day. The agreement amounted to the missing piece of the Good Friday Agreement jigsaw. One of its significant details was that neither the DUP nor Sinn Féin would provide the first justice minister for Northern Ireland's power-sharing government. That important role would go to David Ford, the Alliance leader.

10

The Queen and the changing of the guard

During some of the very days when Iris and Peter Robinson were struggling with their issues, the Sinn Féin president, Gerry Adams, was being confronted with personal matters from his past. In December 2009, a UTV television programme alleged the daughter of Gerry Adams's brother, Liam, claimed that, as a child, her father had sexually abused her for a decade. Áine Tyrell waived her right to anonymity to make her allegations. The incidents began in 1977 when Liam Adams was twenty-two. He was seven years younger than his brother and subsequently lived and worked in a number of places including New York, Dundalk and Donegal before returning to West Belfast. The revelations became a major news story. Sinn Féin issued statements urging Liam Adams to give himself up to the PSNI in order to answer the allegations.

But more was to follow. On the Sunday morning before Christmas, I was offered an interview with the Sinn Féin president and was told he would provide significant new information. The location for our appointment was a semi-detached house in West Belfast. As cameraman Conor O'Brien set up his equipment in a front room, we could hear Gerry Adams getting physically sick upstairs. During the interview, he told how some of his siblings had been subjected to emotional, physical and sexual abuse by their father, Gerry Adams Senior. Gerry Adams was born in 1948. He said he only discovered about his father's behaviour when he was fifty. He also talked about his conflicted feelings when his father, Gerry Senior, died in 2003. He was a former member of the IRA, a founder of the Felons Club, a Republican social centre, in West Belfast. The Sinn Féin president said he was conflicted at the prospect of the tricolour being draped over his father's coffin because he had besmirched the flag. He also said that within the family circle his father was an isolated figure in his final years because of his history of abusive behaviour. During the interview, he also called on his brother Liam to give himself up to the authorities for questioning.

The day after the Gerry Adams interview was transmitted, I went home to Sligo to spend Christmas with the family. But the story was far from over. With huge interest in where he might be hiding, Liam Adams turned up in a bed and breakfast on Pearse Road in my Sligo hometown. He made an appointment at Sligo garda station, and the process began that led to his extradition to Northern Ireland to face charges in 2013.

I attended the trial in Belfast. After several days of evidence, for legal reasons, proceedings halted and a second trial took place. Áine Tyrell gave graphic evidence of her allegations of abuse. Liam Adams's second wife, Bronagh, and their daughter, Claire, provided evidence in his defence. The legal team for the accused was led by barrister Eilis McDermott. In 1974, she and two other Catholic women from Belfast, Mary McAleese and Patricia Kennedy, broke through a glass ceiling of sorts when they were called to the bar. Her junior counsel was the former Derry footballer and pundit Joe Brolly.

In the first trial, Gerry Adams was one of the prosecution witnesses, and he gave evidence against his own brother. He said that he had admitted the past abusive behaviour to him during a walk in the rain in Dundalk in 2000. Eilis McDermott had a number of sharp exchanges with the Sinn Féin leader during his time giving evidence. After the first case collapsed for legal reasons, the prosecution did not require Gerry Adams as a witness during the second hearing.

The jury found Liam Adams guilty on ten counts, including three of rape and four of indecent assault. He died from cancer in February 2019, five years into his sixteen-year prison term. Immediately after the verdict, his daughter Áine made a statement, welcoming the conviction and saying she would now try to get on with her life. I had contact from Co. Donegal with Liam Adams's wife, Bronagh, a number of times afterwards, and she maintained right up to her husband's death and beyond that he was innocent of the charges.

The terrible saga gave me an insight into the circumstances of Gerry Adams's childhood and the West Belfast where he grew up. He was one of thirteen children, ten of whom survived into adulthood. Both his parents were from Republican families. His grandfather, also Gerry Adams, was a member of the Irish Republican Brotherhood during the War of Independence. Two of his uncles were interned. He was at school with my colleague in the RTÉ Belfast office, Gerry McCann, but after earning six O levels, he left St Mary's Christian Brothers' Grammar School at sixteen and became a barman. Significant parts of the rest, including the extent of his involvement with the IRA, will never be known.

A year after the admissions about his father's history as an abuser, he gave me another significant story. On 14 November

2010, I interviewed him at the Ballymascanlon House Hotel outside Dundalk. He announced he would be resigning his seat in the Northern Ireland Assembly and contesting the Louth constituency for Sinn Féin in the next general election. His calculation was that Sinn Féin were in real danger of bouncing off the glass ceiling. They had won five Dáil seats in the previous general election. They were in danger of going down to four. His hope was that by crossing the border to run in the South he could energize the Sinn Féin campaign. He recognized it was a gamble but felt it was required.

Brian Cowen's thirty-four-month term as Taoiseach was dominated by his coalition government's struggle to keep the country solvent during the world economic crash. He and the five cabinet colleagues who came to Armagh on 21 January 2011 had the look of an administration on its last legs. They had crossed the border for a North–South ministerial meeting with their Stormont counterparts.

When I met Enda Kenny, the Fine Gael leader, in Co. Antrim the following day, he was keen to get an account of the Armagh event. While in Northern Ireland as a guest speaker at the annual Alliance conference, Kenny was preoccupied with Dáil politics. He sensed the government was about to fall apart. He hoped that, after so many years on the sideline, his chance to become Taoiseach was approaching. The following day, in Dublin, the Green Party withdrew its ministers, effectively pulling the plug on the coalition. Brian Cowen set the general-election date for 25 February.

I first heard of Brian Cowen during my first year in the Rathmines School of Journalism. Two second-year students acted like older brothers to us there. Joe O'Brien was from Carlow, PJ Cunningham was from Clara, Co. Offaly, and they were keen to look out for the younger ones 'up from the country'. They introduced us to weekend dances in the Leinster Cricket Club, where PJ's standard advice for the crowded dance floor was to 'lie in and hold tight'.

PJ occasionally had 'a visitor from home', Brian Cowen, a son of the local TD, Ber Cowen, who was also a publican, auctioneer, butcher and undertaker. PJ had stories of the Cowens' hearse sometimes being used to attend greyhound meetings and dances. He and Brian were playing for the Clara GAA club. Brian was a handy footballer and could kick with both feet. He was getting his place on the Offaly underage teams.

A qualified solicitor, his life changed dramatically in 1984 when his father died suddenly. He was twenty-four at the time. His father was fifty-one. He contested and won the 1984 by-election caused by his father's passing. He too was fifty-one when he announced he was standing down from politics. Of the twenty-seven years he served in the Dáil, the three final ones, when he was Taoiseach, were the most bruising.

One historic initiative during his final difficult twelve months was the decision to allow preparations for the first state visit to Ireland by the British monarch, Queen Elizabeth. The deal to transfer responsibilities for justice and policing from Westminster to Stormont was agreed during Cowen's time as Taoiseach. It had a significance in terms of British–Irish relations as it was the unfinished business from the 1998 Good Friday Agreement. With that outstanding matter resolved, the Irish government felt the time was right to formally welcome the head of state from the neighbouring island.

Mary McAleese was in the final of fourteen years as president. Throughout both terms, she had faithfully pursued her stated priority to act as a bridge-builder. She had developed a close personal relationship with Queen Elizabeth, and the government was keen that history would be made on her watch.

On 4 March, Buckingham Palace, in consultation with Áras an Uachtaráin, formally confirmed that the first state visit by a British monarch to Ireland would take place in May. But the detailed planning began long before the official announcement. I reported on those events and made two RTÉ television documentaries about them. *The Queen and Us* was transmitted the night the queen arrived, and *The Queen's Speech* was screened seven months later, on 27 December.

It was a fascinating time, when some of the people and activities offstage and behind the scenes were as interesting as the events taking place in public view. Edward Young, then the deputy private secretary at Buckingham Palace, was an important official on the British side. The British ambassador in Dublin, Julian King, was another key player. He later served as the final UK representative of the European Commission in Brussels before it terminated its membership of the EU.

Edward Young made a number of trips to Ireland to help with the early planning. On some of the visits, he was accompanied by Angela Kelly, the queen's personal assistant. Angela has an interesting backstory. She was raised in Liverpool, where her father worked on the docks, and had west of Ireland roots.

She was working as the housekeeper at the British embassy in Bonn when, during a visit by the queen, her skills were noticed. In 1994, she was invited to a job interview in Windsor Castle, and she was appointed the queen's dresser. Her official title is 'Personal Assistant, Adviser and Curator to Her Majesty the Queen (Jewellery, Insignias and Wardrobe)'. She is recognized as a fashion designer, dressmaker and milliner. Her responsibilities include researching the venues for royal visits to help with her decision-making about appropriate outfits. When Edward Young and Angela Kelly made some of those discreet reconnaissance trips to Ireland, they often took Ryanair flights. To avoid baggage delays and costs, they sometimes opted to use hand luggage and wear a number of layers.

I attempted to make a case to Edward Young for permission to interview Angela Kelly. As someone with her emigrant Irish background who spends so much time in the queen's company, she would make for very interesting television. But, despite my pleadings, Edward explained to me that he couldn't grant the request. He offered an alternative interviewee, explaining it was someone who had contact with the queen on a regular basis – the British prime minister, David Cameron.

Brian O'Driscoll was asked out of retirement to help with the preparations. In 1976, he was driving the British ambassador, Christopher Ewart-Biggs, from his south Dublin residence, when an IRA landmine exploded, killing the diplomat and another passenger, twenty-six-year-old civil servant Judith Cooke. It was cathartic for Brian, forty-five years later, to have a role in the planning of events that would signify the improved relationship between the neighbouring islands.

The writer and journalist Colm Tóibín had a role in the preparations. A British civil servant, Richard Cushnie, approached him in confidence and sought his views about what the queen might say in her speech at Dublin Castle. The Enniscorthy-born former editor of *Magill*, the author of novels including *Brooklyn*, *The Heather Blazing* and *The Magician*, submitted his handwritten thoughts. The speech delivered by Queen Elizabeth at the banquet in Dublin Castle included many of his suggestions.

The option of Sinn Féin's leader in Northern Ireland, the deputy first minister Martin McGuinness, attending some of the events of the four-day itinerary was explored. A place at the table in Dublin Castle was kept open for him until twenty-four hours before the dinner. I talked to him, off the record, a number of times. In keeping with his record on power-sharing, his instinct was to make the gesture. His problem was that he couldn't get the backing of his party to do so.

In the February 2011 Dáil elections, Sinn Féin had made incremental but significant advances. With Gerry Adams as one of its candidates, it increased its representation from five to fourteen. Assembly elections were due in Northern Ireland in early May. Rather than risk a fuss about Martin McGuinness featuring in formal dress code at a Dublin Castle dinner along-side the royal family, the Sinn Féin policy decision was to keep him grounded north of the border.

But during the royal visit one Sinn Féin representative broke ranks. Michael Browne was the Mayor of Cashel. He was struggling with cancer. When the queen went to the Rock of Cashel on her final morning in Ireland, in his wheelchair, wearing his mayoral chain, Michael Browne was among the local dignitaries to meet her. He said afterwards he was 'probably' the first Sinn Féin elected representative to shake her hand, and 'sooner or later it was going to happen anyway'. He died from his illness two months later.

The decision of Martin McGuinness to not attend the Dublin Castle event was flagged in advance. His main partner in government, the DUP leader, Peter Robinson, accepted the invitation and crossed the border. He was accompanied to Dublin by his wife, Iris, who had not been seen in public since the controversy about her private life at the beginning of the year. Several of the guests made a point of welcoming her, including the Co. Louth businessman Martin Naughton. He remarked on the colour of her dress: 'Aer Lingus Green'.

A week before the four-day visit began, two invitations arrived at our home for the dinner in Dublin Castle. It was a surprise and an honour to be asked. The best part was that Ceara was going to be with me, witnessing history close-up. We saw the queen's speech that opened with the words 'A Uachtaráin agus a chairde' (President and friends). We heard her say, 'With the benefit of historical hindsight we can all see things which we would wish had been done differently or not at all.'

In the idiosyncratic place that is Ireland, we had some connection with the five other couples seated around our table. David Cooney was the secretary general in the Department of Foreign Affairs. His wife, Geraldine, once lived in Strandhill, two miles from us in Sligo. David's father was an emigrant from Wexford who found work on the buildings in England. Growing up in London, David's ambition was to become an Irish diplomat. When he was posted to Brussels, we played indoor football together. Once, during a break in a meeting in Luxembourg, he found himself in the gents beside John Major, and the Irish diplomat surprised the British prime minister by greeting him in his English accent. His job before returning to run the Department of Foreign Affairs in Dublin was Ireland's ambassador to Great Britain, based in the city where he was born.

Frances Fitzgerald, accompanied by her husband, Michael, was two months into her job as minister for children. Our paths had first crossed in Brussels in 1990, when she was head of the National Women's Council of Ireland, and we filmed her celebrating Mary Robinson's presidential election victory. The minister for health, James Reilly, was sitting with his wife,

Dorothy, a former colleague in RTÉ's make-up department. DUP friends once told me of a most unusual North–South interaction with Reilly. Maurice Morrow, the DUP chairman, was down from Dublin to participate in a live RTÉ *Prime Time* debate. Dr Reilly was also a panellist. Afterwards, while having a cup of tea, the health minister offered to guide the visitors from the unfamiliar roads around Donnybrook to their route north. He proved to be a man of his word, and their parting memory was of a government minister hanging out the window of a state car as he indicated their correct direction of travel.

Adrian O'Neill and his wife, Aisling, had become our friends during his many journeys north in the British–Irish division of the Department of Foreign Affairs. He had been heavily involved in the visit preparations as secretary general to the president. A quintessential diplomat, his final posting before he retired in 2022 was as Ireland's ambassador to Great Britain.

The wealthiest and most influential couple at our table was the most understated: US ambassador Dan Rooney and his wife, Patricia Regan. Her family came from Co. Mayo. Being in their presence reminded me of a story the Ardoyne-based Passionist Order priest Father Gary Donegan tells against himself. He was beside Dan Rooney once at a function in Belfast. Father Gary arrived late to the meal and was directed to a seat beside the stranger. They struck up a conversation about sport, and Father Gary said his team were his native Fermanagh but that he was supporting Tyrone as they were going well in the All-Ireland Championship. He then asked if his fellow guest had a team. The reply came rather hesitantly: 'Well, yes, the Pittsburgh Steelers. They're an American football team.' When the meal concluded, the elderly gentleman made his exit, and, after he left, Father Gary made some inquiries about his identity. He soon learned that he had been sitting beside the US ambassador to Ireland, Dan Rooney, and that the Steelers really were his team because he owned them!

During those four days, there was a sense of healing in British–Irish relations. The bow by the queen as she laid a wreath at the Garden of Remembrance was a powerful moment. Danny Murphy, the Ulster secretary of the GAA, had a significant part in the decision to facilitate the visit to Croke Park, scene of Bloody Sunday in November 1920, when crown forces shot dead fourteen people. After they laid wreaths at the Irish National War Memorial Gardens in Islandbridge, President McAleese introduced the visitors to journalist Kevin Myers. When it was unfashionable, he was one of the first to draw attention to the forgotten valour of the 50,000 Irishmen who gave their lives during the 1914–1918 war. Possibly with a nod from Martin McAleese, some of the former leaders of Loyalist paramilitary organizations, including Jackie McDonald, had come south for the day. They were strategically placed along the exit route from Islandbridge. But as the first drops of rain fell, an umbrella was raised over the heads of the royals, their walking pace quickened and they passed without stopping.

The evening after her speech at Dublin Castle, the queen and her husband were guests at a concert in the national Convention Centre in Dublin. At the end of the programme, compère Gay Byrne invited the VIPs onto the stage. The reception they received was most un-British – it was more akin to the gush that follows the sounding of the final whistle on All-Ireland final day, and it caught them by surprise. Minutes afterwards, when they were outside, the McAleeses approached them to say a formal goodbye as they would be leaving early from Farmleigh House the following morning. Martin McAleese sought to engage with the queen, but she seemed to be still processing the wave of warmth she had received moments before. She politely diverted Martin, suggesting, 'Talk to him.'

Dubliner Mick Devine got a better view than most of the royal visitors during those historic days. Over decades, Mick built a reputation as the driver of choice for international celebrities visiting Ireland – actress Julia Roberts included. When the singer-songwriter Christy Moore is on the concert circuit, Mick always looks after his transport arrangements. For the queen's visit to Ireland, Mick was contracted to drive her ladies-in-waiting. He obviously made an impression on his passengers because one morning he was asked to come to a room at Farmleigh House, where the main VIPs were based. As Mick waited there alone, the queen came in and greeted him.

On the fourth and final day of the visit, as the queen and her husband travelled from Cashel to Cork, her view was sought about an unscheduled walkabout among the crowds gathered on Grand Parade. She gave her approval to the proposed change. Pictures of her banter with the people in Cork and with fishmonger Pat O'Connell received widespread coverage. O'Connell told me afterwards that the queen looked at one of the species resting on ice at his stall in the English Market and said to her husband, 'The fish looks like you.'

On the Sunday after the visitors left, the funeral took place of Garret FitzGerald. As Taoiseach, FitzGerald had negotiated the 1985 Anglo-Irish Agreement with British prime minister Margaret Thatcher. The following day, US president Barack Obama and his wife, Michelle, arrived on a two-day visit to Ireland. It was a hectic but wonderful time to be working in RTÉ – at full stretch. On the night the Obamas departed, I phoned the director of news, Ed Mulhall. He was relieved about how the organization had stepped up to its role as host broad-caster for three major news events, two planned and then the unexpected death of Garret FitzGerald.

By nature, Ed is meticulous, and he told me about the inci-dent when, outside the Central Bank, to the consternation of his security team, President Obama accepted the invitation of a woman in the huge crowd to say hello to her mother on her mobile phone. The pictures featured on RTÉ's live coverage. By the time of the 9 p.m. bulletin, RTÉ colleagues, including journalist Martina Fitzgerald, had actually tracked down the mother who was on the other end of the line in the Obama phone call. She was included in a news bulletin report. Ed said to me, 'It's the little details that can make the difference.'

We were having our conversation after the 9 p.m. news bulletin at the very moment the *Prime Time Investigates: Mission to Prey* documentary was being screened. It contained unfair and untrue allegations about an Irish-born priest during his time working in Africa. It caused a major crisis in RTÉ. Ed Mulhall subsequently resigned from his position. By falling on his sword, in such a public way, he took responsibility for those above, below and around him. He was fifty-six at the time. He was the most talented and most honourable boss during my four decades working in RTÉ.

*

Hosting the historic visit of a reigning British monarch was a meaningful way for Mary McAleese to conclude her fourteen years in Áras an Uachtaráin. Sinn Féin decided it was going to test the political waters by running Martin McGuinness as its candidate to succeed her. In the February 2011 general election,

Sinn Féin had taken almost 10 per cent of the first-preference vote, increasing its Dáil representation from five to fourteen seats. The presidential contest would test if McGuinness could build on that momentum.

I was in Derry's Bogside the evening his campaign was launched, close to his home in the Brandywell. His wife, Bernie, worked in a local café, Frankie Ramseys (known locally as Swanky Frankie's). She usually stayed away from his public life, but she stood beside him that night on the makeshift podium beside the Free Derry wall. He had his bags packed, aware he was heading to what for him was unknown territory, politics south of the border. It proved to be a bruising campaign. He came third on first-preference votes – 13.7 per cent, almost 4 points up on the Sinn Féin general-election figure but less than half the support of the independent Seán Gallagher (28.5 per cent) and a huge distance behind the eventual winner, Michael D. Higgins (39.6 per cent).

On the hustings, McGuinness was tackled a number of times about IRA issues. He was pressed on whether he had a role in encouraging an alleged informer, Franko Hegarty, to return to Derry from MI5-provided facilities in Britain in 1986. After Hegarty's return, the IRA interrogated and killed him. Another damaging encounter happened in front of television cameras at an Athlone shopping centre. McGuinness was quizzed by the son of Private Patrick Kelly, who was shot dead near Ballinamore, Co. Leitrim, in 1983, when Don Tidey's IRA kidnappers were confronted. Chastened by his experiences in the south, McGuinness was relieved to return to his role as Northern Ireland's deputy first minister.

Thirteen months after Sinn Féin refused to sanction his meeting with Queen Elizabeth in Dublin Castle, it agreed to a dramatic change in policy. In Belfast's Lyric Theatre, standing beside Peter Robinson, his partner in government, Martin McGuinness and the British monarch, both smiling, shook hands. Their historic, stage-managed meeting was constructed around the Silent Testimony exhibition of the artist Colin Davidson, whose portraits capture the human cost of the Troubles. The event organizer was the charity Co-operation Ireland. Its joint patrons are Queen Elizabeth and President Michael D. Higgins.

The organization has a Co. Fermanagh-born chief executive, Peter Sheridan. He is a Catholic, whose previous job was assistant chief constable of the PSNI. When he retired from his role in the police, he applied for a position in An Garda Síochána and wasn't offered an interview. The Co-operation Ireland chairman, Christopher Moran, had an Irish father. He is a wealthy London-based businessman, with lines into Buckingham Palace, Clarence House and the Conservative Party, and for the Lyric Theatre staged handshake event, he was the chief fixer.

Four years after they began leading a power-sharing government, Peter Robinson and Martin McGuinness had developed something much deeper than a working relationship. They were spending huge chunks of their waking lives together. Familiarity brought them closer. That very personal bond was required to keep the power-sharing administration intact during difficult times.

On the four or five days he travelled to Belfast each week, McGuinness was regularly on the road by 7 a.m. to avoid the worst of the traffic. While he and Robinson were mostly based at Stormont Castle and in Parliament buildings, they regularly attended events together, and the public noted their standard practice of using first names when referring to each other. They had a shared interest in sport, and they would often talk to each other about their families. McGuinness was the more outgoing. He would bring anecdotes from his family life into his Belfast workplace. One of the stories he shared for a time was how his young grandson pulled him aside and asked, 'Martin, what's in a head?'

After the crisis in her personal life, Iris Robinson stood down as MP for Strangford and retired from public life. Bernie McGuinness rarely left her native city, but she would often walk by the Foyle with her husband in the late evening.

The McGuinness–Robinson chemistry needed to be strong because it was challenged by active forces and factors in their orbit.

Peter Robinson had the instincts of a modernizer. In 2011, he said publicly that he wanted to make the DUP more attractive to Catholics by building its centre-right, pro-business credentials. But some in his support base saw nationalism as a threat to their constitutional position. They viewed Sinn Féin as the enemy that could never be trusted or forgiven. Jim Allister's TUV championed such views. Even though he won just 2.5 per cent support in 2011, during the first Assembly election he contested, and never managed to take more than one Assembly seat for the next decade, Allister's presence continually unnerved the DUP. The cautious side of Robinson had him constantly struggling to accommodate the two conflicting DUP strands: the modernizers and the traditionalists.

Just like Robinson, Martin McGuinness was content to concentrate on the challenge of making power-sharing work on a day-to-day basis. But his party often had different aspirations and priorities. At community and local-government levels in Northern Ireland, Sinn Féin and nationalism were regularly at loggerheads with the DUP and Unionism. Sinn Féin believed that, North and South, it was on a journey that would lead to a united Ireland, knowing such an outcome would sever ties that were sacred to Unionists.

The bond between the two men was stretched to breaking point many times. The Union flags saga that erupted in December 2012 was one severe test. Traditionally, the flag was flown every day over Belfast City Hall. With nationalists outnumbering Unionists on Belfast City Council, they sought to change that. In an effort to avoid a row, the middle-ground Alliance party floated a compromise that would allow the use of the flag on eighteen designated dates, in keeping with the practice on many public buildings elsewhere in the UK. Unionists, including the DUP, viewed the change as one more example of the undermining of their culture and history.

The division was exacerbated by a very personal issue involving Peter Robinson. In 2010, he had lost his East Belfast Westminster seat to Alliance's Naomi Long. Some within the DUP saw the flags row as an opportunity for retribution. They printed thousands of leaflets, highlighting Alliance policy on flags. On the night of the controversial vote, protestors surrounded Belfast City Hall. Some Unionists claimed the flags issue was part of a wider campaign against their Britishness. Months of unrest followed the Council vote. Demonstrators clashed with the police in several areas. The attacks on the premises and homes of Alliance representatives included the petrol-bombing of Naomi Long's East Belfast constituency office.

Loyalist anger found a stage during the marching season – the period between April and August when Unionists celebrate the victory of William of Orange over the Catholic King James II of England and Ireland, VII of Scotland, at the Battle of the Boyne

in 1690. One of the most contentious parades in North Belfast
has Unionists marching past Catholic homes on 12 July and
returning the same route after a day's parading and celebrating.
In the tense summer 2013 environment, Northern Ireland's
Parades Commission imposed strict conditions on the planned
parade in North Belfast. Severe street violence followed.

Early on the morning of the march, I watched the DUP deputy
leader and MP for North Belfast, Nigel Dodds, gather with
bandsmen and members of the Orange Order. I counted more
than the numbers stipulated by the Parades Commission as
they set off to march past the interface with nationalist homes,
at Ardoyne, on their way to the city centre. Several hours later,
after parading hundreds strong up the Loyalist Shankill Road,
they were preparing to return past Ardoyne, contrary to the
Commission's stipulations. Lines of PSNI Land Rovers, flanked
by police officers in riot gear, blocked their route, and rioting
began. At one stage, Nigel Dodds approached the police lines
to have a discussion with one of the senior officers. He was
struck by a missile fired by one of the demonstrators and fell to
the ground. He was unconscious for several minutes and was
brought to hospital by emergency-services personnel.

I got to know Nigel Dodds and his wife, Diane, during my
years in Belfast, and their story is illustrative of the complexities
of Northern Ireland. Nigel was born in Derry, but the family
moved to Fermanagh because of his father Joe's work with the
customs authorities. Diane was from a farming family in Co.
Down. Nigel graduated with a first-class honours degree in law
from St John's College, Cambridge, and during further studies
at Queen's, they met. He qualified as a barrister, and she began
teaching history and English in Lisburn. As a twenty-nine-year-
old councillor, he became Belfast's lord mayor in 1988. In 1993,

he began a fifteen-year period as DUP general secretary, and, along with Ian Paisley and Peter Robinson, he was recognized as a powerful figure in the party.

Their son, Andrew, was born in 1989 with a spina bifida and hydrocephalus condition. They modified their home in Banbridge, Co. Down, to help with his care. In December 1996, the boy was seriously ill, on a ventilator at Belfast's Royal Victoria Hospital. The IRA had suspended the ceasefire, announced in August 1994. Acting on police advice that he might be targeted by paramilitaries, Nigel Dodds was varying visiting routines to the children's ward. The parents were waiting to see a surgeon when hospital staff became suspicious of some people in a corridor. Two policemen shoved the Doddses into an anteroom, and shortly after that shooting began. One of the officers was wounded in the foot. During the firing, two IRA members sprayed areas of the ward with bullets before making their escape.

Two years later, Andrew Dodds died from his illness. Nigel Dodds won the North Belfast Westminster seat in 2001. Unionists had a majority in the constituency, but the balance was shifting. Some of the most notorious sectarian murders took place in the area during the Troubles, and even after the Good Friday Agreement paramilitaries continued to operate there. Diane Dodds joined her husband in front-line politics by winning a West Belfast Assembly seat in 2003, but Sinn Féin defeated her at the first attempt. In 2009, she won the European Parliament seat vacated when Jim Allister left the party. Given their history, they were always likely to have reservations at delicate phases in power-sharing.

In August 2013, while on holidays, Peter Robinson dispatched what became known as the letter from Florida. It told how he was withdrawing his participation from the cross-party support needed to build a peace and reconciliation centre on the site of the old Maze prison. Convicted paramilitaries, including the IRA hunger-striker Bobby Sands, had been jailed there during the Troubles. McGuinness took the decision and the manner in which it was delivered as a personal slight, and it was one of the low points in his relationship with Robinson.

If the conditions around the flying of the Union flag became a sensitive issue for Unionism, the promotion of the Irish language exercised sections of nationalism. This issue formally surfaced as far back as the 1998 Good Friday Agreement. The document that emerged from the negotiations stated that, 'All participants recognize the importance of respect, understanding and toler-ance in relation to linguistic diversity, including in Northern Ireland, the Irish language, Ulster-Scots and the languages of the various ethnic communities.' There was also a Good Friday Agreement clause committing to 'explore urgently with the relevant British authorities, and in cooperation with the Irish broadcasting authorities, the scope for achieving more wide-spread availability of Teilifís na Gaeilge in Northern Ireland'.

In the pre-satellite and pre-broadband era, before Teilifís na Gaeilge existed, the only way to receive RTÉ television signals in Northern Ireland was via a rooftop aerial. During the most violent years of the Troubles, particularly in interface areas, there was risk attached to living in a house with an RTÉ aerial overhead. It was possible to identify homes that had the special aerial type required to access the RTÉ service. Those Good Friday Agreement references to Teilifís na Gaeilge and the absence of any mention of access to RTÉ services indicated the priorities of some of the participants in the negotiations. It also gave notice that the Irish language would become a contentious issue between some sections of nationalism and Unionism in future years.

In my dealings with Peter Robinson, it was never in doubt that he wanted to move the DUP towards the middle ground. He is suited to that space. He is a Christian and regularly attends Newtownbreda Baptist Church, but he is not a member of the Free Presbyterian Church founded by Revd Ian Paisley. Nor is he a member of the Orange Order. And he doesn't participate in the Twelfth of July Parades. There was a menacing phase in his past life during some of the worst years of the Troubles. In the mid-1980s, when Unionists were exercised by the Anglo-Irish Agreement, he appeared in a beret and sunglasses alongside his party leader, Revd Paisley, at a rally of a paramilitary group, Ulster Resistance. In another episode from that time, he was part of a protest group that crossed into Clontibret, Co. Monaghan, daubed slogans on a garda station and became involved in scuffles with garda reinforcements.

But he bought into the significance of the 1994 IRA ceasefire and the direction of travel set by the Good Friday Agreement. He was indispensable in the pirouetting of the DUP towards power-sharing. The pragmatist in him believed that during his lifetime a majority of voters would support Northern Ireland remaining part of the United Kingdom, provided it became a more tolerant society, committed to a positive relationship with its next-door neighbour.

As Gerry Collins articulated when he once urged Albert Reynolds not to 'burst up the party', Robinson worried about a factor that stalks all political organizations: the danger of a split. Day-to-day experience kept reminding him that Sinn Féin, his partners in government and his rivals for the largest party system, were more cohesive and less likely to splinter than the

DUP. He also understood that he was probably the one best placed to restrain the DUP from imploding. It was a dubious, challenging honour.

He and his wife, Iris, worked at dealing with the consequences from the brief but very public crisis in their family life. It hurt his political pride that during that time Naomi Long of Alliance replaced him as the Westminster MP for East Belfast. The DUP and its leader were determined to reverse the result in the 2015 general election. It wasn't an option that he would contest the seat, due to the end of the double-jobbing practice. The party selected a thirty-year-old member of Belfast City Council as its candidate. Gavin Robinson is no relation of his party leader, but they have the same surname and many of the same middle-ground instincts. He won almost 50 per cent of the votes cast in the May 2015 general election, almost 17 per cent more than the performance of his leader five years before. The UUP not fielding a candidate helped him. Naomi Long's vote was actually up by 4,000, but it wasn't enough to catch Gavin Robinson.

For Peter Robinson, the result was a boost and a relief. The seat regained in East Belfast was offset by one lost in South Antrim to the UUP's Danny Kinahan. Another positive was that the DUP replaced Sinn Féin as the party with the largest number of votes: 25.7 per cent compared to 24.5 per cent. With that baggage addressed, Robinson was ready to return to his day job, heading up the power-sharing administration with Martin McGuinness. But on Monday, 25 May, two weeks after the elections, he came close to dying. He was due to leave for Dublin early that morning, with his official police driver, to attend a series of events in Dublin. In typical Robinson fashion, he sent an email to his advisers at 3.56 a.m., and there followed a clammy, sleepless period. Doctors subsequently told him that he probably would have died during the car journey south if he had decided to leave with his driver at the 7.30 a.m. scheduled departure time. Instead, a call for advice to his GP led to the arrival of an ambulance at his home and confirmation that he was having a heart attack.

During emergency care at Belfast's Royal Victoria Hospital, Robinson had three stents inserted and his condition was stabilized. During his post-treatment discussions with the medical team, Robinson listed off his eating habits in the seven-day run-up to the heart attack. It included two Chinese meals, a Kentucky Fried Chicken and another Northern Ireland fast-food dish, a Cowboy Supper (sausages, beans and chips). Much of that dining was done at Stormont or at the DUP's Dundela Avenue office, in the company of his hand-picked back-room team, constantly in his orbit.

In the calm of the summer months, Robinson engaged in a period of private reflection. He was sixty-six and would turn sixty-seven on 29 December. He decided he would retire and that Arlene Foster was the best person to replace him. The decision was formally announced on 19 November. As often happens in such situations, warm tributes are paid to the departing individual but attention rapidly shifts to the successor.

There was a tender, public occasion in Armagh that celebrated some of what happened during the closing phases of Robinson's public life. The North–South Ministerial Council, one of the structures established by the Good Friday Agreement, has its offices in the city at the distinctive address 58 Upper English Street. It is where the administrations from North and South gather to hold discussions and review cooperation at least once a year. Robinson was in relaxed mood, verging on demob happy, when he arrived for what would be his final such meeting that Friday morning, 15 December. During his remarks inside, he said that relations between Northern Ireland and the Republic had never been better.

Enda Kenny, almost four years in the role of Taoiseach, and foreign-affairs minister Charlie Flanagan were his main points of contact in the South. Kenny presented Robinson with *The Dictionary of Irish Biography*, a project of the Royal Irish Academy, which features the stories of prominent men and women from Ireland, North and South, from the earliest times to the twenty-first century. Almost 10,000 lives are listed in the heavy volumes, with biographies varying from 100 to 15,000 words. Robinson was taking stock of the gift when Kenny reached into his pocket for a final, unexpected surprise. It was two quality tickets for the next Spurs v. Arsenal match. The present had been requisitioned by Department of Foreign Affairs staff from contacts in the Tottenham Hotspur football club. Robinson would ask his wife, Iris, to accompany him to the match. As happened at the presentation of the wooden bowl from the site of the Battle of the Boyne to Ian and Eileen Paisley, eleven years before at St Andrews, the Irish government had come up with the imaginative present.

McGuinness told how he and Robinson were the only two ministers remaining in office from the Stormont Executive of 1999, and he reflected on his own situation. 'Very shortly I will be the last, so my day too will come at some stage,' he said. With his gift of Irish biography lists, his Spurs match tickets and his sense of time passing, Robinson interjected, 'It's *Tiocfaidh ár lá*, isn't it?' he said. McGuinness had the final word: 'I'm glad to see your Irish is improving.'

*

During the days immediately after the death of her eighty-one-year-old father, John Kelly, in December 2011, I learned about some of the complexities of Arlene Foster. She was travelling to a tourism function in London in her role as minister for enterprise and trade when he suffered a fatal heart attack in Co. Fermanagh. She knew something was wrong when her phone lit up with messages after the flight landed.

When I called to pay my respects to her parents' home in the small town of Lisnaskea, she brought me to the front room where her father was laid out. We were alone beside his coffin. Her grief was deepened by the fact that she never got to say goodbye. As she talked about his life, she pointed to the forehead that had been grazed by bullets when an IRA gang came to kill him in 1979.

Arlene was eight at the time of that attack, one of four children. The family was living on a small farm close to the border, near Roslea. Her father was a part-time farmer whose main income came from his job as a member of the RUC. As he locked up the cows for the night, the gunmen began firing. He crawled into the house with blood streaming from his forehead, and the gang made their escape. John Kelly recovered from his injuries, but the shooting changed his family's life. For their safety, they were moved under a government scheme to a small estate in Lisnaskea, opposite the police station. Missing the farm, Granny Kelly often described their new home as a box.

Terrible visceral patterns stunted rural border communities during the Troubles. Republican paramilitaries had a policy of targeting those who worked for the police or British Army on a part-time or full-time basis and those providing services to the security forces. Nationalists often felt they were treated as second-class citizens by the state. Many had first-hand experience of neighbours who morphed into strangers or worse each time they put on the uniform of a police officer or soldier. Land – how it was acquired and then retained – was often contentious. Catholics would point to examples of where religion was the deciding factor in the sale of a field. Protestants had the evidence of tombstones in rural graveyards and what they saw as a strategy to remove them from the landscape.

When she was sixteen, violence interrupted Arlene Kelly's life a second time. She was a student of Enniskillen Collegiate Grammar School, twelve miles away. The IRA carried out a bomb attack on her school bus, hoping to kill the driver, Ernie Wilson, because he was a part-time member of the Ulster Defence Regiment. The girl sitting beside her, Gillian Latimer, was seriously injured. The bus driver's son, James, usually searched the vehicle several times a day for suspect devices. He blamed himself for not spotting the bomb and took his own life shortly afterwards.

Arlene Foster was shaped by such events. She could never forget about them or set them aside. She remained troubled by the suspicion that some of her neighbours had supplied information to the IRA gang that tried to murder her father. When she was in government with Sinn Féin's Martin McGuinness, she struggled with the knowledge that he gave the oration at the funeral of an IRA member linked to that attack. Yet there was a restless, questioning side of her that would not let her remain rooted within her own traditions or settle for a one-sided view of history.

In his poem 'Ceasefire', Michael Longley captures the sometimes impossible challenge that is at the heart of Northern Ireland's peace process, a dilemma constantly confronting those who seek to shape it and keep it alive.

I get down on my knees and do what must be done
And kiss Achilles' hand, the killer of my son.

For Foster, her dealings with Sinn Féin, and specifically with Martin McGuinness, involved that Longley test. Like a Shakespearian tragedy, there was a pattern that circumstances intervened, at critical junctures, with detrimental consequences.

Arlene was the first member of her family to go to university, studying law at Queen's University, Belfast. She was considered 'bright' by one of her lecturers, Mary McAleese, a future president of Ireland. While there, she joined the university branch of the UUP and became its chairman. After graduating, she returned home to Co. Fermanagh and worked for a decade as a solicitor in Enniskillen. Her boss in the legal firm, James Cooper, was a future chairman of the UUP, and she continued to be an active member. When she defected to the DUP in January 2004, less than two months after she won a Fermanagh–South Tyrone Assembly seat as a UUP candidate, she burned a lot of bridges.

Part of her believed the dream job would be representing the Fermanagh–South Tyrone constituency as its MP in Westminster. But that was unlikely to ever happen for her because of the strong nationalist numbers in the constituency and the bad blood with UUP voters as a result of her decision to switch parties. Some in the DUP saw her as a blow-in, but Peter Robinson and Ian Paisley regarded her highly.

From the day in 2007 that the party began power-sharing with Sinn Féin in Stormont, she was always given a senior role. First as minister for the environment (2007–8), then as minister for enterprise, trade and investment (2008–15), briefly as minister for finance and personnel (May 2015–January 2016) and finally as first minister as well as DUP leader, for over five years until she resigned in 2021.

She had a deserved reputation as a hard worker. She and her husband, Brian Foster, and their three children lived outside Fivemiletown in Co. Fermanagh. Both parents had demanding jobs outside the home. Each time I travelled the main road between Sligo and Belfast I would pass their house. Because of the traditional links between our native counties, Fermanagh and Sligo, in casual conversations I'd often call her 'neighbour'. Several mornings a week she was on the road early and home late, making the 160-mile round trip to Belfast. She travelled in a reinforced vehicle with a police driver because the security assessment was that her family was a potential target for dissident Republicans.

In 2018, she made headlines with her comment that if a united Ireland happened she would probably move. The remark was made to the Co. Down-born comedian Patrick Kielty, for his ITV television documentary to mark the twentieth anniversary of the Good Friday Agreement. His father, Jim, was murdered by Loyalist paramilitaries in 1988, the year the IRA bombed the school bus of Arlene Foster and her classmates.

But a decade earlier she had expressed different views about whether Irish unity would force her out of her native province. At a forum in West Belfast, after the issue was raised, she said the only way she would be leaving would be in a box. One of her aides with her heard someone in the audience mutter, 'That could be arranged.' The remark wasn't a thought-through threat but it was a reminder of the suspicions, below the surface, in a society still affected by trauma.

During public occasions on executive as well as party business, she regularly took the opportunity to affirm her British identity. But in two North–South political relationships, a milder persona emerged. Both involved border women: Fianna Fáil Donegal TD Mary Coughlan and Cavan–Monaghan Fine Gael TD Heather Humphreys, a fellow member of the Church of Ireland. In Arlene Foster's seven years as enterprise minister, when their paths crossed formality was often abandoned.

Other Southern politicians sought to engage with that softer side. As Taoiseach, each November Enda Kenny made a point of travelling to Enniskillen to stand alongside Arlene during the Remembrance Sunday service at the town's war memorial. His successor, Leo Varadkar, made that journey too. But Arlene noted and filed away comments he and Minister for Foreign Affairs Simon Coveney made about the aspiration for a united Ireland in their lifetime.

She had a solid relationship with Simon Coveney's predecessor, Charlie Flanagan. For her first meeting in Dublin with Micheál Martin after he became Taoiseach she brought a present of fresh eggs that her young son, Ben, had collected from the chickens he kept in the family garden.

The year 2016 started well for Arlene Foster as the first female first minister of Stormont's power-sharing Executive as well as the first woman to lead the DUP. In those early days of change, she had no sense of the storms that lay ahead. Northern Ireland was heading into the most turbulent political year since the restoration of power-sharing and beyond.

Arlene's priority in her new position was to prepare for the scheduled May Assembly election. On so many levels, she was different. A former UUP, female, Church of Ireland member from West of the Bann. The contest would test her standing as the formal successor of Peter Robinson and Revd Ian Paisley before him.

To avoid the danger of mischief-making from some of her rivals, she quickly made it clear that she would not be attending the Easter Monday ceremonies in Dublin to mark the centenary of the 1916 Rising. Ben Lowry, the deputy editor of the *Belfast Newsletter*, thought it was a mistake on her part. In his account of the event, he told of seeing Sinn Féin's Martin McGuinness there and wrote, 'It was the first time I have seen him look almost old.'

11

Brexit

In February 2016, the British prime minister, David Cameron, announced that the UK would hold a June referendum on its membership of the EU. It was a decision dictated by internal Conservative Party politics. He was following through on a promise he had made in 2013 to calm the Eurosceptic minority in his parliamentary group. He was also keen to curtail electoral support for Nigel Farage's United Kingdom Independence Party. Cameron made it clear his government would recommend a Remain vote.

The day of that statement, Arlene Foster told me, in an interview in the Killyhevlin Hotel, close to her home, that the DUP would take the opposite stance. There was very limited debate within the DUP's Northern Ireland, Assembly-linked structures about the party's referendum policy. The driving force on the DUP Brexit position was its team of eight Westminster MPs, elected the previous year, and the party's House of Lords members.

With 330 seats, David Cameron had just secured the first overall Conservative Party majority for twenty-three years. In the afterglow of his election success, the DUP's minuscule presence didn't figure on his priority list. Several of the DUP's Westminster contingent had friendships and shared political views with Eurosceptic MPs who had been a minority but dogged presence in Tory machinations for decades.

There was another reason why the DUP opted to be the only one of the five main Stormont parties to adopt a Vote Leave strategy for the referendum campaign. Jim Allister, the TUV leader, was advocating that stance. He had been a DUP member of the European Parliament but left the party over its decision to share power with Sinn Féin in 2007. He tried twice and failed to be re-elected as an MEP. A one-man party in Stormont, he became its most active campaigner to sever the links with the European institutions. In Assembly elections season, the DUP was wary of entirely ceding that space to him.

The Conservative Party was split on its future within the EU. A breakaway group, led by Boris Johnson and managed by Dominic Cummings, was campaigning for a Leave vote. The possible consequences of a Leave victory for Northern Ireland's peace process, North–South and British–Irish relations barely figured in the UK's Brexit debate. As they geared up for the Assembly elections, in their occasional contacts with David Cameron's team, some of Arlene Foster's key advisers continued to get the message that the Remain campaign would triumph in the referendum.

In the 5 May Assembly election, the DUP retained its thirty-eight seats. Sinn Féin dropped one and returned twenty-eight members. It was a satisfying outcome for Arlene Foster in her new leadership role. But in the days immediately afterwards, the UUP and SDLP said they would be stepping outside the mandatory coalition structure set out in the Good Friday Agreement and going into opposition. Alliance confirmed it would not be providing a justice minister.

For the first time since they became the lead partners in power-sharing in 2007, the DUP and Sinn Féin were being saddled with full responsibility for government. Foster was warily adjusting to her new circumstances. Northern Ireland and the Republic of Ireland had qualified for the June European Football Championship finals in France. Martin McGuinness put it to her that it would be a powerful cross-community gesture if, as leaders in what was now a two-party administration, they together attended matches featuring teams from both side of the border. Foster decided against the idea and would only attend a Northern Ireland game.

Two days before the EU membership referendum vote, the then home secretary, Theresa May, was persuaded to fly to Northern Ireland and visit the North Down constituency of pro-Remain MP, the independent Unionist Lady Sylvia Hermon. Mrs May's very limited involvement in support of her prime minister's referendum stance had been noted by several commentators. BBC Northern Ireland's political editor, Mark Devenport, was offered the interview opportunity with her. A short clip of what she said featured on the lunchtime news but didn't make it to later bulletins. When asked how might the UK leaving the EU affect the island of Ireland, Mrs May said it would be 'inconceivable' that there would not be any changes on border arrangements with the Republic if the UK pulled out of the EU.

She expanded: 'Just think about it. If we are out of the European Union with tariffs on exporting goods into the EU, there would have to be something to recognize that between Northern Ireland and the Republic of Ireland . . . And if you pulled out of the EU and out of free movement, how could you have a situation where there was an open border with a country that was in the EU and has access to free movement?'

In the final days of the referendum campaign, the DUP provided almost £300,000 to fund a pro-Brexit advert that was wrapped around millions of copies of a freesheet newspaper in Britain but did not circulate in Northern Ireland. The DUP's spend in the EU referendum campaign was seven times greater than the amount it used for the Assembly elections. The last-minute injection of cash wasn't sourced in Northern Ireland. The DUP's then chief whip in Westminster, Jeffrey Donaldson, said it came from the Constitutional Research Council and described the group, chaired by the former vice-president of the Scottish Conservative party, Richard Cook, as 'a group of businessmen that promotes pro-union politics'.

I was in the Titanic election centre in Belfast when the results of the 23 June referendum were announced: 55.8 per cent of Northern Ireland voters wanted to remain in the EU, and 44.2 per cent were in favour of leaving. But the overall UK result had 52 per cent support for Brexit, making historic change inevitable.

The only prominent DUP figure from its Assembly and Westminster representatives celebrating in the Belfast count centre after the result was announced was Edwin Poots. It was like the final moments of a poorly attended event in a parish hall. There was no sense that Northern Ireland was on course to become the most difficult element of negotiations between London and Brussels, that an important element of the Good Friday Agreement architecture had been removed or that the Brexit decision had launched a new phase in the debate about a united Ireland.

David Cameron resigned the day after he failed to deliver his promised Remain victory. Theresa May was chosen by the Conservative Party to succeed him. Within a fortnight of taking over as prime minister, she came to Stormont Castle to meet Foster and McGuinness. She spoke of her determination to avoid a 'return to borders of the past'. The DUP leader told

Mrs May, 'There must be no internal borders within the UK.'
McGuinness referenced how a majority of Northern Ireland
voters had wanted to remain in the EU and said, 'There is no
good news whatsoever about Brexit.'

The following month, helped by senior civil servants, Foster,
McGuinness and their advisers spent two days preparing a document for Mrs May. Rather than focus on what divided them
about Brexit, they tried to concentrate on the Northern Ireland
issues that required attention in the pending negotiations between
the British government and Brussels. One of the sentences in
their two-page letter said, 'We need to retain as far as possible
the ease with which we currently trade with EU member states
and also more importantly retain access to labour.'

With the summer over and an Assembly with a new mandate
under way, the first minister and deputy first minister were
aware of the difficult realities of their circumstances. They
had very limited influence over the British government as it
prepared for what would be difficult negotiations with Brussels.
Under scrutiny from a three-party opposition in the Stormont
Assembly chamber, they would be expected to deliver on local
issues. And they each had sections in their own support base
complaining that power-sharing was not working for them.

*

The events of Tuesday, 8 November 2016, will remain with me
for the rest of my days. It was like an unexpected burst of sunshine
and warmth. After it, things began to fall apart. I had worked on
a half-hour television programme for RTÉ's *Nationwide*. One of
the wonderful benefits of working as a journalist is you sometimes see exceptional people at close quarters. Colin Davidson

has an ability to capture on canvas a sense of his subject's inner self. We had been to Colin's studio to film the finishing stages of his portrait of Queen Elizabeth. The work to mark the queen's ninetieth birthday had been commissioned by the chairman of the Co-operation Ireland charity, Christopher Moran.

Christopher is a multimillionaire. From humble beginnings, starting as a runner, he made his fortune among the traders in London's financial services centre. He owns Crosby Hall, once the sixteenth-century residence of Sir Thomas More, and several adjacent buildings beside the Thames. That's where the queen came to see the finished portrait.

Moran was keen to acknowledge how the queen's state visit to Ireland in 2011 gave a lift to British–Irish relations. The Co-operation Ireland organization was also aware of the uncertainties created by Brexit and was glad of a timely opportunity to publicly reprise the achievements of the peace process. Representatives of all the main parties in Northern Ireland came to what effectively was a celebration. Northern Ireland secretary James Brokenshire and tánaiste Frances Fitzgerald represented the British and Irish governments. Martin McGuinness stood alongside Arlene Foster as the queen saw the Davidson work for the first time.

McGuinness came to the function directly from Heathrow Airport. We chatted about his hectic weekend transatlantic journey to attend a function honouring Irish-American Bill Flynn. He was disappointed that illness had prevented the recipient from attending the ceremony. He was excited by the prospect of Hillary Clinton becoming the first female president of the United States as Ireland, North and South, would have a proven friend in the White House. He had a slight wheeze in his voice and told me he was low on energy and intending to visit his GP in Derry.

Within twenty-four hours, Donald Trump would debunk the Clinton calculation. Also, on the very next day, a Stormont committee would hear evidence about a Renewable Heat Incentive scheme, introduced on Arlene Foster's watch, that would lead to the collapse of power-sharing. And within a week Martin McGuinness would begin a health battle that would see a rare blood disorder end his life the following spring.

While Arlene Foster was making her way back from the function in London, a senior civil servant, Andrew McCormick, was preparing his presentation for Stormont's Public Accounts Committee. The Assembly members were delving into the operation of a green-energy scheme that had been controversially closed over fears that it could leave taxpayers exposed to a bill amounting to hundreds of millions of pounds or more. In his evidence, McCormick explained how it was a 'cause of great concern' to him that officials had not believed allegations of abuse raised by a whistle-blower in 2013. The controversy exploded into life early in December after a BBC Northern Ireland *Spotlight* investigation, presented by Conor Spackman. It suggested that participants in the scheme were offered government subsidies higher than their wood-pellet fuel costs and the more they burned the greater their profits.

The DUP was in the firing line for most of the criticism. What was now known as 'the cash for ash' scheme had been introduced when Arlene Foster was the enterprise minister and then taken over by her party colleague Jonathan Bell when she switched to the finance portfolio. Allegations of insiders 'in the know' 'filling their boots' were spreading like wildfire.

McGuinness came back from London to criticisms from some Sinn Féin supporters. They cited a front-page *Irish News* photograph of him standing beside Queen Elizabeth and

Arlene Foster and pointed to the absence of funding for an Irish-language school in his native Co. Derry. In an unforgettable television programme presented by BBC Northern Ireland's Stephen Nolan, Jonathan Bell prayed with a pastor before the cameras as he prepared to make serious allegations about members of the Foster team. McGuinness was privately digesting the news that he had a serious medical condition requiring urgent attention.

On 16 December, Sinn Féin issued a statement from Martin McGuinness calling for an independent inquiry into aspects of the Renewable Heat Incentive scheme, urging Arlene Foster to stand aside pending its findings. The DUP quickly put out a response, saying she would not be doing so. The Assembly was about to go into recess for Christmas, and doubt was growing about its future. I phoned McGuinness to get his views on the escalating political crisis. He was in a taxi in London after receiving expert opinion about his amyloidosis condition.

At her home in Co. Fermanagh, Arlene Foster was facing into the bleakest Christmas of her public life. I called in to see her when driving home to the family in Sligo. A year that opened with her creating political history was ending in disaster. The DUP and some of those closest to her were under scrutiny and the party was riven with division. Her competence and her very integrity were being questioned. And, most galling of all, Sinn Féin, led by Martin McGuinness, were assuming the roles of judge and jury about her actions and her future.

On New Year's Eve, instead of taking the direct road from Sligo back to Belfast, I detoured to Derry and called to the home of Martin McGuinness. He answered the door, wearing tracksuit bottoms and a casual top. His wife, Bernie, was out visiting family members so we were alone in the house. He had been cooking. We talked about his amyloidosis illness and his treatment arrangements in the local Altnagelvin hospital. He knew about my chronic cancer condition and the way I was dealing with it. I had made some checks about his disease. We both believed there was a good chance the problem could be curtailed and that he would be able to live with it for a long time.

We also talked about the political crisis. He didn't want to see Arlene Foster removed from office or her career ended. He had full trust in her integrity. He said he hoped that she would stand aside while an investigation was set up into the Renewable Heat Incentive scheme and that she could then return to her first minister role. He mentioned how Peter Robinson had stood aside, temporarily, seven years before, when propriety issues were raised after his wife's affair became known. At the time, Arlene Foster replaced him while a government-appointed lawyer investigated the situation. Robinson resumed his duties a month later.

Even though McGuinness had spent almost ten years sustaining an often-difficult power-sharing partnership with the DUP, the relationship was heading for the rocks. One act signalled inevitable breakdown. On 23 December, the DUP communities minister, Paul Givan, announced that he was ending a £50,000 bursary scheme that allowed Irish-speakers from disadvantaged backgrounds to improve their language skills at courses in Irish-speaking areas over the border. He made the announcement in a two-line statement: 'Because of efficiency savings, the Department will not be providing the Líofa bursary scheme in 2017. Happy Christmas and Happy New Year.'

Most of Sinn Féin's elected representatives, Martin McGuinness included, were not fluent Irish-speakers. But many of them had friends and relations who were keen to learn and use Irish who saw it as part of their identity. The Irish-language lobby is one of the most active movements in Northern Ireland. The decision to cut the scheme was seen as a deliberately provocative gesture by Sinn Féin's partners in government.

McGuinness was dressed in his jumper and jeans the afternoon he came to formally announce his resignation as deputy first minister on Monday, 9 January 2017, a decision that would cause the collapse of the power-sharing government. My Derry cameraman colleague, Peter Doherty, hadn't seen McGuinness since the start of his chemotherapy treatment, and he was shocked by the frail figure making his brief statement at his office in Stormont House. McGuinness looked healthier nine days later when we met in Ratoath, Co. Meath. With Gerry Adams and Sinn Féin's Richard McAuley, he had come to attend the funeral of a former secretary general of the Department of Foreign Affairs, Dermot Gallagher. This time he was formally dressed, and we talked as he made his way from the churchyard.

Just two days later, he seemed thinner and more vulnerable when he gave a number of one-on-one interviews to journalists, in Derry's Bishop's Gate Hotel, announcing his decision to retire as a full-time public representative to concentrate on dealing with his health issues. One of his brothers, Declan, and other family members stayed close to him in the hotel room as he fulfilled his media duties. That night, outside his home, he told a gathering that he wouldn't be physically capable of leading Sinn Féin into the March Assembly elections because of his illness. He ended his remarks saying, 'My heart lies in the Bogside and with the people of Derry.'

The following week, he made what would be his final journey over the Glenshane Pass from Derry to Belfast. On 23 January, he stood alongside Michelle O'Neill upstairs in Stormont as she was announced to succeed him as Sinn Féin's leader in Northern Ireland. There was no selection process or election contest. McGuinness wanted O'Neill to replace him, and nobody, from the party president, Gerry Adams, down, challenged that. Other capable members within the Assembly team, including Conor Murphy and John O'Dowd, had significant ministerial experience, but the appointment was made decisively.

O'Neill had served under McGuinness for almost six years as a member of the Executive, mainly as minister for agriculture and for a brief period in health. An important part of the bond between them was how she stood up to dissident Republicans for a period of his sixteen-year tenure as MP for the Mid-Ulster constituency. Even though his treatment was affecting his energy levels, he insisted on coming to her home area, Clonoe, to attend the celebration of her appointment.

The Assembly elections set for 2 March meant that for the second time in ten months Arlene Foster was under scrutiny. In a bitterly fought contest, she and her party were on the defensive about their handling of the Renewable Heat Incentive scheme. The resignation of Martin McGuinness had caused the contest. Their relationship had broken down, but when I met Foster during campaigning, she asked about his health. I told her how I was in text contact with him and he seemed hopeful that the treatment would be successful. She asked me to pass on her good wishes to him.

In the 2017 elections, for the first time, the number of Assembly members was being reduced from 108 to ninety. Each of the eighteen constituencies was returning five rather than six members. Unionism took the hit for most of the seat losses. The DUP, led by Arlene Foster, went from thirty-eight to twenty-eight members. The UUP also suffered significantly, falling from sixteen to ten members. Sinn Féin dropped only one seat from twenty-eight to twenty-seven. The SDLP retained twelve seats in the reduced Assembly, and Alliance also held its eight seats. The consolation for the DUP was that it still emerged as the largest party, just a single seat ahead of Sinn Féin, and therefore it retained its right to provide the first minister. For Arlene Foster, this was the significant achievement from a bruising campaign.

The last contact I had from Martin McGuinness was a text on 22 February, acknowledging Arlene Foster's message. It said, 'Many thanks, Tommie. Still in hospital. Pass on my appreciation to Arlene. Hope you are well. Love to Ceara and your clann. Martin.' After that, his wife, Bernie, took charge of his phone as his condition weakened. I still struggle with how the combination of his illness and the severe treatment caused such a rapid decline. Up to his final days some of those closest to him believed he was going to recover.

Arlene Foster wrestled with whether to travel to his funeral in Derry on 23 March. Huge numbers, including former US president Bill Clinton, were due to attend. The Assembly elections were over; there seemed no immediate prospect of the DUP and Sinn Féin under Michelle O'Neill resuming power-sharing. When Foster's father had died suddenly, six years before, McGuinness had made discreet inquiries about travelling to the funeral. One of Foster's aides advised against it, warning that if he turned up his safety might be an issue.

That Thursday morning, as Foster set off with her security driver towards Derry, a close friend phoned her and implored her not to make the journey. During the Troubles, her friend's life had been scarred by the actions of the IRA, and she couldn't countenance the idea of the DUP leader attending the funeral of Martin McGuinness. Foster reflected on the conversation but stuck by her decision. Among those she met inside the Long Tower church was Michelle O'Neill. The two women shook hands.

In the fraught decade of DUP and Sinn Féin power-sharing, on occasions of loss rivalries were sometimes suspended. On 6 April 2011, the then first minister, Peter Robinson, became the first DUP leader to attend a Catholic Mass when he attended the funeral of Ronan Kerr, a PSNI constable killed by a car bomb planted by dissident Republicans. The following week, McGuinness surprised some of the congregation at Bethany Free Presbyterian Church, in a Loyalist area of Portadown, when he attended the funeral of Marie Duffield Malloy, the mother of Iris Robinson. Two months later, Sammy Wilson, the DUP finance minister, crossed the border to attend the funeral of his counterpart and friend, Brian Lenihan. Foster left Derry after the McGuinness funeral, content that she had made the right decision.

*

'Is this a problem without a solution?' That's the recurring question I've failed to answer since the Brexit saga began. As she thought out loud during that interview with BBC Northern Ireland's Mark Devenport in North Down, just days before the referendum vote in June 2016, Theresa May seemed to have a light-bulb moment. She suddenly twigged that the UK leaving the EU would have significant consequences for the island of Ireland and for Northern Ireland in particular.

Pulling out of the EU meant ending something that the Conservative icon Margaret Thatcher had championed during her time as prime minister. In the 1980s, she was one of the most forceful advocates of establishing a single European market, with purchasing power bigger than Japan and the United States. That policy, getting rid of tariffs and border checks between EU member states, was enshrined in the Single European Act that came into force on 1 January 1993. As part of it, the customs posts on the island of Ireland were removed, twenty months before the IRA 1994 ceasefire and six years before the Good Friday Agreement.

The UK leaving the EU could not avoid creating issues for the only place where it has a land border with an EU member state: the island of Ireland. To date, all of the possible solutions proffered involve negative consequences. Reimposing border checks and varying tariffs between North and South would disrupt trade on the island and antagonize the majority of Northern Ireland voters who wanted to remain in the EU. Imposing some form of border controls in the Irish Sea would see Northern Ireland treated differently than other regions of the UK and anger Unionists. Negotiating a soft departure from the EU that would allow the UK continued access to the European single market would leave Brexiteers arguing that the referendum promise to 'take back control' had been abandoned. Trying to frame a special deal that would allow Northern Ireland to have the best of both worlds – continued access to the European single market and internal UK markets – could create suspicion in many quarters, including Scotland, Wales and other EU member states.

It was a tragedy that during the referendum campaign and the immediate aftermath the former SDLP leader John Hume had no role in the discourse. He had a track record of respect and influence on domestic and international stages. But, as the Brexit debate raged, he was in Derry, in the care of his wife, Pat, coping with a dementia condition. One morning in Brussels, in the 1990s, I saw the first signs of his declining health. When chatting with Hume outside the European Parliament Hemicycle, he became ill and I accompanied him to the infirmary on the ground floor. The staff immediately recognized him. It was obvious that he had been there before.

Hume was the most impressive influencer of Irish history I observed close-up during my working life as journalist. Instinctively he sought imaginative solutions to problems. Early in his public life, in response to the struggle and unfairness he witnessed in his home town, he was involved in the Derry Housing Association. He started the credit-union movement, and he campaigned for a Derry university. He became prominent in the civil-rights movement but never condoned the use of force. As the Troubles raged, he sought to internationalize the search for solutions by courting the political and economic clout of Irish America.

Hume's masterstroke was his initiative to Europeanize Ireland's challenge. As a former teacher of history, he was inspired by some of its lessons. Even the very name of Hume's birthplace is disputed. For nationalists, it is 'Derry', taken from the old Irish name 'Daire' – oak wood. Unionists call it 'Londonderry', celebrating its links to the London guilds who came there during the Plantation of Ulster by English and Scottish settlers in the early seventeenth century. In 1689, Derry was a battle site of a major European war when forces of the dethroned Catholic King James, supported by the French, fought against the armies of his successor, the Dutch-born Protestant William of Orange.

Four hundred years later, Hume sought to mine a positive feature of difference. As a member of the European

Parliament, he found hope in its political experiment and its ideology that emerged as a response to the destruction of the Second World War. He noted how Ireland, North and South, and every region of the UK, were members of those European structures. He brought that non-threatening, shared European identity into the architecture and the philosophy of the 1998 Good Friday Agreement.

In Northern Ireland, Unionists could be European and British. Nationalists could be European and Irish. The British could be British and European. The Irish could be Irish and European. Ireland's peace process, including the reconciliation between two of its member states, became the most successful example of internal peacemaking in the EU's history. In February 2016, when he was mayor of London, as Boris Johnson mulled over what stance he would take in the UK's EU membership referendum, that European dimension in Ireland's peace process is unlikely to have figured in his calculations. As Dominic Cummings and his team devised slogans, including 'Take Back Control', to drive their Brexit campaign, the economic and political consequences for the island of Ireland and British–Irish relations didn't affect their strategy.

They convinced a majority of the UK's electorate to vote Leave. The Brexit decision propelled Johnson to the job of prime minister. History may not be kind to him. Cummings subsequently left his job as Johnson's most influential adviser, and their relationship turned toxic. But as their day-to-day influence fades, the consequences of the Brexit campaign they championed continue to destabilize British–Irish, North–South and internal Northern Ireland relations.

The trickle-down effect began immediately after the referendum vote. The British prime minister, David Cameron, resigned the day after the UK's Brexit decision. Theresa May was chosen by the Conservative Party to succeed him. With difficult negotiations due in Brussels, to bolster her authority she quickly decided to seek her own mandate. The UK general election held on 8 June 2017 turned out to be a disaster for her. The overall Conservative majority, won by Cameron two years before, disappeared. Faced with a hung-parliament dilemma, in order to form a government May needed a partner. Her search brought her to the DUP. Arlene Foster's party had ten MPs after the election, an increase of two. Sinn Féin had seven members, up three. The SDLP and the UUP presence had been wiped out.

Sinn Féin's abstentionist policy meant its seven MPs would continue to do constituency work and travel to London but would not speak or vote in the House of Commons. The three SDLP casualties were its leader, Alasdair McDonnell, and two former leaders, Margaret Ritchie and Mark Durkan – the latter had effectively been John Hume's chief of staff during the Good Friday Agreement negotiations. The changes in Northern Ireland's representation meant responsibility for presenting a case in Westminster debates for the 56 per cent of the electorate that favoured remaining in the EU was left to one of its eighteen MPs: the independent Unionist, Lady Sylvia Hermon.

As a result of Theresa May requiring DUP support to stay in office, its Westminster Ten were transformed from peripheral characters to VIPs, with access to all areas of government. A fortnight after the election, before the cameras in Downing Street, DUP and Conservative teams signed a formal confidence and supply agreement. It committed the DUP to supporting the government in important Westminster votes. Mrs May's promises included the British government providing £1 billion funding for Northern Ireland projects. This finance would prove important for under-pressure areas including health and education. It would also fund the rollout of broadband to rural as well as urban areas.

Within the DUP organization, the balance of power tilted towards its Westminster cohort. It became dominant at the expense of party's Assembly members. Sammy Wilson, the DUP East Antrim MP, was one of its ten members enjoying increased influence at Westminster. Over the years, I saw several of his decent traits. One Christmas Day, when it was my turn to work the news shift, I came across him at a Salvation Army centre in East Belfast among the volunteers providing turkey and ham and plum-pudding dinners for dozens of people. Sammy wasn't seeking attention or acknowledgement for his efforts. He was on duty in the kitchen.

He never turned down my requests for an interview, even though it often involved a story when he was at the centre of controversy. Sometimes I'd drive to his home near Larne, and we would exchange anecdotes about our shared interest in wood-chopping before getting down to formal business. On other occasions, we'd agree a rendezvous point, he would arrive, on time, in a weather-beaten van, deliver the required comment and head off.

We were chatting candidly about Brexit one day. I told him that I felt membership of the EU was such a positive factor in Ireland's development, the peace process included. I explained how I'd probably be dead but for medical treatment received in Sweden thanks to my rights as an EU citizen. Sammy knew I was 100 per cent sincere when I told him of my worries about the consequences of Brexit. He responded with similar honesty. 'Tommie,' he said, 'I know what you are saying, but I just hate the EU.' That was, and remains, Sammy's position. Like the

Eurosceptic MPs in the Conservative Party who have featured in British politics since Margaret Thatcher's time and before, he sees membership of the EU as incompatible with the UK's past and future. No economic, political or social arguments will change that view.

In November 2017, Gerry Adams confirmed that he planned to stand down as Sinn Féin president the following February. He and Martin McGuinness had an agreed exit strategy, but the death of the latter in March ended that plan. After twenty-four years in the party leadership role and seven years as a TD, commuting between Belfast, Louth and Dáil Éireann, Adams was tired. He was keen to spend more time with his wife, Colette. He was also still grieving McGuinness.

In the weeks before his formal retirement date, Adams became involved in a push to restore power-sharing at Stormont. Simon Coveney had replaced Charlie Flanagan as minister for foreign affairs. James Brokenshire was still the secretary of state for Northern Ireland. The British side concentrated on attempting to deliver the DUP while Irish diplomats focused on Sinn Féin. It was the last time that Adams, in his role as Sinn Féin leader, assembled the crew of his contemporaries, sometimes described as 'shadowy figures', to assist in sensitive political negotiations. Many, possibly all, of them had been in the IRA. Like Adams, they are all likely to go to their graves without giving a full account of their past. They had been part of his trusted circle as he oversaw the Republican movement's sometimes stuttering journey to exclusively peaceful means.

Adams was aware of Sinn Féin's incremental progress south of the border. Mindful of the damage caused by a closed Stormont, he was keen to make an effort to change that before his influence waned. For their last manoeuvre, anticipating what it expected would be lengthy talks, the unit arrived to the Stormont Estate with elaborate home-made food provisions. During their regular meetings with Simon Coveney's team, they'd sometimes depart with their stocks of fizzy water replenished.

The issue of an Irish Language Act became contentious in the discussions. During campaigning for the March 2017 Westminster elections, Arlene Foster elaborated on her objections to such legislation, saying, 'If you feed a crocodile they are just going to keep coming back for more.' She was heavily criticized for her comments. In one more example of Foster's habit of making a mistake and then seeking to make up for it, a month after the election she visited a class of Irish-speakers at Our Lady's Grammar School in Newry, Co. Down. The painting presented to her by students had an inscription, 'Together we are strong', and Foster replied to them, 'Go raibh maith agat' (Thank you).

In the days before Adams was formally replaced by Mary Lou McDonald at a Sinn Féin event in Dublin, the attempts to restore power-sharing in Stormont collapsed. Within her own party, particularly from some of the Westminster MPs, Foster didn't receive the support to compromise and cut a deal. The DUP was basking in its clout at Westminster and couldn't be persuaded to resume the difficult business of power-sharing. It would be a further twenty-three months before agreement was reached to recommit to Stormont.

The Conservatives–DUP liaison in London had started with the intensity of a holiday romance. But it hit difficulties as soon as the British government engaged in its detailed Brexit nego-tiations with the European Commission. In December 2017, Theresa May was in Brussels, on the cusp of shaking hands with the European Commission president, Jean-Clauder Juncker, on what she believed were acceptable terms when Arlene Foster phoned her and said the DUP wouldn't back her. It was the beginning of the end of the May–DUP relationship.

During 2018, when the prime minister struggled with the hard-line Brexiteers within her party, the DUP grew closer to Boris Johnson. He was at loggerheads with Theresa May as she sought to resolve the Northern Ireland issues that were now the most contentious element of the Brexit negotiations with Brussels. In July, Johnson resigned as foreign secretary from May's cabinet, suggesting that her latest plans amounted to 'a semi-Brexit', with large parts of the economy 'locked into the EU system, but with no UK control over that system'.

The switch in DUP loyalties was made public in dramatic fashion at their annual party conference in November 2018. Boris Johnson turned up as a guest speaker. He was accompanied to Northern Ireland by Christopher Moran, the chairman of Co-operation Ireland who had hosted the unveiling of the queen's portrait at Moran's London home two years before. The pair sat together in the front row of the conference hall.

When his turn came to address the delegates, Johnson said that Theresa May was 'on the verge of making a historic' mistake with her latest offer to Brussels. He predicted that the Westminster parliament would reject it. Before concluding his speech, he floated the idea of building a bridge from Scotland to Northern Ireland. The DUP's deputy leader, Nigel Dodds, described the latest May offer as 'pitiful and pathetic'. Immediately after the formalities, upstairs in the Ramada Hotel, I met Boris Johnson, who was with Christopher Moran. Our paths hadn't crossed since our days in the Brussels press corps in the 1990s. One of the conference organizers, John Robinson, was amused by the unlikely combination and we stood together for a photograph.

Embarrassing publicity awaited Christopher Moran when he returned to Britain. Newspaper stories alleged that high-class prostitution services were being provided in some of the properties he owned in Chelsea. One headline suggested a particular building involved '10 floors of whores'. His lawyers issued a statement asserting the building 'operates a zero policy towards prostitution on its premises'. Moran suspected that some of his political enemies within a warring Conservative Party had a role in creating the unwanted attention.

Theresa May bowed to the inevitable in May 2019 and resigned as prime minister. Opposed by the DUP and by a section of her own Conservative Party, she failed to get the support of the Labour opposition for her latest Brexit compromise offer to Brussels. On 23 July, Boris Johnson had a comfortable victory in the contest to succeed her. But DUP hopes that they now had a reliable ally in Downing Street hit a wall. The new prime minister was determined he would deliver on his promise to 'get Brexit done'.

In his contacts with Washington, Brussels and with EU member-state leaders, including Germany's Angela Merkel, Johnson was confronted by a consistent pattern of solid support for Ireland. At the time of the Conservative Party annual conference in Manchester, British government officials were having discreet discussions with their Irish counterparts. On 10 October, Johnson met the Taoiseach, Leo Varadkar, for talks at Thornton Manor, in the Wirral. They said afterwards they could see the pathway to a Brexit deal.

A week later, in Brussels, at a news conference alongside Jean-Claude Juncker, the president of the European Commission, Johnson announced a new withdrawal agreement that 'represents a very good deal for the UK and the EU'. The

DUP immediately put out a statement saying its members would oppose the deal. The terms Johnson was accepting included a version of the Northern Ireland protocol, with elements of border controls in the Irish Sea, that rankled with Unionists then and since.

Johnson knew he didn't have the required numbers in Westminster to vote through his deal. He called a general election in an effort to strengthen his mandate. But, unlike Theresa May, in December 2019 he won a landslide victory, increasing Conservative seats in the 650-member parliament to 365. The result was a disaster for the DUP on two levels. Their votes were no longer required by the Conservative prime minister to form a government so their brief phase of significant influence at Westminster was over. Mindful of the election victory secured by their leader, Conservative MPs endorsed Johnson's Brexit deal, despite the objections of the DUP.

The other negative election consequence for the DUP involved two of their MPs, Nigel Dodds and Emma Little-Pengelly, failing to retain their seats. The defeat of Dodds was a body blow for the party. He had represented the North Belfast constituency since 2001 and had seen off the challenge of Sinn Féin's Gerry Kelly four times. His career as an MP was ended by Sinn Féin's John Finucane, whose father, Pat, was murdered by Loyalist gunmen in controversial circumstances at the family home in 1989.

As the leader of the DUP's group in Westminster and a driver of its stance on Brexit, Dodds was targeted during the election campaign. An important factor in the Sinn Féin victory was the decision by the SDLP to not run a candidate and so avoid splitting the anti-Dodds vote in a first-past-the-post contest. With Diane Dodds having to vacate her seat in the

European Parliament, Brexit was delivering a double rebuke to the household.

That Westminster election lifted the morale of the SDLP and Alliance parties. In the Foyle constituency, Colum Eastwood regained from Sinn Féin's Elisha McCallion the seat once held by former SDLP leaders John Hume and Mark Durkan. In South Belfast, the SDLP's Claire Hanna replaced the sitting DUP representative Emma Little-Pengelly. Alliance deputy leader Stephen Farry replaced the retiring independent Unionist Sylvia Hermon. Those results meant that ten of Northern Ireland's contingent of eighteen MPs opposed Brexit (seven Sinn Féin, two SDLP, one Alliance), compared to the eight DUP members who supported it. The House of Commons situation mirrored the outcome of the 2017 Assembly elections when a majority of those returned were from pro-Remain parties.

The increased level of productive contacts on Brexit issues between the British and Irish governments and their officials was a factor in renewed efforts to restore power-sharing at Stormont. Julian Smith had replaced Karen Bradley as the secretary of state for Northern Ireland when Boris Johnson took over as prime minister from Theresa May. There was speculation that Theresa Villiers, who had the role from 2012 to 2016, might be returning. A prominent Brexiteer, sending her back to Northern Ireland would have been a controversial appointment.

Smith was chief whip for Theresa May during most of her term as prime minister. He had lots of contact with the DUP during that time, linked to its confidence and supply agreement with the government. It was a solid relationship even though he was a Remain supporter during the Brexit campaign. Senior DUP figures often say they were supportive of Smith when Boris Johnson was selecting his ministerial team after May. The new northern secretary quickly bonded with the Irish minister for foreign affairs, Simon Coveney. They began a talks process with the Stormont parties. Smith wasn't part of Boris Johnson's circle, and there was speculation the prime minister would drop him after his election victory in December 2019. But he was left in post to continue his role in the negotiations.

There was another factor forcing all the political factions to focus on restoring power-sharing. Lyra McKee was a twenty-nine-year-old journalist and writer, shot dead in Derry in April 2019. She was observing rioting in the Creggan area when she was fatally wounded by a bullet fired by dissident Republicans targeting the police. Her death caused outrage. She had been planning to propose to her partner, Sara Canning, and had purchased an engagement ring. At her funeral service, in a packed Anglican Belfast Cathedral, a Catholic priest, Father Martin Magill, drew attention to the consequences of the political vacuum.

On Thursday, 9 January 2020, with the Stormont building in the background, Smith and Coveney announced at a news conference they had the basis of a deal to recommence devolved government. It was three years to the day since Martin McGuinness resigned as deputy first minister and initiated the collapse of power-sharing. A week later, Boris Johnson and Leo Varadkar travelled to Belfast to acknowledge the new administration led by the DUP's Arlene Foster and Sinn Féin's Michelle O'Neill.

Our RTÉ Belfast office team decided that after three years of closed doors at Stormont and several failed attempts to resume business, we would celebrate the change. We headed for the Errigle Inn on the Ormeau Road. We told the two special advisers of Julian Smith – Ross Easton and Lilah Howson-Smith – about our plans. Prior to his appointment, they had never worked in Northern Ireland. In our dealings during the negotiations, they were helpful and good company. They arrived to our corner of the Errigle with their boss.

A quiz for some of the bar's clientele was in full flow. Before the night ended, the quizmaster arrived over to the secretary of state and told him that although he hadn't taken part in the competition he was being presented with a bottle of wine in thanks for his work at Stormont. The spontaneous gesture indicated how, during his six months in the job, Smith achieved more than many of his predecessors. The following month, in a reshuffle, Boris Johnson sacked him and replaced him with Brandon Lewis.

Six weeks after power-sharing resumed, Northern Ireland's first case of COVID-19 was confirmed. Like most governments in the world, the Stormont Executive was ill prepared for the unprecedented pandemic. Attempting to deal with it became the priority of the power-sharing administration. In June 2020, as the COVID challenge deepened, a senior Republican, sixty-four-year-old Bobby Storey, died. At that stage of the pandemic, the practice in place allowed a maximum of thirty mourners to attend a funeral. Thousands, including the leadership of Sinn Féin, North and South, turned up in West Belfast for the Storey ceremonies. The term is a contradiction, but if there is such a grouping as Republican royalty, Bobby Storey was a member. The controversy over his funeral happened a year before attendance at a golf outing south of the border led to the resignation of Ireland's member of the European Commission, Phil Hogan, and the Partygate saga at Downing Street that badly damaged the British prime minister, Boris Johnson. But Sinn Féin did not yield to pressure over the Belfast events, and eventually it went away.

As the COVID emergency continued, the British government pressed ahead with its Brexit plans. Formally, the UK left the EU on 31 January 2020. The rules governing the new relationship did not take effect until 1 January 2021. That's when it became clear that Northern Ireland was at the centre of a conundrum, and the power-sharing administration would struggle to deal with the weight of its consequences.

The deal Boris Johnson struck with the European Commission allows Northern Ireland to have access to EU as well as internal UK markets. No other part of the UK has such a unique arrangement, and, in return, Brussels sought actions from the British government. Both parties agreed that the border on the island of Ireland, the only land frontier between the UK and the EU, should remain open, without customs infrastructure. In order to avoid breaches of the EU's internal market, Brussels required a system of checks and inspections on goods entering Northern Ireland from Britain. This part of the Brexit agreement, the Northern Ireland protocol, is the basis for the claim that a border is being created down the Irish Sea, between Britain and the Northern Ireland.

Within the Northern Ireland Executive, the minister for agriculture, the DUP's Edwin Poots, had responsibility for oversight of the controversial new controls. Over several months, in discussions between London and Brussels, options to fine-tune the operation of the new measures were explored. Boris Johnson was pressed by the DUP and sections of the Conservative Party to end British government support for the Northern Ireland provisions. He had to balance that pressure with the understanding that resiling from an international agreement would have consequences.

*

After two decades as RTÉs northern editor, during the last week of March 2021, my two final interviews were with Arlene Foster and Michelle O'Neill. COVID-19 was still a huge challenge, but a vaccine had been found to counteract the disease. No formula had been agreed to defuse the tensions over Brexit in Northern Ireland. But, like their predecessors, Paisley, Robinson and McGuinness, the leaders of the two main parties seemed committed to the concept of power-sharing. In my last on-air comment before handing over responsibilities to my successor, Vincent Kearney, I said I was full of hope about the future.

I set aside the month of April for a final RTÉ project, a television documentary detailing the improved cancer services in Ireland for patients like me. I was in Belfast, editing the programme, the day it emerged that the DUP had turned on its leader. I found out that Arlene Foster was in the North Belfast office used by Nigel Dodds as his base when he was MP and went to see her. The issue that caused her demise was loaded with irony. In 2004, she left the UUP and was led by a piper into a DUP gathering, alongside two fellow defectors, Jeffrey Donaldson and Norah Beare.

The person who unwittingly pulled the first thread in her unravelling, seventeen years later, was the current UUP leader, Doug Beattie. With a colleague, John Stewart, Beattie tabled a motion in the Stormont Assembly seeking support for a ban on all forms of conversion therapy in Northern Ireland. Gay rights and other social provisions, including access to abortion services, had proved contentious for the DUP throughout the party's history. In the Assembly vote the previous day, Tuesday, 21 April, most of the DUP members voted against the Beattie motion. But Foster and four of her colleagues – the economy minister, Diane Dodds; the education minister, Peter Weir; and two others, Pam Cameron and Paula Bradley – abstained. All of the five participated in an effort to move on from the split by supporting a DUP amendment. It sought to include a provision that any therapy ban would have to include protections for 'legitimate religious activities'. But that amendment was defeated, and, besides, those wanting to get rid of Foster now had the issue of her abstention as their rallying call.

I sat with her, listening, in that upstairs office room on Belfast's Shore Road, as she assessed her options. She was bruised, almost broken. Earlier that day, Stephen Nolan's BBC Northern Ireland radio programme had suggested a majority of her Assembly colleagues wanted her gone. She believed she could rely on the support of some but not all of the Westminster MPs. This meant the numbers were against her.

Aware of the pressures of her job, some of her close family members were encouraging her to resign. What rankled with her – indeed, hurt her – was that her decision to abstain on the conversion therapy issue was influenced by her knowledge that some of her DUP colleagues had gay family members. She believed at least one of them was among those moving against her. She returned to Fermanagh that evening, resolved that her days as first minister and her political career were over. The next day, she announced her plan to stand down. It was the latest twist in the ongoing DUP internal struggle between traditionalists and modernizers.

Edwin Poots quickly emerged as the front-runner to replace her. Jeffrey Donaldson was his main challenger. On the night Poots won the contest by nineteen votes to seventeen, one of his backers, Ian Paisley Junior, told of his family's experience of leadership transfers. Referring to how his father was ousted

as leader of the party thirteen years before, he told reporters,
'If anyone in this party can talk about difficulty it is me. I
saw what happened to my father. It killed my father.' Poots
was less than three weeks in the role before a majority of his
colleagues turned on him and forced his resignation. At the
second attempt, Jeffrey Donaldson defeated him; thirty-two of
the party's Members of the Legislative Assembly (MLAs) and
MPs backed him.

Some of those who successfully plotted to oust Arlene Foster
also had other targets in their sights. Timothy Johnston, the
party's chief executive, had been working with the party for
twenty years. John Robinson, its director of communications,
and press officer Clive McFarland had been on the full-time
staff for more than a decade. They are the lynchpins of Northern
Ireland's most experienced political team. All were recruited by
Peter Robinson. In the substance and style of some of their work
in a difficult environment, they accumulated enemies. When the
cohort fronted by Edwin Poots and Paul Givan took over, they
quickly realized how important the back-room team was for the
day-to-day running of the DUP machine. If anything, the tenure
of the incumbents was strengthened.

The decisive scale of Donaldson's victory confirmed he had
the support of a majority in the different camps of the divided
party. He is one of the politicians I came to know best over the
past two decades. With his quota of subtleties and contradic-
tions, he has chameleon-like qualities that have helped him to
survive and thrive in the challenging landscape. From a distance,
he is sometimes mistaken for the Donegal-born singer Daniel
O'Donnell. He plays on the doppelgänger status.

A former member of the Ulster Defence Regiment and a
proud member of the Orange Order, he lives on the Dublin

Road near Banbridge, Co. Down. In the days before his then leader, David Trimble, signed up to the Good Friday Agreement in 1998, he walked out of the UUP's negotiating team. During subsequent years he would publicly criticize Trimble for his compromises before moving to the DUP in 2004. Soon after he defected, he became one of the most active supporters of the Paisley and Robinson journey towards power-sharing with Sinn Féin.

His career advanced, and he was knighted while working as a Westminster MP, although he is an enthusiastic believer in devolved government. He has an extensive network of good relationships with all the main parties in Northern Ireland, including the UUP he left. He developed and retains contact with many leading politicians and diplomats in the Republic. Frequently, at a time of crisis, Donaldson was first choice of the DUP's back-room team to publicly present a reasonable version of chaos.

He was to the fore in some of the DUP's Brexit manoeuvrings, prior to the referendum vote in June 2016. As the party's chief whip in Westminster, he was a signatory to the party's confidence and supply agreement with British prime minister Theresa May. The consequences of the referendum outcome, including the unresolved questions it created for Northern Ireland, helped propel him to the leadership of the DUP. He became the first person in the role to face into Northern Ireland Assembly elections after the UK had formally left the EU. His past is a successful history of balancing competing and often contradictory factors. But that Donaldson trait will be tested like never before by the repercussions of a referendum result he championed but might not have expected. In this instance, imperfect coexistence might not be an option. For Donaldson and Unionism, Brexit may necessitate a binary decision between creating sustainable arrangements around the Northern Ireland protocol or giving significant momentum to the campaign for a united Ireland.

12

The journey made and the road ahead

I kept a copy of the book *Lost Lives* in the RTÉ Belfast office and on a bedside locker throughout my Northern Ireland years. It lists the details of each of the men, women and children who died as a result of the Troubles. It is an authoritative reference source. But, for me, it had a more significant value. On the many days when the different political factions were indulging their verging-on-limitless capacity to argue, it served as a reminder of the wondrous in our midst: the awful killing that was a blight on our island and beyond for three decades is over. That's the miracle of our times that flowed from the Good Friday Agreement.

Paul Connolly and his wife, Mary, lived next door to me on Belfast's North Parade. One couldn't wish for better neighbours. Poor health forced Paul to retire from the ambulance service. He rarely talked about his everyday difficulties with walking and breathing. He carried an even more onerous burden with ingrained understatement. When he was a child, his mother was shot dead by British soldiers. She was one of eleven civilians killed during what's known as the Ballymurphy massacre.

Like many of her fellow residents in West Belfast, Joan Connolly had welcomed the soldiers when they were first posted to Northern Ireland. But, as the conflict deepened, the relationship between the local people and the army soured. On Monday, 9 August 1971, large numbers of the Parachute Regiment flooded areas of nationalist Belfast and mayhem followed. Based on inadequate planning, they were seeking to arrest and intern members of the IRA.

Joan Connolly had eight children. She was out looking for two of her daughters when she was killed. She went to the aid of nineteen-year-old Noel Phillips, who was fatally wounded on waste ground near a British Army barracks. She was struck a number of times by high-velocity bullets, including the one that hit her face. In our many conversations, Paul never once talked about how the loss of his mother affected his family.

I was reminded of Paul's dignity when in the company of Alan Black. One January night in 1976, Alan was among a group of workers returning home from their shift at a textile factory in Co. Armagh. On a dark country road, their minibus was ordered to stop by what the driver mistook to be a British Army patrol. Several gunmen emerged from the hedges, and the Catholic among the workers was asked to identify himself. His Protestant colleagues feared he was being targeted by Loyalist paramilitaries who were shooting Catholics in border areas at that time.

But the gang was made up of IRA members who had come to kill Protestants. They lined up all eleven of them and fired on them at close range. One of the assailants walked among the dying and shot each of them in the head. Alan Black was the only victim to survive. He was wounded eight times and lived only because the final bullet, meant to finish him off, just grazed his forehead. At anniversary times of what became known as the Kingsmill massacre, when debate would recur about the incomplete investigation of the murders, Alan would reluctantly make himself available to the media. I visited him at his home in the village of Bessbrook. He wanted the unanswered questions addressed, but his ability to not be overwhelmed by bitterness is extraordinary.

Twenty-one-year-old Aidan Gallagher went to Omagh to buy boots and a pair of jeans one August Saturday in 1998. He never came home. He was among the twenty-nine people and two unborn twins killed by the car bomb planted by dissident Republicans in the town centre. Forty-eight-year-old Ann McCombe was another of those who died. She was on a tea break with her colleague Geraldine Breslin, from Watterson's drapery shop, when the explosion took place. Both women were killed. Ann's husband, Stanley, was in Glasgow with the older of their two boys, performing with band members in the World Piping Championships, when news of the bombing reached them.

Stanley and Aidan Gallagher's father, Michael, were prominent in the campaign to establish if the security forces on both sides of the border could have done more to prevent the atrocity. The families were determined to bring all those responsible before the courts. The efforts of Police Ombudsman Nuala O'Loan encouraged them to continue their work. One night, after Michael and Stanley featured in an RTÉ programme from Belfast, I gave them a lift back to Omagh. In the confined space of the car, the dignity and the woundedness of the two men was inescapable.

Sometimes at night, when I'd be scripting a radio news preview of one more round of talks about talks, or on a morning walking from the car park in the rain towards the Stormont entrance, I'd remind myself that another day had passed without the killing that damaged the lives of so many families like the Connollys, Blacks, Gallaghers and McCombes.

*

What happened in an imperfect way was that the antagonisms, loathing and suspicion that fuelled the Troubles for thirty years were compressed and transplanted into the Assembly Chamber of Parliament Buildings on the Stormont estate. Scratchy, imperfect politics replaced the killing. That's the achievement of much-maligned, flawed Stormont. That unique model of mandatory coalition power-sharing absorbs and requires huge amounts of energy. It was harsh on those who were consumed and later tossed aside by the process. But their contribution was vital in putting an end to the slaughter.

Monica McWilliams, Avila Kilmurray, Pearl Sagar and Jane Morrice were among the leading figures of Northern Ireland's Women's Coalition party during its brief decade of existence from 1996 to 2006. McWilliams and Morrice were elected to the 108-member Assembly in the 1998 contest that followed the Good Friday Agreement. They failed to hold their seats in the 2003 elections. The misogyny they encountered and confronted would not be tolerated in any Northern Ireland political forum today.

The Progressive Unionist Party (PUP) never denied its links to the Loyalist paramilitary organizations, the Ulster Volunteer Force and Red Hand Commando. In the same way, the Loyalist Ulster Democratic Party (UDP) was associated with the paramilitary organization the Ulster Defence Association. The PUP and the UDP had a role in the Loyalist ceasefires, and their representatives took part in the negotiations that led to the Good Friday Agreement and then publicly backed it.

Both Loyalist micro-parties sought to mirror what Sinn Féin was doing within nationalism and secure an electoral mandate from their own community. But, after a brief flickering, they failed to make the breakthrough. Most Unionist voters took politics to be the exclusive preserve of the DUP and the UUP. The arrangement suited the two main Unionist power blocs. Although the PUP and UDP sought to challenge it, they failed to make inroads.

If the Women's Coalition and the two small Loyalist parties had grounds for disappointment with their cameo walk-on, walk-off role, the two parties who took lead roles in the Good Friday Agreement negotiations, the SDLP and the UUP, suffered an even more humiliating fall from grace. In the 2001 Westminster contest, three years after the Agreement was signed, UUP leader David Trimble almost lost his Upper Bann seat. He and his wife, Daphne, were jostled by DUP supporters as they left the Banbridge count centre. Three police officers and three civilians suffered crush injuries. In a jibe suggesting that Republicans were making fools of the UUP, the DUP campaign included the message that they didn't want gunmen in government. In the next Westminster election, Trimble lost his seat and resigned as UUP leader.

At their home between the Creggan and the Bogside in nationalist Derry, the SDLP leader, John Hume, and his family were sometimes subjected to similar intimidation and worse. They lived behind reinforced windows and doors, in fear of attack from Republicans who disagreed with Hume's politics.

UUP members like Trimble, his successor Reg Empey and their contemporaries Dermot Nesbitt and Danny Kinahan were helpless as the DUP first berated them for the compromise they had made with nationalism and then moved into the political space that they had created. In the twelve years after Empey stood down, five different leaders tried and failed to arrest the slide.

The SDLP suffered a similar dilution of influence. It stead-
fastly remained faithful to democratic values and never blinked
in its opposition to violence from any quarter. It saw its mandate
challenged and usurped by Sinn Féin. For some who were active
in the most difficult days – the likes of Bríd Rodgers, Sean
Farren, Denis Haughey and Margaret Ritchie – it was difficult
to stomach. As SDLP leader from 2011 to 2015, Dr Alasdair
McDonnell was another who tried and failed to halt the slide.
He was MP for the South Belfast constituency where I lived.
During one election campaign, on the day before polling, I was
due a monthly injection and suggested a deal with him. He is
a qualified GP, with a good sense of humour. He gave me an
injection and I acknowledged the kindness in the polling station.

Mark Durkan, SDLP leader from 2001 to 2010, lost his
Foyle Westminster seat to Sinn Féin in 2017. He was a respected
contributor to debates in the London chamber. The electorate
replaced him with Sinn Féin's Elisha McCallion, who would
follow her party's abstentionist policy. One MP told me of
seeing Durkan struggling to hold back the tears as he gathered
his belongings in the House of Commons. He had been John
Hume's most trusted adviser during the Good Friday negotiations. He tried to resurrect his political career south of the
border, in the 2019 European elections, when selected as a
Fine Gael candidate for the Dublin four-seat constituency. He
received 16,473 votes, less than a third of the support won by
his successful running mate, Frances Fitzgerald.

In West Belfast, Sinn Féin remorselessly chipped away at
the support base of SDLP Assembly member Alex Attwood.
Eventually they squeezed him out, in the same way that Gerry
Adams had once ousted the SDLP's Dr Joe Hendron from his
Westminster seat.

The SDLP's Seamus Mallon was buffeted by those turning tides when he and David Trimble led the first power-sharing executive. The pressure they both faced from rival parties may have been a factor in their strained relationship. Mallon retreated from politics in 2001 to help with the care of his wife, Gertrude. In the final years of his life, I met him a number of times. To mark his eightieth birthday in 2016, a function was organized and I compèred the event in the packed huge function room of the Armagh City Hotel. The audience included many of Mallon's Protestant neighbours and political rivals.

After the publication of his autobiography, *A Shared Home Place*, I interviewed him as part of the Clifden Arts Festival in Co. Galway in September 2019. The function room of the town's Station Hotel (the venue that featured in the Golfgate political controversy in August 2020) couldn't accommodate the huge crowds. The event was switched to the town's Catholic church, and it was a full house.

Four months later, one of Mallon's friends, Kevin Loughney, contacted me with the news that Seamus was losing his battle with cancer. On a Sunday afternoon, I called to see him at his home in Markethill. Seamus was in bed, watching a GAA match on TG4. We had a long chat about his life. He was a man at peace with himself and his times. When we talked about David Trimble, Seamus made clear that his respect and affection for the former UUP leader outweighed his memories of the difficult times in their relationship. Earlier that day, when I called to Bríd Rodgers at her home near Portadown, she told me how, when she was parting with Seamus days before, unusually he leaned forward to kiss her.

I said goodbye to him, knowing we were unlikely to meet again.

Back in Belfast, I found a number in my phone for David Trimble and called him. My dealings with him had been limited over the years because the political tide was turning when I moved back from Brussels and he began spending more time in London. He always seemed shy, but decency was never an issue. I told him how I had called to see Seamus Mallon and how he had talked fondly about him. Trimble said he would like to visit his old friend, and I shared Orla Mallon's number with him. Even though David Trimble made the follow-up phone call, Orla was surprised when she looked out the window and saw the former UUP leader arriving to visit her father. The two men spent a long time together talking. In fact, Trimble had plans to make a second visit when the news came through that Seamus had died.

RTÉ's managing director of news and current affairs, Jon Williams, decided the Requiem Mass at St James' Church, Mullaghbrack, would be carried live on the RTÉ News Now channel, and David Trimble was one of the many dignitaries in attendance.

The following year, when Martin McGuinness was dying, Trimble, now a Conservative Party member of the House of Lords, wrote to him. In the letter, he told McGuinness that he had been 'indispensable' in helping Republicans move towards power-sharing. He also said in the letter that McGuinness had 'reached out to the Unionist community in a way some of them were reluctant to reach out to you'.

I observed a pattern with several politicians in the autumns of their lives, including those like Trimble and Mallon, whose parties experienced painful rejection at the ballot box. The hurt had not disappeared, but there was a recognition that they had lived to see an end of the killing and that they had contributed to that change.

*

In 2007, Sinn Féin and the DUP both came to their new status as the dominant political forces in Northern Ireland politics with troublesome baggage. Sinn Féin's issue was its links to the IRA and the paramilitary activities that were the core function of the Republican movement during the Troubles. With the DUP, the impediments blocking its evolution as a political party included its history of opposing change on social issues. It also has a deep-rooted hankering to return to its secure space within an era of British Empire that will never return.

Sinn Féin had no choice but to embrace change. That reality, and some of the decisions made by the DUP, have contributed to Sinn Féin now having significantly better medium- and long-term future prospects than its Unionist rival. The more Sinn Féin became involved in politics, the more it realized that 'the Armalite in one hand and ballot box in the other' strategy of the 1980s wasn't just a hindrance. It was halting the party's growth.

A number of times, as Taoiseach and minister for foreign affairs, Brian Cowen lost patience in his dealings with Gerry Adams and Martin McGuinness. When the Sinn Féin leaders put it to Cowen that the views of the IRA would have to be sought on some sensitive issue, Cowen's tendency was to ask, 'Why don't you go to the toilet and look in the mirror?' Cowen's attitude was in tune with reality. From 2007 onwards, for Sinn Féin, as a lead partner in government at Stormont, IRA links and any ambivalence on paramilitary activities became synonymous with trouble. The Sinn Féin mindset became 'That was then, now is different, and we are different.'

Sinn Féin has another dimension that makes it unique. It is active on a second front, over the border, an area with even greater growth potential than Northern Ireland. And in the South the need to shed the IRA baggage and put distance between the present and the past is even more imperative. I was in Belfast on 6 May 2022, the day of the Stormont Assembly election results. By retaining its twenty-seven seats, for the first time Sinn Féin was on course to overtake the DUP as the largest party in the Stormont chamber. A day of historic change in the history of the party and Northern Ireland politics had arrived.

With just a 21 per cent share of the first-preference vote but 27.8 per cent of the Assembly seats – twenty-five elected members – the DUP had the consolation that the outcome could have been worse.

Compared to election counts from Northern Ireland's past, the absence of hostilities was striking. Some back-room teams were actually sharing tally figures with rival parties. There was no sense that the PSNI might be required to maintain order during the speeches of the winners and losers. Union flags and Irish tricolours, once a standard prop, were gone. As the count unfolded, Sinn Féin prepared for the triumphant arrival at the Titanic Centre of its president, Mary Lou McDonald, and the first minister elect, Michelle O'Neill. But there was no sign of the party's former leader, Gerry Adams. He didn't feature in the victory speeches in the same way that he no longer figures in Sinn Féin's narrative in the South, as it consolidates its position as the most popular party in Dáil Éireann.

In my view, Adams, even more than McGuinness, is the most significant person in Sinn Féin's history. Following the election to Westminster of hunger-striker Bobby Sands, the pair led the Republican movement's slow-motion journey towards politics. They were crucial in the 1994 ceasefire, the Good Friday Agreement and IRA weapons-decommissioning. Adams recognized that McGuinness was better suited for the power-sharing relationship with the DUP and the deputy first minister role. He was also the one who decided to cross the border and seek a Louth Dáil seat in the 2011 general election. The increased Southern presence is, arguably, the most important factor in Sinn Féin's evolution and growth.

As an outsider in Leinster House, 'down from Belfast', Adams was vilified and ridiculed. Often in what were unfamiliar surroundings, he didn't fully understand the issues. At times he displayed a very limited grasp of economics and the workings of government and state. Routinely in Northern Ireland, on public occasions, he attempted to make use of his limited Irish. But in the Dáil chamber there were others more fluent in the language. He knew it. And they knew it. (Among Oireachtas members, prior to his retirement, Adams may be the one who made the most progress in his efforts to improve his Irish.)

His past was his most obvious vulnerability. Few, including many Republicans closest to him, believed his denial of past IRA membership. The reality was that if he varied one syllable from his stated position he was likely to be arrested and prosecuted. He persisted with what many dismissed as fiction. He became the lightning conductor, sponge and punchbag when allegations of Republican duplicity and criminality surfaced. As the party leader, he was in the eye of the storm when Máiría Cahill made public her account of rape by an IRA member in Belfast in the late 1990s. Her description of the IRA internal inquiry that followed heaped further pressure on Sinn Féin. With his past north of the border, and his present as Sinn Féin's leader in Dáil Éireann, Adams was the obvious candidate for accountability. The full truth about parts of his earlier life will never be known.

Those seven Dáil Éireann-based years as Sinn Féin's leader (2011–18) were probably the most difficult period in Adams's public life. In the Southern political arena, he encountered challenge and hostility that were different but at least equal in severity to what he was accustomed to in Northern Ireland. And yet, the Adams move south coincided with Sinn Féin smashing through the glass ceiling in Dáil Éireann. It had five seats after the 2007 election. In the first contest after his switch, 2011, Sinn Féin representation increased to fourteen. In the 2016 election, Adams's final one as leader, twenty-three Sinn Féin TDs were returned. By the time Adams retired from Dáil politics, in 2020, under McDonald's leadership, Sinn Féin won thirty-seven seats and the highest share of the first-preference vote.

A significant section of the electorate now regards the IRA as part of Sinn Féin's past. When Adams and some of those closest to him exited the stage, the most toxic electoral elements of the Republican movement's history left with them.

*

Compared to the potential that Dáil Éireann offers to Sinn Féin, Westminster provides no such opportunity to the DUP as its second activity front. Northern Ireland sends eighteen members to the 650-seat London parliament. In the 2019 UK general election, the DUP won eight seats. Even when its ten members held the balance of power during Theresa May's minority government, the DUP's influence was always going to be limited and brief. Mathematics ensures that it can aspire to no more than minnow status at Westminster.

Over a twenty-year period, I observed the DUP attempting to adapt to change. Gay rights was one of the problematic issues for the party. At an August 2017 Pride march in Belfast, there was a placard and balloons with the message 'Fuck the DUP'. The organizers confiscated a poster, and one participant was interviewed by the PSNI but no prosecution followed.

Peter Robinson, the main strategist in the party's fifty-one-year history, is a modernizer at heart. But even he became cautious about change at critical junctures.

In the 2022 Assembly election campaign, one more time the DUP's dilemma between the centre ground and its conservative roots reared its head. The identity crisis took its toll. The DUP managed to confine its main threat from the right, the TUV, led by Jim Allister.

He secured just his one seat (1.1 per cent of the Assembly total) even though his party received 7.6 per cent of the first-preference votes. But two of the DUP's senior outgoing Assembly members, Mervyn Storey and Peter Weir, were defeated by Alliance party candidates. The constituencies involved, North Antrim and Strangford, were once DUP heartland. Alliance, a middle-ground party, made progress at its expense.

On issues like the establishment of abortion services, similar to those available elsewhere in the UK, and formally recognizing the rights of the Irish-language community, the British government has found a mechanism to help the DUP. By introducing the necessary legislation through Westminster and bypassing Stormont, London gives the DUP the option to tell the hard-line sections of its support base, 'We fought the good fight, but the matters were taken out of our hands.' In the 2022 Assembly elections, several outgoing DUP Assembly members from the conservative wing of the party were replaced by younger candidates more attuned to the views of the electorate. Those personnel changes may facilitate a process of renewal within the party.

But the DUP remains stuck on the Brexit hook. It championed the Brexit cause without fully carrying out the due diligence on its possible consequences. Brexit really is the poisoned apple, and the DUP ate it. In the 2016 Brexit referendum, a majority of those who voted in Northern Ireland favoured remaining in the EU. In the Assembly elections of 2017, and again in May 2022, parties that campaigned to remain won a majority of seats.

The DUP has helped to persuade the UK government that it should prepare to ditch elements of the Northern Ireland protocol arrangements it negotiated and agreed with the EU. Such action would leave London and the DUP at odds with a majority of the elected members of the Assembly. Jeffrey Donaldson's best outcome would be a tweaked version of the protocol, acceptable to the EU, and the continuation of the arrangement that uniquely allows Northern Ireland access to all UK and EU markets. If that workable compromise can be achieved, there is a realistic prospect of power-sharing being restored at Stormont, with Sinn Féin in the first-minister role.

If the issue of Northern Ireland's problem with Brexit is resolved, in their role as co-guarantors of the Good Friday Agreement, the British and Irish governments could explore whether elements of the Agreement need to be revisited. But if the Brexit row rumbles on and deepens, and if the DUP persists in avoiding responsibility for the situation it created, Northern Ireland will risk fuelling the theory that it is a failed political entity.

Unionism's best prospect of maintaining the current constitutional position centres on making Northern Ireland a success. That would include harnessing its unique 'best of both worlds' status within the Brexit settlement, having a harmonious relationship with the neighbouring jurisdiction and pursuing policies that reflect the views of a majority of Northern Ireland's citizens.

*

Two cultural festivals, *feiseanna*, take place in my home town, Sligo, thirty miles south of the border, each year. They are held in the days immediately after Easter Sunday, when the young participants for most of the competitions are on holidays from school. The organizers of Feis Shligigh often came from a Fianna Fáil party background while Feis Ceoil was linked to Fine Gael.

The Noble Six Trophy and the Seamus Devins Cup are two of the most important Irish-dancing events of the Feis Shligigh programme. They commemorate six members of the anti-Treaty forces who were shot dead by Irish Army soldiers on Ben Bulben mountain during the civil war. Brigadier Seamus Devins was the leader of the six IRA men killed. One of the others, Brian MacNeill, was a son of Eoin MacNeill, the then education minister in the government Brian opposed. Brian MacNeill's nephew, Michael McDowell, would serve as a Progressive Democrats minister for justice from 2007 and is currently an independent member of the Senate.

Like many incidents in the two-and-a-half-year War of Independence and the eleven-month civil war that followed it, the controversial circumstances of the killings on the Co. Sligo mountainside were never fully clarified. A ring was removed from the body of Brigadier Devins. After representations from his widow, it was recovered and returned to her. His grandson, Jimmy Devins, a Sligo–Leitrim TD from 2002 to 2011 and a Sligo-based general practitioner, wears that ring today. Those civil-war enmities were transferred to Dáil Éireann and to local-authority chambers throughout the country. Remarkably, democratic politics, sometimes including bitter arguments, replaced killing, as would happen many decades later in Northern Ireland after the Good Friday Agreement.

From the tumult that followed the 1916 Rising, Sinn Féin was the only significant faction to refuse to participate in the democratic structures of the new state. It didn't accept partition and remained committed to achieving a united Ireland, free of a British presence in the north. It considered the armed-struggle strategy of the IRA legitimate, even when that campaign was funded in part by robberies, kidnapping and other criminal activities, carried out by IRA members, on both sides of the border.

Caoimhghín Ó Caoláin, elected in the Cavan–Monaghan constituency in 1997, made history by ending Sinn Féin's policy of not taking its Dáil Éireann seats. Sinn Féin received 2.5 per cent of the national first-preference vote in that contest. Twenty-three years later, for the first time, it was returned as the most popular party in the 2020 general election with a 24.5 per cent vote share. A direct consequence of that Sinn Féin success saw Fianna Fáil and Fine Gael agreed to park their rivalry, dating back to the civil war, and form a coalition government, with the assistance of the Green Party.

Opinion polls during the two years since indicate that Sinn Féin's popularity with the electorate continues to grow. There is no solid pattern suggesting that it will receive the level of support required to form a single-party government after the next election.

But, unless a dramatic change of trends takes place, Sinn Féin will return the most representatives to the next Dáil.

The party that chose outsider status at the time of the formation of the state is on course to centre stage and power. If the outcome of voting in 2020 forced Fianna Fáil and Fine Gael to put aside their traditional hostilities, the next election may prompt even deeper soul-searching for them.

In Northern Ireland, the largest parties from nationalist and Unionist traditions are guaranteed the right to lead a power-sharing government. The Good Friday Agreement prevents Sinn Féin from being excluded if it is returned as the largest party. No such conditions apply to government formation after Dáil elections. But if very different practices continue to occur in neighbouring jurisdictions, the contrast won't go unnoticed.

Exercising power competently is always a challenge. Micheál Martin is leading the coalition administration in Dublin for the first half of the five-year cycle. His main coalition partner, the Fine Gael leader Leo Varadkar, will soon replace him.

Early into the coalition's term in office, it was ambushed by the COVID-19 pandemic challenge and the outworkings of Brexit, including the Northern Ireland protocol. Then came the war in Ukraine, the challenge of accommodating refugees from the conflict and now the biggest cost-of-living increases and highest inflation rates in thirty years.

Sinn Féin has become such a vocal and active opposition to the under-pressure coalition that many government policy initiatives now attempt to 'second-guess the Shinners'. The spectacle of a nervous coalition adds to the status of Mary Lou McDonald and her Sinn Féin colleagues.

It is an imperfect version of soft power because it involves a level of influence, at arm's distance, without accountability. McDonald has spent two decades contributing to Sinn Féin's growth. She succeeded Gerry Adams as president in 2018. I can't envisage the circumstances after the next general election where she would be content to settle for a five-year term as leader of the opposition.

Fianna Fáil and Fine Gael may again have the numbers to cobble together a coalition with others. It is highly unlikely, though not impossible, that one of the two would consider going into government with Sinn Féin. But Sinn Féin as the dominant force in a coalition government for the first time would make for a very demanding partner.

One possibility, favoured by some in both Fianna Fáil and Fine Gael, would have Sinn Féin form a minority government, leaving its main rivals to watch on in judgement from the comfort of the opposition benches.

*

In an interview with Sky News's Beth Rigby on 19 May 2022, McDonald made a statement that is likely to be linked to her for the rest of her political career. She told the forty-six-year-old presenter that 'a united Ireland will happen in our time' and elaborated: 'It will happen in our lifetime . . . without a shadow of a doubt. We will see constitutional change in the course probably of the next decade. Of that there is no doubt and we need to prepare for that. And the appetite for change, across Ireland, would really lift your heart, the opportunity that exists for our country – and we need to bring our Unionist brothers and sisters along that road with us.'

I would be very surprised if border polls, on each side of the frontier, are held within that ten-year time frame. In the unlikely event of them happening, unless there is radical change before then, I would expect the option of a united Ireland to be rejected.

Sinn Féin entered power-sharing, in a lead partner role with the DUP, for the first time in 2007. I observed its performance as a participant in the government of Northern Ireland since then. In the fifteen-year period, it had a significant role shaping, championing and helping to implement just one major and unique policy initiative: the devolution of justice and policing.

The party had very obvious self-interest in that legislation because it helped Sinn Féin's evolution as a post-Troubles political force, North and South. The three most important drivers of that project were Gerry Adams, Martin McGuinness and Gerry Kelly – all with connections to the IRA. One of the trio is dead. A second has retired from public life.

Kelly remains an active member of the Assembly. He is seen as 'old guard', but he remains important.

Within the party he has the role of six-counties chairperson. As part of his responsibilities, in advance of the 2022 Assembly elections, he was dispatched to the Foyle (Derry) constituency to oversee the retirement of two sitting MLA members and the selection of their replacements.

Some of his IRA past is known, including his involvement in the bombing of the Old Bailey in London and the IRA mass breakout from the Maze during which a prison officer died.

In 2004, when three frightened British soldiers were surrounded by an angry crowd in Ardoyne and were on the point of using their guns, I saw Kelly intervene to rescue them and suffer a broken arm during the scuffles. Nowadays, he is now probably the most effective example of the Republican movement's journey from paramilitarism to politics.

Conor Murphy, another who served a prison sentence for IRA activities, was minister for regional development from 2007 to 2011 and took over as finance minister in 2022 when his party colleague Máirtín Ó Muilleoir retired. Like Gerry Kelly, he is able. Yet Murphy was bypassed by Martin McGuinness when he preferred Michelle O'Neill to succeed him. McGuinness was impressed by the support she gave him during some of his years as an Assembly member and MP for the Mid Ulster constituency. He took note of how she faced down dissenting voices within the republican movement who were keen to undermine him.

John O'Dowd was a competent education minister from 2011 to 2016 but fell out with the party leadership when seeking to challenge Michelle O'Neill. She held two senior positions, agriculture and rural development minister (2011–16) and health minister (2016–17) before taking up the deputy first minister role.

Policing and justice changes aside, I saw no evidence of this senior group of Sinn Féin ministers pioneering policy change in the Northern Ireland Executive. The same observation applies to all the parties in the successive power-sharing administrations. Stormont receives the bulk of its finance from Westminster through a block-grant system.

It and Northern Ireland are a branch office, at a significant distance from London headquarters. The default position of the devolved administration, support staff included, is to function like an end-of-the-line outpost. On most occasions when the opportunity arose to make tough policy decisions that might trigger significant change, the chance was ducked or postponed.

The standard response, usually supported by all the main parties, when financial difficulties arise, is to make a case for Northern Ireland's unique circumstances and ask Westminster for more money.

Health is an example of an important policy area affected by the procrastination malaise. An expert panel, chaired by

Professor Rafael Bengoa, was appointed to recommend a sustainable way forward for the provision of health and social care. Its recommendations, issued in October 2016, remain no more than that.

Northern Ireland has the UK's longest hospital appointment waiting lists. Even before COVID-19, its health system was creaking at the seams.

Education is another area requiring reform, but there, too, the big decisions are on hold. One project epitomising the reluctance to implement change is the case of the former British Army barracks at Lisanelly, near Omagh, Co. Tyrone. It is supposed to be a spectacular example of post-conflict Northern Ireland, involving the development of its biggest-ever education building project, catering for six schools and 4,000 pupils on a shared education site. To date, just one of the six promised centres, the Arvalee Special School, has opened.

The campus was due to be completed in 2020. The projected costs have risen substantially. The current completion estimate is 2026 and that deadline is unlikely to be met.

In the fifteen years since it became a lead partner in government, Sinn Féin has never held the economy portfolio, charged with responsibility for enterprise, trade and investment.

Máirtín Ó Muilleoir, who had a business background in the publishing sector, became a Sinn Féin finance minister in May 2016. He quickly announced that he wanted to start a major public-housing programme, mainly financed by borrowing. The plan was affected by the collapse of power-sharing in January 2017. He formally resigned as an Assembly member in December 2019 before Stormont reopened.

Sinn Féin has indeed cut its teeth as a participant in government at Stormont, and its elected representatives and their party officials have gained experience in challenging circumstances. But it cannot point to a significant record of policy making or a track record of implementing difficult decisions.

*

In the Republic, the obvious is worth stating. All of Sinn Féin's Dáil experience is as a party of opposition, growing spectacularly from its one-member status in 1997 to thirty-seven TDs after the 2020 elections. It has no hard-earned track record in government.

Opinion polls suggest that the party leader, Mary Lou McDonald, makes a better connection with voters than her predecessor, Gerry Adams. One senior civil servant told me when Fine Gael's Michael Noonan was finance minister, from 2011 to 2017, the practice was to always treat queries from Sinn Féin's spokesman, Pearse Doherty, with urgency. He continues to be held in high regard.

Other consistently impressive performers include Louise O'Reilly (enterprise, trade and employment) and David Cullinane (health).

Eoin Ó Broin has possibly the most eclectic curriculum vitae of the prominent Sinn Féin politicians, North and South. Born in South Dublin, he was educated in Blackrock College, the University of East London and Queen's University Belfast. He was a member of Belfast City Council from 2001 to 2004. He worked for Sinn Féin in Brussels for three years. After unsuccessful election attempts to the Dáil and the Seanad, he was co-opted onto South Dublin County Council by Sinn Féin in 2013. He finally made his Dáil breakthrough in the 2016 general election in the Dublin Mid-West constituency. His increased majority in 2020 helped to elect a second Sinn Féin candidate, Mark Ward. As the party's housing spokesperson, Ó Broin consistently achieves traction over what is a priority issue with voters.

Sinn Féin's Dáil cohort compares favourably with its main rivals. It has experienced campaigners like Pádraig Mac Lochlainn and Matt Carthy and first-time TDs including Rose Conway-Walsh, Claire Kerrane and Mairéad Farrell.

It also has able officials who have contributed to the party's growth and can at least match the teams of rival organizations. Wexford-born Dawn Doyle, a former general secretary, is McDonald's *chef de cabinet*. Ken O'Connell is the Dublin-based general secretary and former political director. In Belfast, Stephen McGlade is the special adviser to Michelle O'Neill, and he previously worked for Gerry Adams in Dublin. Conor Keenan is the Belfast-based deputy general secretary. Ciaran Quinn spent several years working for the party at Stormont before moving to Dublin, where he is now Sinn Féin's representative for North America.

The party's track record in fundraising, including its connection to emigrant communities in the United States and Australia, leaves its rivals in the slipstream.

But Sinn Féin has never been a major or minor party in a sovereign government, interacting from that position of authority with civil servants and consistently making difficult decisions.

When that opportunity comes for Sinn Féin, based on the experience of all previous newcomers to power, it will be a case of a very steep learning curve.

May 2032 is the deadline identified by Mary Lou McDonald for 'constitutional change'. Given that Fianna Fáil and Fine

Gael show no appetite for such a historic challenge in that time frame, she must be banking on Sinn Féin being in government from the next general election onwards to drive those complex preparations.

It would be an achievement, unparalleled in the history of the state, if an Irish administration manages to complete such radical groundwork within that time frame.

*

The second part of the project, having the two neighbouring but very different administrations ready for successful fusion and able to attract the support of a majority of voters in each jurisdiction, will require statecraft well beyond the miraculous.

Health is a priority for most citizens, regardless of their political views. In Northern Ireland, services are provided through a faltering version of the National Health Service model. Its citizens have free GP care, free hospital care and free prescriptions – but the longest waiting lists in the UK. It is a single-tier system. Less than 5 per cent of the population have private health insurance. The model operating in the South is an imperfect two-tier hybrid, with up to 50 per cent of citizens prepared to pay for private health care in order to bypass the queues in the public system.

A number of Ireland's best-known entrepreneurs are shareholders in the network of private hospitals. Some health professionals, used to an income stream from the public and private systems, are wary about giving up the practice. Administrative staff of the HSE expend significant time and resources trying to identify and retrieve revenue due to the state from the complex hybrid system.

In May 2017, a cross-parliamentary committee published its Sláintecare (healthcare) report, mapping out a ten-year plan to achieve universal health care in Ireland. It has the support of all the main political parties. In theory, its timetable could neatly dovetail with Mary Lou McDonald's timeline for constitutional change by May 2032. But there is little chance of the radical change advocated for in the Sláintecare plan being completed on time.

In May 2022, controversy broke out in the Dáil over the proposed new National Maternity Hospital. The €1 billion facility is due to be built alongside St Vincent's Hospital on lands owned by a religious order, the Sisters of Charity. A row raged for several days over whether the proposed legal ownership structure left open the danger of religious interference in the future. The Taoiseach, Micheál Martin, argued that the site would 'essentially' be state-owned because of the 300-year lease secured at €10 per year. The project is due to be completed in 2030 but may run beyond that.

The latest completion date for the new National Children's Hospital in Dublin is the second half of 2024 – ten years after its original promised date and significantly over budget.

Merging the different health-service models, North and South, to the satisfaction of a majority of voters is one of those challenges facing those advocating a united Ireland. I can't see it happening within Mary Lou McDonald's 2032 time frame.

There are different systems, in so many areas, north and south of the border. The Motability Scheme was one of the features of Northern Ireland I learned about during my Belfast-based years. It provides those who qualify for certain levels of disability payments with a new car, scooter, power wheelchair or wheelchair-accessible vehicle, free of charge, with all insurance, service and tyre-replacement charges covered. The vehicle can be used by up to three named drivers. It is replaced with a new one free of charge to the recipient every three years.

In the four-year period from 2018 to 2021, the Motability Scheme accounted for 32 per cent of all the new cars sold in Northern Ireland. It is a huge factor in the number of new Northern Irish cars and the quality of used cars in circulation.

In some postcode areas, including in Sinn Féin heartlands, three out of every four cars purchased during 2018–21 were Motability vehicles. At its network of advice centres, Sinn Féin often provides practical information about how to access the scheme.

When the detailed debate gets under way about how a united Ireland might work, the future of the Motability Scheme is an example of those thousands of policy issues that will have to be addressed.

Would such a scheme be extended to the Republic of Ireland, or would it be scrapped or changed to the less generous provisions that apply in the South?

Third-level education fees is an interesting example. Students at Northern Ireland institutions pay annual fees of £4,600 (£9,250 in England) compared to the €3,000 third-level charges in the Republic of Ireland. For decades, generations of Northern Irish and British students received grants to cover the cost of third-level education. But that UK grants model has been replaced by a system of repayable student loans. In the Republic a system of means-tested grants, as well as lower annual fees, operates.

Corporation tax varies significantly between south and north. The current UK rate, Northern Ireland included, is 19 per cent, compared to Ireland's figure of 12.5 per cent. Significant voices within the Conservative government want to increase the rate to 25 per cent – double the Republic's figure.

The Northern Ireland secretary, Brandon Lewis, stated in October 2021 that the British government was providing £15 billion annual funding for the Northern Ireland Executive – the largest-ever settlement. He claimed that Stormont was receiving around £121 per person for every £100 per person of equivalent UK government spending in England.

In the event of a united Ireland, would that UK subvention to Northern Ireland disappear or would Britain be pressurized to provide several years of 'balloon payments' following constitutional change?

Would the 7,000 PSNI officers and 2,600 support staff be subsumed into An Garda Síochána? The current garda commissioner, Drew Harris, is a former deputy chief constable of the PSNI. His late father, RUC superintendent Alwyn Harris, was killed by an IRA car bomb in 1989. Drew Harris crossed the border to take charge of a garda force with 14,000 personnel. Since then, PSNI chief superintendent Paula Hilman made the same journey to become an assistant garda commissioner. The pair have experience of working with Sinn Féin on both sides of the border.

How would such an amalgamation of the police services work?

In Northern Ireland, 40 per cent of the voters in the 2022 Assembly elections supported Unionist parties who favour remaining part of the UK. Convincing significant numbers of them to change their loyalties won't be easy.

It may well be that a majority on both sides of the border can be persuaded to support a new start as an island nation of 7 million people, a member of the EU, with huge goodwill from the USA and a special relationship with Great Britain.

The ambition to unite Ireland has been central to Sinn Féin's existence since its foundation in 1905. The constitutional change by 2032 predicted by McDonald is one yardstick by which she and her party will be judged. But there will be others, too.

If Sinn Féin makes its way into government on both sides of the border, it will be assessed on how it exercises power and delivers on the many promises made from the opposition benches.

If or when Sinn Féin enters government, the electorate, including the growing cohort of those born after the 1994 IRA ceasefire, will exercise their democratic right to decide on Sinn Féin's effectiveness and future.

But there can be no doubt that unfinished business from the foundation of the state a century ago will present itself for attention during the next decade.

*

Just as new factors are at play in politics North and South, a new phase in British–Irish relations is under way. In May 2022, Michelle O'Neill sent a personal letter to Queen Elizabeth II in advance of her Platinum Jubilee celebrations.

In the correspondence, the Sinn Féin deputy leader acknowledged the significant contribution the queen has made 'to the advancement of peace and reconciliation between the different traditions on our island, and between our two islands during those years of the peace process'.

The writing style suggested that the drafting work was done by back-room team member Stephen McGlade. Like a lot of what Sinn Féin does, the O'Neill correspondence was part of a strategy. The party's newly elected Sinn Féin lord mayor of

Belfast, Tina Black, was mandated to attend a number of Jubilee events. The Sinn Féin finance minister, Conor Murphy, was cleared to attend a Jubilee service at St Patrick's Church of Ireland cathedral in Armagh.

Thirty-five summers before, information came my way that the IRA had obtained a sensitive garda document with advance knowledge of the British ambassador's travel plans to Co. Kerry. For my inexperienced shoulders, the story nearly proved too awkward to handle. At the time, the IRA was actively targeting and killing people. How our island has changed since.

In Michelle O'Neill's letter to the queen, she also said, 'As incoming first minister of the Northern Ireland Executive, I, like you, will take every opportunity to strengthen the bonds of friendship and renew the spirit of co-operation between those of us in the world of politics and public life from different traditions, and also the people and communities we proudly represent.'

Not just Sinn Féin but the two other main parties in the Republic, Fianna Fáil and Fine Gael, and diplomats from the Department of Foreign Affairs believe the senior members of the royal family are important players in the ongoing relationship between the neighbouring islands.

I saw a spectacular example of the dynamic in May 2015. Prince Charles and the Duchess of Cornwall came for the first time to the place I know best, my home county, Sligo.

For him, it was an emotional journey because, for the first time, he was visiting the village of Mullaghmore, where his grand-uncle and mentor, Lord Mountbatten, was one of four people killed by the IRA in 1979.

The first stop on their itinerary was a former Protestant school, now The Model arts centre, in Sligo. Harpist Michael

Rooney had composed a beautiful piece of music for the occasion. He performed it with violinist Niamh Crowley and members of her Sligo Academy of Music. Our daughter Moya was one of the cellists.

Late in the afternoon, the prince and his wife were brought through the front doors of Classiebawn Castle, near Mullaghmore, by Timothy Knatchbull and his wife, Isabella. All the other members of the entourage remained outside, in their cars. Thirty-five years before, Lord Mountbatten breakfasted there for the final time. Timothy Knatchbull's fourteen-year-old twin brother, Nicholas, was one of those killed when the IRA bomb detonated in Mountbatten's fishing boat outside Mullaghmore harbour. Timothy suffered a serious eye injury and would also have died if two locals, Dick and Elizabeth Wood-Martin, had not spotted him floating among the debris in the water and rescued him.

A neighbour who lived two doors down from our family home in Sligo, Kevin Henry, was a garda on duty that August Monday morning in 1979. His job was to accompany Lord Mountbatten and his party from Classiebawn Castle to his small boat, *Shadow V*, in the harbour. He would then monitor them from a vantage point as they fished in the Atlantic and accompany them back to Classiebawn when they returned. Kevin was sitting in the garda car, with a perfect view of the fishing boat in the sea below, when it blew up.

The McHugh family owned the Pier Head Hotel in Mullaghmore harbour. After the explosion took place, they converted bedroom headboards and bedsheets into make-shift stretchers and bandages as the wounded and dying were brought ashore. Many years later, the singer Leonard Cohen staged two magical concerts in the grounds of nearby Lissadell

House and he stayed in the McHughs' hotel. He posed for photographs with the hotel staff, and his presence was a great lift to their business and the village. But it was the visit of Lord Mountbatten's grand-nephew all the years later that brought a very special sense of healing to the entire area.

*

In the Sligo of my childhood, Tessie Jinks was a larger-than-life character. She and her family lived in a local-authority house close to the centre of the town, near the Garavogue river. She was constantly on the go, rearing her children and working outside the home to help pay the bills.

A public house she liked, owned by the Gilmartin family, was nicknamed 'Shoot the Crows'. Some of its patrons enjoyed singing and it then got a second nickname, 'The Opera House'.

One morning before Christmas, a local gift-shop owner, Nina O'Brien, was busy getting her stock in order for the festive season. She felt under pressure from the volume of work she knew was coming and, in small talk to her customer, said, 'Christmas can be very stressful. Do you like Christmas, Mrs Jinks?' The reply was delivered instantly. 'The way it is with us, Miss O'Brien, we have Christmas every Friday night in Shoots.'

I was at school with two of the Jinks boys, Frank and Cyril. They had their mother's spirit and energy. Frank became a busy agriculture contractor. Cyril joined the Irish Army, learned to be a chef and afterwards set up a catering business with his partner. They had a younger brother, Noel, who was nick-named 'Mousey'. When we were running fundraising discos in Summerhill College, we were wary of Mousey's gang. After that phase, he graduated from driving a Honda 50 motorbike to travelling with a group of friends across the USA on Harley-Davidsons. Noel and his partner settled in Mullaghmore and have a house above the village, with a view of the sea.

After Prince Charles and the dignitaries met the invitees on the guest list in the grounds of a convent close to Classiebawn Castle, he came out to the main street of the village, where large crowds had gathered. There in his eyeline, wearing a distinctive cowboy hat, was Noel 'Mousey' Jinks.

The image of the pair of them shaking hands provided the opening shot for my report into the RTÉ 9 p.m. television news bulletin that night. There could not have been a better example of the people-to-people bond and reconciliation in Mullaghmore that memorable day.

During April 2014, President Michael D. Higgins made a point of acknowledging such threads of connection. He was on the last day of what was the first official visit by an Irish head of state to Britain. He decided that Coventry would be the final venue of his busy itinerary. He knew from personal experience how the city's building sites and factories had once provided jobs for West of Ireland emigrants.

In August 1939, nine days before the outbreak of the Second World War, an IRA bomb left in the basket of a bicycle exploded on a busy Coventry street. Five civilians, ranged in age from fifteen to eighty-two, died, and over seventy more were injured. Two Irishmen convicted of the bombing were hanged. Several others brought before the courts were acquitted. A number of the perpetrators escaped. In the aftermath of the IRA attack, anti-Irish sentiment flared, but, over time, relations recovered.

In his remarks at St Mary's Guildhall, near Coventry's famous cathedral, President Higgins made reference to the Irish community living in Britain. He said, 'I thank you for your fidelity to your homeland of origin; for your solidarity to each other; and for the contribution you have made to the warm friendship that now exists between Ireland and the United Kingdom.'

I'm comfortable living in a republic and can readily see the downsides of royalty and privilege. But I admire the queen and what she has done to foster friendship between Britain and Ireland through her engagement with our three most recent heads of state: Michael D. Higgins, Mary McAleese and Mary Robinson.

If and when Prince Charles succeeds his mother as monarch, I expect he will be keen to build on her work. I've listened to him speak about Irish and British relations. Like his mother, he shows an understanding of our complex history. The castle he came to in Mullaghmore, where his grand-uncle holidayed before he was assassinated, was part of an estate of 10,000 acres owned by a British prime minister, Viscount Palmerston, in the nineteenth century.

Prince Charles's role could grow in importance as the problems build in the intergovernmental aspect of our relationship as next-door neighbours.

It's difficult to find evidence to suggest that, in its determination to leave the EU, the Conservative government gave any significant thought to how their actions might affect not just Northern Ireland but the entire island of Ireland.

We've had such a difficult past. For centuries Britain was the colonizer and we were the colonized.

The 1821 census estimated that the population of England, Scotland and Wales was 14.4 million compared to 6.8 million on the island of Ireland. Against the backdrop of the industrial revolution, Britain's population continued to grow dramatically. In 1841, before the Famine, over 8 million people were living in Ireland. Hunger and disease killed an estimated 1 million people, and millions more were forced to emigrate. The April 2022 census detailed how, for the first time since the aftermath of the Famine, Ireland's population exceeded 5 million.

Consistently, over hundreds of years, there was an edge to the relationship. Up to and including the Troubles, we did terrible things to each other.

And yet, as far back as the fourteenth century, some descendants of the Anglo-Norman settlers became 'more Irish than the Irish themselves'. After the Famine, a constant flow of Irish workers and their families sought in the neighbouring island a livelihood that their own country could not provide. They put down roots in Britain and reared families there.

Those layers of kinship found expression when both countries joined the Common Market in 1973 and sat, as neighbours and friends, around the members' table. The relationship was reflected in a very practical and positive way when, as equals, both countries assumed a co-guarantor role of the Belfast (Good Friday) Agreement in 1998.

But those truths don't appear to merit even afterthought status in the post-Brexit behaviour of the current British government.

It's easy to forget that the British Empire covered a quarter of the world when the Irish Free State of twenty-six counties was established in 1922. In the Second World War, Britain was a major force and made huge sacrifices fighting Nazism while Ireland remained neutral.

For much of the twentieth century, Britain was locked in a pattern of decline. In 1963, and again in 1967, the French president, Charles de Gaulle, blocked the UK's application to join the EEC. It succeeded (at the third attempt), along with Ireland and Denmark, in 1973.

Decline in status and influence, past quarrels on mainland Europe and the wish to re-establish the UK as a world power were factors in its Brexit referendum campaign and the outcome.

Time will provide the verdict on the wisdom of the UK deliberately reducing its access to an EU market of 450 million citizens. The campaign promising a sunlit uplands and a better life outside the EU was devised and driven by Dominic Cummings. He used Boris Johnson as the chief salesman and armed him with slogans, including 'Take back control of our borders, money and laws' and 'Get Brexit done, unleash Britain's potential'.

Initially, Cummings's work was a complete success, bringing victory in the Brexit referendum and helping Johnson become prime minister. But the pair fell out, with Cummings leaving Team Boris in November 2020 and, after the bitter parting, playing a role in his downfall in July 2022.

I wasn't surprised that the Johnson phase in Downing Street ended abruptly. In the 1990s, when we were colleagues in Brussels, I'd observed his early engagements with Tory eurosceptics. 'Almost true' was a factor then and would continue to be. The fact that Boris wondered which side he would support, right up to the formal start of the Referendum campaign, was telling.

On centre stage, the Brexit project and its main promoter struggled under scrutiny. I have no doubt that Boris will resurface, in a new chapter. He has two young children. He is fifty-eight. He needs to generate income. He will earn a big cheque for his account of his time in power. His personality and talents will create opportunities. He could become a force in the *Strictly, I'm a Celebrity, GB News* world of television.

When I retired from RTÉ in April 2021, Boris wrote to me, wishing me well. I suspect that Adrian O'Neill, Ireland's ambassador in London, suggested much of the text for the two-page letter that arrived from 10 Downing Street. But the 'Yours affectionately, as ever, Boris Johnson' sign-off was handwritten and I could imagine him having that 'you know yourself' half-smile as he added it to the typed script.

While the Conservative Party has dispensed with Boris, it remains committed to the vision of a post-Brexit Britain that he championed. During the contest to select his replacement, each candidate had to provide proof of Brexit credentials. Even the Labour party leader, Keir Starmer, felt it prudent to place on the record that, if elected prime minister, he would not seek to have the UK rejoin Europe's Single Market.

The three Irish government members who have had most dealings with London since the Brexit decision acknowledge the British–Irish relationship is stuck in its most difficult phase for decades. Micheál Martin, Simon Coveney and Leo Varadkar take no satisfaction from their downbeat assessment. They watched a line of British ministers, in the House of Commons and elsewhere, argue that the Northern Ireland protocol element of the UK's Brexit Treaty must be dropped because it endangers the Good Friday Agreement. Many of those making the assertion have no history of understanding the contents of the said Agreement or the journey made in British–Irish relations over the past two decades.

A striking change in the first half of 2022 is London's willingness to opt out of its role with Dublin as co-guarantor of the Good Friday Agreement. While the behaviour doesn't register in Britain, it causes significant offence in Ireland because it creates questions about the reliability of a partner to act in an honourable way.

Going back to Margaret Thatcher's time, through the Major years, into the terms of David Cameron and Boris Johnson, the Conservative Party has struggled to agree a coherent, robust political philosophy. Brexit has added to that challenge.

A consequence of the Tories' preoccupation with in-house argument and bloodletting is, in Ireland, it revives the premise of 'Perfidious Albion', the next-door neighbour that cannot be trusted. It also undermines a relationship that was significantly reshaped during the past three decades.

The next British general election must be held before January 2025. It may not figure in a major way in Conservative Party calculations, but the behaviour of the current and the next British government will influence Irish hearts and minds.

Under Micheál Martin and Leo Varadkar, Fianna Fáil and Fine Gael have practically swapped positions on the Irish unity question. The Fianna Fáil leader is a champion of a 'shared island' vision. It suits his 'small steps, no rows' disposition. Varadkar (and Simon Coveney) make plain their hope that a united Ireland would be achieved in their lifetime.

Varadkar is likely to be Taoiseach for the phase of Tory government in the run-up to the British general election. His form to date suggests that if he feels a Conservative government is putting party interests above commitments to solid British–Irish relations, he is unlikely to hold back. Nor does Varadkar show any sign of ceding the lead role in the 'Whither Ireland' debate to Sinn Féin. The evidence increases that his stance is based on conviction, not just pragmatism.

The SNP leader, Nicola Sturgeon, has already started the push for a second referendum on Scottish independence. London is resisting it. In the 2014 referendum, almost 55 per cent of Scottish voters opted to remain part of the UK. Sturgeon believes that a second referendum would produce a different result. She sees Brexit as the game-changer, as the UK's 2016 decision to leave the EU was not supported by the majority of voters in Scotland.

The SNP's talk of independence is guaranteed to unsettle some Northern Ireland Unionists because the Scots taking their leave from the UK would add to their vulnerability.

Some within the EU might balk at the notion of admitting a newly independent Scotland into the Brussels club. The Catalans and Basques in Spain and communities in other EU regions might be inclined to follow the Scottish example.

As with Ireland, the behaviour of the British government in Westminster will influence the judgement of Scottish voters in the run-up to any referendum.

In this new chapter of British–Irish relations, many factors are at play, all of them linked, in one way or another, to the UK's Brexit decision.

For five decades Ireland has been a member of the EU, and, arguably, it has been the most transformative factor in the history of the state. The contrasting attitudes to EU membership on neighbouring islands could not be greater.

I like to believe that the people-to-people bonds, those layers of connection established over the centuries, run deeper than current, fraught politics and will sustain the relationship. One vivid example of those genes of shared identity is captured each time the Kop at Liverpool FC modifies Pete St John's 'Fields of Athenry' Famine anthem and breaks into a chorus of 'All Around the Fields of Anfield Road'.

But on constitutional matters, the lesson of the Good Friday Agreement, confirmed by the Brexit decision, is that actions have consequences, some intended, some not. The border poll and unity questions are now part of general discourse in Ireland. Emotions as well as economic calculations will influence how Irish citizens assess the issues. It may not preoccupy the administration in power in Westminster, but its behaviour will be a factor in determining the stability or the break-up of the United Kingdom.

*

When I first went to work in Brussels in 1989, Ireland was one of twelve European Community member states. Austria, Finland and Sweden joined in 1995. By the time I left Belgium to work in Belfast in 2001, there was a long queue of countries seeking to join the Brussels club. The end of the Cold War and the break-up of the Soviet Union had prompted those changes. Today the European Union has twenty-seven members, with a fresh queue of applicants.

I reported on the introduction of the euro to world financial markets as an accounting currency on 1 January 1999 – Ireland was among the first wave of eleven EU member states to adopt it, while our neighbours, the UK, decided to stick with sterling. Physical euro notes and banknotes first entered into circulation on 1 January 2002.

In the first decade of the new century, the EU had the self-confident swagger of a victor, epitomized by the Portuguese-born president of the European Commission from 2004 to 2014, José Manuel Barosso. A reunified Germany, with 83 million citizens, was powering ahead. The low-cost finance freely available throughout the euro zone facilitated the massive infrastructure investment required in its eastern territories. Unhealthy amounts of that cheap money were accessed by Irish financial institutions and dispersed with gusto.

A friend working for one major bank told how he had given out his annual loans budget at the halfway point of the financial year and was then encouraged to begin again and shell out more loans, with new bonuses for his diligence. One former Brussels colleague said to me at the time that the Irish seemed to have discovered a magic get-rich-quick formula by selling houses to each other. His caustic observation proved to be painfully true.

When the EU admitted ten new member states in 2004 – eight former countries from behind the Iron Curtain as well as Malta and Cyprus – I wondered was this the end of Ireland's best days in the Brussels club.

As one among twelve and then fifteen members, the EU had the feel of a delicatessen. Now it was becoming a crowded supermarket. The energy and excitement were being generated by the new arrivals from the east. Ireland, which had benefited so much from EU fund transfers, was now more affluent than most of the new members and would become a net contributor to the Brussels kitty. With just 1 per cent of the EU's population, it was at risk of becoming peripheral.

My wariness was not justified, and I failed to anticipate a significant consequence of EU enlargement for Ireland. As the new members were being admitted, some EU member countries feared they would be flooded by migrant workers, and they imposed temporary labour-market restrictions. Ireland and the UK didn't adopt such measures. Even though tiny Ireland is the most distant EU country for many of the new EU citizens, a pattern began of workers and their families arriving, finding employment and putting down roots. Many were drawn to the cities – the main source of jobs. But, over time, most Irish rural towns and villages gained new residents.

The phenomenon of the New Irish, drawn mainly but not exclusively from countries that form part of the enlarged EU, is one of the most significant changes I've noticed in my home country during the past decade.

Another driver of change is the role played by the citizens' assembly model. The vehicle has been successfully used to facilitate discussion and action on important political and legal issues that politicians find too hot to handle. Policy initiatives started at citizens' assembly level and the contribution of immigrants are two of the most transformative influences in today's Ireland.

When the UK followed through on its referendum decision to leave the EU, I thought it would prove to be an unwise decision. I also worried about the possible consequences for the European Union. With 67 million citizens – 13 per cent of the EU's population – the UK is a big unit. It has been an influential presence on mainland Europe for hundreds of years. It made a significant contribution to victories in two world wars. It was a founder member of the Council of Europe. It hosted the Treaty of London from which the European Convention of Human Rights and the European Court of Human Rights flowed.

After it was admitted, at the third attempt, to what is now the EU, some of its officials and politicians made important contributions to the different institutions. The Conservative Party prime minister Margaret Thatcher was a champion of the European single market, without customs barriers or tariffs.

Part of me worried how the EU would cope after the loss of such an able and respected member state. When I worked in Brussels among colleagues who included Boris Johnson, French was the working language of the press room. Gradually that changed and English became the norm. After German reunification and EU enlargement, which included several countries whose citizens have fluent German, I wondered might pressure come from Berlin to change the practice in the Brussels press room. But French was replaced by English, and that practice continues today, even though the UK has left.

In so many aspects of day-to-day European life – on flights, in the cinema and at international conferences – English is now the main working language. It is a potent example of the UK's soft but influential power in the same way that rock 'n' roll, movies and brands such as Coca-Cola were tools that spread US weight and influence in earlier decades. The fact that the EU communicates mainly through English had little impact on UK voter thinking as it headed for the Brussels exit door. English is registered as an official language in just two of the twenty-seven member states, Ireland and Malta. (They have also registered Irish and Maltese as their official languages for EU purposes.)

The EU is a lesser place without the UK. It is like a football team that is less effective without a difficult but talented player.

Even before Russia invaded Ukraine, government actions and attitudes in Hungary and, at times, Poland were creating significant angst within the EU. On occasions, the European Commission president, Ursula von der Leyen, a former defence minister, seemed out of her depth. The problems now posed by Vladimir Putin could well be the EU's greatest challenge since its foundation.

During a recent visit to Brussels, I noticed the enormous new NATO building near Zaventem airport. Europe's defence and security challenges are now on the agenda. Putin's wariness of an expansionary NATO presence is understandable. But he may be more even more unhinged by the prospect of countries bordering Russia seeking admission to the EU. That could lead to his own citizens being able to compare their situation with the conditions of their next-door neighbours. The conclusions might have negative consequences for the Kremlin. Ukraine is hoping the hardship it has suffered might gain it preferential treatment in the queue for EU membership.

The first of January 2023 will be the fiftieth anniversary of Ireland joining the EU. On so many levels membership has been a transformative experience. But a new, more complex phase is under way and the questions remain around whether bigger is better.

Bonus years

After retiring from RTÉ in April 2021, Sligo became my base again. I'm spending more time with Ceara than ever before. We had both become used to our space. Forty years after we first met, it's like beginning again. Our house at Lisheen is close to the sea, under Knocknarea mountain with the distinctive cairn on top where the legendary Queen Maeve is buried. Ransboro church, where we were married and where our children were baptised, is close by. I try to walk the quiet back roads or at Rosses Point every day. The landscape is beautiful and constantly lifts the spirits. Our two adult children are gone, but technology takes the edge off separation. Moya lives in Brussels and works there as a translator. After studying at DCU and Boston's Northeastern University, Joe is working in the USA. In time, the pull of Europe may take him back across the Atlantic.

Twenty thousand people live in Sligo town, five miles away. The county has a population of 65,000. Every time I'm out, I meet someone I know. Often when walking the familiar streets, I slip into humming the chorus of the Bruce Springsteen song 'My Home Town'. Increasingly there are moments when I feel that I am becoming my father.

From childhood days, the Showgrounds, the home of our League of Ireland football club, Sligo Rovers, is a place that brings colour to our lives. The 12-acre site, close to the centre of the town, is owned in trust for the people and can never be sold. The ground provides spectacular views of Ben Bulben mountain. On match nights, when the floodlights are switched on, the venue can be seen for miles around. It is the beating heart of our community.

Keeping a soccer club of full-time professionals solvent in the north-west corner of Ireland is a constant struggle. There is no wealthy patron. The fans are the owners. In times of crisis, when funds are required, door-to-door collections always draw a generous response. When my mother was a young girl, living with her aunt, one of the greatest centre-forwards of all time, the England international Dixie Dean, signed for the club. He was greeted by huge crowds at Sligo railway station. He was thirty-two at the time, the outbreak of the Second World War was just four months away, and Rovers bought him for the FAI Cup campaign. He played seven times, scoring ten goals, and won a runners-up medal after defeat in the Cup Final replay.

As happened when the club signed Dixie Dean, through the decades, even in lean times, it tends to gamble on the exotic. Willie Gilmartin and his wife, Kathleen, would sometimes arrive for a visit as we were heading up the stairs to bed before the next school day. Willie worked as a night telephonist in the local post office where the staff often had advance knowledge of the next big-name signing in advance of a Cup campaign. We'd hang on for Willie's prediction about an ex-West Ham striker or a proven goal-scorer from Scotland or Northern Ireland. A former English cricket international cum centre-half was one of the arrivals in the 1960s. One bleak winter Sunday afternoon, a Nigerian trialist fell over in the snow as he attempted to take a corner. Once, after an opposition goalkeeper allegedly struck a youngster behind the goals, the pitch was invaded. Another time a referee was persuaded to reverse his decision and accepted that Sligo had scored a goal before the ball exited through a large hole in the frayed net. Hundreds of such true stories are lodged in the memory.

Rovers have won the League twice and the FAI Cup five times during my life. In between those peaks we content ourselves with what one League of Ireland manager, Mick Cooke, once described as 'mid-table supremacy'. Relegation to the division below is the fear that hovers during a run of bad form. The national side in soccer or rugby or a favourite team from the Premier League might be playing, but the result that decides the mood in our town is the one featuring Sligo Rovers. That will never change. The club will celebrate its centenary in 2028. One pleasing task during this new phase of my life is to help with fundraising for the refurbishment of the Showgrounds in time for the anniversary.

RTÉ has a policy of retiring its staff when they reach sixty-five. When my birthday came, I wasn't fully ready to leave. But there was a good team in Belfast lined up to take over. I was also conscious of other younger colleagues, in Dublin and elsewhere, patiently waiting for jobs to become vacant. They are entitled to their time in the orchard. I can explain to myself that my formal working life really is over. But it is impossible to completely stop being a reporter. More than a year after leaving, I'm still having dreams in which I'm happily employed by RTÉ. It doesn't surprise me because I was so fulfilled during my time there. It is painful to watch from the sidelines how a government lets public-service broadcasting wither on the vine.

During my final years as northern editor, I began writing for the RTÉ website. Before agreeing to do so, I wrongly thought that it would be an extra pressure in an already busy working life. Once I began, it was like rediscovering an old love: the written word. Sometimes I'd go to bed still not sure how to fill the gaps in a piece under construction. During the night, the elves would deposit a solution under the pillow, and I'd wake up refreshed, keen to get to the keyboard with new ideas in the fingers. What I had once resisted as a chore became a passion. James McNamara and Paul Ferris had responsibility for the RTÉ online service and we had a few great years together.

I asked about the chances of continuing to write for the RTÉ website after retiring, but that wasn't possible. Fortunately, a new online publishing venture called The Currency was interested in using my work, and a new relationship began. Two able and well-known journalists, Tom Lyons and Ian Kehoe, founded The Currency in 2019. Its main focus is on business, finance, economics and public policy. The model is funded by subscriptions and, at a time of unprecedented flux in the sector, they have already established what is a viable business. My main Currency contact is Dion Fanning, a journalist I met very early in his career, attending press conferences at Manchester United Champions League matches. I enjoy working with him. I provide long reads for The Currency, mainly about politics – North and South, British–Irish and EU – and occasionally about sport.

It's a pleasure to have an involvement with the project because the energy reminds me of John Healy and Jim Maguire and their start-up provincial newspaper, the *Western Journal*, where I got my first job in 1977. Healy was the person who said to me that first time we met in the living room of his home in Dublin that a person should try to do three things in a life: plant a tree, father a child and write a book. For a long time,

I parked that third element of Healy's advice. The decision to revisit it took its first steps after a gathering of friends in Galway on 9 June 2021.

The seven of us had worked as colleagues for many years. Because of roots or emotional bonds with the West of Ireland, we call our WhatsApp group 'Westawake'. The other six had all passed through the retirement door before me: Jim Fahy, Joe O'Brien, Charlie Bird, Sean O'Rourke, Michael Lally and Ray Burke. The bonds run deep. When I retired in pandemic times, they each wrote an essay about memories of our times together and sent it in book form to me.

A number of times, COVID thwarted our plans for a get-together. But an easing in the restrictions allowed us to gather in Galway. We walked along the Prom by the Atlantic in Salthill and then sat down together for food at the Ardilaun Hotel. Michael Lally was frail but in good spirits because of the positive readout from his ongoing cancer treatment. We all congratulated Charlie Bird for his innovative podcast work in the *Irish Times* the previous weekend.

Charlie told us that he was having trouble with his speech and said he was worried about it. Medical investigations were scheduled in Dublin the following week. I was sitting beside him, and he told me that he was frustrated because he couldn't properly participate in the conversation. He was due to travel to the Aran Islands the following day so he headed for bed early. Typically, he tried to discreetly pay the food bill for the group. Charlie said to us that night that he feared he might have motor neurone disease. We knew two deceased colleagues who had battled with the condition: Colm Murray and Kevin Dawson. Sadly, over the following weeks, Charlie's suspicions were confirmed to be true. Immediately after he was diagnosed, he and his wife, Claire, began their response that has earned the admiration of the country and beyond.

Jim Fahy drove away from our gathering that night to his home at Garden Field, outside Tuam. None of us knew that it would be our last time in his company. His daughter, Aideen, had a baby boy the following month. We decided that Jim and Christina were revelling in their role as grandparents and that this was the reason for his sudden absence from our social-media exchanges. He sent me a message, in confidence, on Tuesday, 7 September 2021. He had been diagnosed with bowel cancer and was receiving treatment at Galway University Hospital. He had beaten a version of the disease thirty-seven years before and was hopeful he would do so again.

Jim was my best friend in RTÉ. He was the ultimate story-teller. His *Looking West* series of half-hour radio programmes featuring the characters he unearthed in the parishes of rural Ireland is gold-standard public-service broadcasting. An American relation who heard he was a legend at his craft once came home to see him in action but was underwhelmed, describing him as 'a beat reporter'. Jim was chuffed with the assessment because that's what he aspired to be. After years trail-blazing in the West of Ireland, he applied for the job of RTÉ's Washington correspondent but wasn't successful. It would have been an inspired appointment because Fahy would have taken Irish America by storm, right into the Oval Office. He dusted himself down, and, with producer Caroline Bleahen, he went on to make a string of award-winning television documentaries with an Irish core, from Haiti to Argentina to Chernobyl, while continuing with his Galway day job as the beat reporter.

With the country in COVID lockdown, Jim's cancer treatment continued. He had a very private side. When he retired from RTÉ on the last day of 2011, my wife Ceara came up with the idea that we buy him an oak tree. On several nights, when I knew he was at home in Christina's care, I was tempted to go and stand by the tree in his garden and whistle up to him or send prayers in his direction. In late October, he sent a message, telling me for the first time about a project he had been working on quietly for several years.

While making a *Looking West* radio programme thirty years ago, he heard about a man called Michael McGovern, born in Williamstown, Co. Galway, in 1847. McGovern emigrated to the USA and became a champion of iron and steel workers in the Midwest. He published a collection, *Labour Lyrics and Other Poems*, and persuaded a local newspaper-publisher in Ohio to print 50,000 copies. For several years, Jim had been quietly working on researching McGovern's story with Leo and Eileen Finnegan from the Heritage Society in Williamstown. On 7 December, he sent me an email with some of the material. He didn't know if it would ever get to print but wrote that he would be very happy if it made it online, where local people could read it. That was the last contact I had from Jim. I sent him a message on Sunday, 9 January 2022, promising that the Williamstown work will be completed, sure in the knowledge that he would be the one directing it. Five days later, with his family at his bedside, Jim died. We laid him to rest in view of an old round tower at Kilbannon cemetery, near his home.

In the void that followed his passing, I began reflecting on my times as a beat reporter and John Healy's advice about leaving behind some account of them. I've lived to see the ballot box replace the Armalite, the resilience of democracy, the power of generosity and the liberating force of forgiveness. Today's Ireland is a better place, more willing than it once was to address its failings. I'm thankful for a health service that has kept me alive to witness such change. With a sense that these are bonus years, the first thought I have on waking, most mornings, is 'Never better.'

Acknowledgements

When I retired from RTÉ, Caroline Bleahan gave me a list of my forty years of television reports, logged in the RTÉ system. It served as a useful guide-track when working on this project. Simon Hess introduced me to Will Atkinson and editor Clare Drysdale from publishers Allen & Unwin. Working with them is a pleasure. Copy editor Liz Hudson kept me between the ditches. Journalist Mark Simpson was a constant friend. Ed Mulhall, Dermot O'Toole and Mary and Martin McAleese were trusted sounding boards.

Ceara, Moya and Joe stuck with me during the wobbles.

Index